Re-Enchanting the Earth

Re-Enchanting the Earth

Why AI Needs Religion

ILIA DELIO, OSF

ORBIS ✦ BOOKS
Maryknoll, New York 10545

Founded in 1970, Orbis Books endeavors to publish works that enlighten the mind, nourish the spirit, and challenge the conscience. The publishing arm of the Maryknoll Fathers and Brothers, Orbis seeks to explore the global dimensions of the Christian faith and mission, to invite dialogue with diverse cultures and religious traditions, and to serve the cause of reconciliation and peace. The books published reflect the views of their authors and do not represent the official position of the Maryknoll Society. To learn more about Maryknoll and Orbis Books, please visit our website at www.orbisbooks.com

Copyright © 2020 by Ilia Delio, OSF

Published by Orbis Books, Box 302, Maryknoll, NY 10545-0302.

Manufactured in the United States of America

Manuscript editing and typesetting by Joan Weber Laflamme

Library of Congress Cataloging-in-Publication Data

Names: Delio, Ilia, author.
Title: Re-enchanting the Earth : why AI needs religion / Ilia Delio, OSF.
Description: Maryknoll, NY : Orbis Books, 2020. | Includes bibliographical references and index. | Summary: Artificial Intelligence (AI), the new frontier of human evolution, holds the promise of reuniting religion and science.
Identifiers: LCCN 2020002329 (print) | LCCN 2020002330 (ebook) | ISBN 9781626983823 (trade paperback) | ISBN 9781608338467 (ebook)
Subjects: LCSH: Religion and science. | Artificial intelligence. | Human evolution—Religous apsects—Catholic Church. | Theological anthropology.
Classification: LCC BL240.3 .D455 2020 (print) | LCC BL240.3 (ebook) | DDC 201/.60063—dc23
LC record available at https://lccn.loc.gov/2020002329
LC ebook record available at https://lccn.loc.gov/2020002330

Religion will not regain its power until it can face change in the same spirit as does science.

—ALFRED NORTH WHITEHEAD, 1925

Contents

Acknowledgments   ix

Introduction   xi

1. Holism and Human Evolution   1

2. Axial Consciousness   27

3. The Rise of the Individual   41

4. The Forgotten Openness of the Closed World   63

5. In Search of Relational Wholeness   87

6. The Posthuman Social Imaginary   113

7. Teilhard and Life in the Noosphere   133

8. Second Axial Religion   157

9. Posthuman Spirituality   177

10. Church of the Planet   189

Conclusion: Where Are We Going?   211

Index   227

Acknowledgments

I am grateful to Villanova University, especially Adele Lindemeyer, PhD, dean of the College of Liberal Arts and Sciences, and Peter Spitaler, PhD, chair of the Department of Theology and Religious Studies, for granting me a research sabbatical to complete this work. I would also like to acknowledge support from the Institute for Buddhist Studies, University of California–Berkeley for the Public Theology and Technologies of Presence Fellowship sponsored by the Henry Luce Foundation.

A big thanks to the executive director of the Omega Center, Gregory Hansell, who read this book in its evolving form and offered helpful comments. Greg's keen mind and probing questions were inspirational in navigating the final chapters of the book. I am also grateful to my colleague at Villanova, Mark Doorley, PhD, who was kind enough to read an early version of the book and offer valuable suggestions.

Finally, a special thank you to my good friend Robert Ellsberg and the Orbis team with whom I have had the honor to work for more than a decade. The mission of Orbis is to produce books that make a difference in the world. I hope this book deepens the mission.

Introduction

The United Nations recently issued a troubling report on biodiversity; it indicated that the loss of species is happening "tens to hundreds of times" as fast as the average rate over the past 10 million years, and thereby is posing a dire threat to ecosystems all over the world.[1] With the indelible toxic human footprint on the earth's natural resources, we are truly living in the Anthropocene. According to many environmental scientists we are nearing a crisis.[2] *Crisis* is defined as "a rapidly deteriorating situation that, if left unattended, will lead to disastrous results." Yet even as we take note of these impending disasters, we are neither changing our lifestyles nor slowing down our rate of production.

In fact, we have been on the brink of disaster for over fifty years. In her 1962 book *Silent Spring* Rachel Carson first alerted the world to the toxicity of pesticides, thereby, in effect, launching the environmental movement. Nevertheless, the rate of global warming, species extinction, ocean pollution, and water contamination continues unabated. The roots of this breakdown can be traced to a complex of factors including industrialization, technology, consumerism, capitalism, radical individualism, and religious otherworldliness. We cannot claim to be ignorant of these dangers. Even as the impending crisis worsens, we have more information about these changes than ever before, all

---

[1] United Nations, Intergovernmental Science-Policy Platform on Biodiversity and Ecosystem Services (IPBES), "Nature's Decline 'Unprecedented'; Species' Extinction Rates 'Accelerating'" (May 6, 2019).

[2] See, e.g., Jonathan L. Bamber et al., "Ice Sheet Contributions to Future Sea Level Rise from Structured Expert Judgment," *PNAS* (May 20, 2019).

delivered quickly and efficiently to our computer devices. Something is amiss.

What does the environmental problem have to do with artificial intelligence (AI)? Is ecology distinctly different from technology, competing for human attention? Have we artificially separated intelligence from nature? These questions are at the heart of this book, but they cannot be addressed by ecology or technology alone. As Lynn White noted in 1967, the underlying problem is essentially religious.[3] To appreciate the reasons that ecology and technology share a root in religion requires that we explore the question of intelligence in nature as well as the evolution of intelligent nature in relation to God. Rather than considering ecology and technology as separate but related disciplines, I focus specifically on the rise of AI in the context of evolution and draw out the ecological implications of AI as the principal factor of evolution in the twenty-first century.

It is not a trivial matter that AI emerged in the midst of a violent century of war. In a 1950 paper British mathematician and cryptanalyst Alan Turing, who played a key role in cracking the German Enigma code, sought to explore whether or not a machine could reason like a human. He was interested in knowing if a machine could "think" objectively, that is, without bias. The term *artificial intelligence* was coined by John McCarthy in 1955 in his proposal for a 1956 conference on artificial intelligence held at Dartmouth College. McCarthy's term evoked ways to explore how a machine could be capable of abstract thought, problem solving, and self-improvement. "He believed that every aspect of learning or any other feature of intelligence can in principle be so precisely described that a machine can be made to simulate it."[4] While McCarthy focused on machine learning, other scientists were exploring how information is generated and shared, such as complex dynamical systems and cybernetic systems, principles undergirding AI yet also found in nature. Such

---

[3] Lynn White, "The Historical Roots of Our Ecologic Crisis," *Science* 155 (March 10, 1967): 1203–7.

[4] Martin Childs, "John McCarthy: Computer Scientist Known as the Father of AI," *Independent* (UK), November 1, 2011.

findings lead me to suggest there is an implicit "intelligence" in nature, raising the question whether or not the adjective *artificial* is helpful to describe machine intelligence. Is artificial intelligence fake intelligence, like a plastic rose compared to a real rose? Or does artificial intelligence simulate biological intelligence and hence extend biological intelligence in a new medium? Some models of quantum physics suggest that intelligence is inherent to nature and that there is nothing fake about intelligence or nature.[5]

Twentieth-century science unveiled a biological holism by which nature dynamically recreates, transcends, and evolves to more complex forms of life. On that basis we can say that the root principles of AI are actually found in nature. But the word *nature* is a fast-and-loose term. We use it so often we do not realize that the term is a smokescreen for the complex interplay of physical, biological, and chemical life. The word *nature* can mean the capacity to become something—a quark, a cell, a bird, or a complex human—which means that nature has the capacity for multivalent forms; it is infinitely malleable and hence "plastic." Despite the penchant to reduce biological nature to verifiable mechanisms, biology can never quite cope with the fact that *nature* is an umbrella term for vital informational flow that often eludes causal mechanisms.

Biological life is anything but mechanistic. Nature is more flow than fixed. There is a dynamic impulse in nature choreographing the various structures through finely tuned regulatory steps and elaborate processes. Steve Talbott points out that structures, once formed, do not necessarily stay that way. This is now true on just about every level of biological life. How the smallest structures of a single cell, such as the nucleus, mitochondria, and golgi apparatus, can work together in a seamless rhythm baffles the search for mechanistic principles. Nature, as Talbott writes, is an "unbearable wholeness of beings."[6]

---

[5] Chapter 1 herein explores the models of mind in relation to matter in detail.

[6] Steve Talbott, "The Unbearable Wholeness of Beings," *The New Atlantis: A Journal of Technology and Society* (2010).

The awareness of relational holism was part of the rebirth of science in the twentieth century. Quantum physics disclosed a relational holism through the discovery of wave-particle duality, and biological systems were found to work as complex dynamical wholes. Every single cell is more than the sum of its parts. Living systems are networks of information, interacting with other systems and giving rise to more complex systems. Every system is a super-system, so that systems exist within systems—an insight that led to the description of a *holon*, something that is simultaneously a whole and a part.[7]

Quantum physics in particular brought holism to new light by identifying the observer as part of the system, pointing to a fundamental role of consciousness in material reality. The significance of consciousness is still highly contested among scientists today because the nature of consciousness is still unknown. Does consciousness emerge from nonconscious matter? Is consciousness the fundamental layer of matter or the governor of matter? Since all physical events are descriptive events that depend on consciousness, there can be no clear answers to these questions. It is impossible to talk about the intrinsic properties of matter apart from consciousness.

One could describe evolution as the emergence of cosmic and biological holism that reaches a peak in the species *Homo sapien sapiens* (hereafter *Homo sapiens*.) The human species is an outflow of biological evolution and part of the overall community of life; hence, the human species is governed by the same principles of nature as the clam or the beaver. On one hand, the complex brain and physiological makeup of the human person recapitulates cosmic life. On the other hand, the development of cultures and societies complexifies holism on a higher level of consciousness. Technology is part of this complexification process.

---

[7] For a discussion of holons, see Judy Cannato, *Radical Amazement* (Notre Dame, IN: Sorin Books, 2006), 94–102; idem,, *Fields of Compassion: How the New Cosmology Is Transforming Spiritual Life* (Notre Dame, IN: Sorin Books, 2010); and Ken Wilber, *A Theory of Everything* (Boston: Shambhala Publications, 2000).

The term *techne* means the act of "bringing forth" what is potentially in nature, the capacity of nature to create structures and relationships toward wholeness, or as Aristotle noted, toward the flourishing of life. *Techne* is as much a verb as it is a noun; it is linked with *poiesis* or the art of making something out of existing materials. In this respect *techne*, which is the root of *technology*, is not artifactual or mere tool making, something inert and extrinsic to biological life; rather *techne* is biology's capacity for whole making.

Among early humans, knives, utensils, and hunting tools—all crafted from nature—became means of participating in flourishing life in the face of environmental pressures. Similarly, the birth of the tribe in early human development followed the communal pattern of nature. Decisions were made within communities in relation to the wider cosmos, and thus the natural world and the human world were sympathetic and symbiotic. As rationality and language began to emerge in complex ways, a new power entered into nature with a new consciousness of self-reflective life: the awareness of finitude. And with the complexification of consciousness that arose with increased brain size and function came a new level of self-reflection; death entered into human awareness, and with that came the rise of religion.

Religion emerged in evolution as part of cosmic holism. Religion is the response of collective consciousness and human action in the process of development. It is about ultimate concern, but even more, it is about cosmic tethering, or what Mircea Eliade called an "umbilical cord" to the whole.[8] The word *religion* has

---

[8] Mircea Eliade, *The Sacred and the Profane*, trans. William R. Trask (New York: Harcourt Inc., 1959), 37. Eliade writes: "Such a cosmic pillar can be only at the very center of the universe, for the whole of the habitable world extends around it. Here, then, we have a sequence of religious conceptions and cosmological images that are inseparably connected and form a system that may be called the 'system of the world' prevalent in traditional societies: a) a sacred place constitutes a break in the homogeneity of space; b) this break is symbolized by an opening by which passage from one cosmic religion to another is made possible (from heaven to earth and vice versa; from earth to the underworld; c)

as its root the Latin *ligare,* from which the English word *ligament* is derived. Hence, religion refers to that which binds us or returns us *(re-ligare)* to ultimate wholeness, in which we find our ultimate concern and value. In this respect religion is not simply an adaptive mechanism for well-being;[9] rather, religion has a deeper function in cosmic life, a "tethering" function, without which no aspect of life can adequately survive, since the fullness of life depends on the whole.

Given nature's holism and the rise of religion as an evolutionary dimension of the search for wholeness, I raise three main questions in this book: (1) Why did AI arise in the process of evolution? (2) What does AI do for us? (3) What do we want with AI, especially in light of the crisis of climate change? Some may wonder whether AI arose in the absence of religion or if AI is supplanting religion. My position is that AI shows the critical need to reconstruct religion for a world of evolution and complexity. The thesis of this book is that religion is the linchpin to the future of AI-mediated cosmic intelligent life and that an AI world, oriented by new religious sensibilities, can bring about an ecological re-enchantment of the earth.

Although I spell out this thesis in the chapters ahead, I here provide a brief explanation of my ideas. In speaking of "new religious sensibilities" I refer to the conviction that something about religion has broken down in contemporary culture and that something new is on the horizon. Lynn White claimed that religion, in particular Christianity, lies at the source of our ecological crisis. He based this argument on Christianity's ambivalence toward nature, its anthropocentric focus, and its otherworldliness.[10] I share his concerns, which I think Pope

---

communication with heaven is expressed by one or another of certain images, all of which refer to the *axis mundi*: pillar, ladder, mountain, tree, vine, etc.; d) around this cosmic axis lies the world (=our world), hence the axis is located 'in the middle,' at the 'navel of the earth'; it is the Center of the World."

[9] See Stephen Asma, *Why We Need Religion* (New York: Oxford University Press, 2018); E. O. Wilson, *Consilience: The Unity of Knowledge* (New York: Vintage, 1999).

[10] White, "The Historical Roots of Our Ecologic Crisis."

Francis tried to address in his recent encyclical *Laudato Si'*. But the problem is compounded by ancient metaphysical principles, patriarchy, and biblical literalism, all of which appear insuperable in institutional religion. In response, I look to the novel insights of the Jesuit priest and scientist Pierre Teilhard de Chardin (1881–1955). Teilhard was a trained paleontologist whose area of expertise was the Eocene period of evolution, 56–34 million years ago. He was also a deeply committed Christian and a mystic.[11] He was bold, creative, and daring in his approach to evolution and the role of religion.[12] He did for religion, in a sense, what Steve Jobs did for the computer: harness it for a new world.

Teilhard anticipated a new level of collective mind, which he called the "noosphere," from the Greek *nous* (mind). Computer technology has initiated this next step of evolution, but according to Teilhard we must take hold of this new level of consciousness and evolve.[13] The noosphere is the natural culmination of biological evolution and not its termination. "Just as Earth once covered itself with a film of interdependent living organisms, which we call the biosphere, so humankind's combined achievements are forming a global network of networked mind, a new intersubjectivity."[14] The noosphere is a sphere of collective consciousness expressed in the way culture is organizing itself around social networks. The age of nations has passed, Teilhard

---

[11] See Kathleen Duffy, *Teilhard's Mysticism* (Maryknoll, NY: Orbis Books, 2014).

[12] James W. Skehan, SJ, "Exploring Teilhard's 'New Mysticism': Building the Cosmos," in *Pierre Teilhard de Chardin on People and Planet* (New York: Routledge, 2006), 21.

[13] Pierre Teilhard de Chardin, *The Future of Man,* trans. Norman Denny (New York: Harper and Row, 1964), 204. "In the 1920s Teilhard coined the word *noosphere* in collaboration with his friend Edouard Le Roy. Derived from the Greek word *nous* or mind in the sense of integrating vision, the noosphere describes the layer of mind, thought and spirit within the layer of life covering the earth." Ursula King, "One Planet, One Spirit: Searching for an Ecologically Balanced Spirituality," in *Pierre Teilhard de Chardin on People and Planet*, ed. Cecelia Deane-Drummond (London: Equinox, 2008), 82.

[14] Michael H. Murray, *The Thought of Teilhard de Chardin* (New York: Seabury Press, 1966), 20–21.

said, and unless we wish to perish, we must shake off our old prejudices and build the earth.

To build the earth is another way to talk about the flourishing of life. How do we move beyond our impasses toward a new intersubjectivity and planetized consciousness? Responses have come from two camps: *transhumanism* and *posthumanism*. Nick Bostrom, a forerunner of transhumanism, claims that human enhancement through AI is the way forward. In this sense AI builds on the Cartesian subject and the perfection of mind. Donna Haraway and Katherine Hayles, who represent critical feminist posthumanism, distance themselves from transhumanism precisely because the latter so closely weds itself to the ideals of modernity and Enlightenment humanism. While transhumanists and critical posthumanists both see that moving beyond the present through AI is a step toward flourishing life, their notions of flourishing life differ. For transhumanists, enhancement is the key to betterment; for critical posthumanists, transgressing boundaries toward complexified relationships is paramount. AI is not perfecting the mind but extending the body beyond narrow boundaries that limit or thwart personhood and community. Critical posthumanists claim we will never flourish if we don't first recognize that our relations with others are integral to who we are. Hence, they argue for a deep and abiding relationality that can extend in and through our electronic devices (Hayles) but must also extend into kinship with the nonhuman biological world (Haraway).

My work builds on the insights of posthumanism but widens this perspective through cosmic and relational holism, building on Teilhard's ideas for a new religion of the earth. If religion means connecting to ultimate wholeness, and AI is seeking to hyper-connect toward seamless unity, then religion is at the heart of AI. Teilhard saw computer technology as the next level of biological life in evolution because it is the next level of religious evolution. From cosmos to life and mind, religion is the energy of life's fulfillment because it focuses on ultimate meaning and concern. As Teilhard recognized, computer technology can extend the outreach of human activity, but it depends on a broader use of human activity and how we control psychic, spiritual energy needs and powers.[15]

Religion grew up in what Karl Jaspers called the axial period, the age of the individual; now it is time to reconceive religion for a new axial period of consciousness, a second axial period brought about by AI technology and the electronically linked globe. Teilhard recognized the emergence of a new electronically mediated hyper-connected person. For this new interconnected person in an interconnected world he posited a new religion of the earth. Such a religion engages the plasticity of nature, the complexity of systems, the fragile boundaries of relationships, and the invaluable role of love in orienting human and biological life toward a future fullness of life. Here is a brief look at the chapters.

In Chapter 1 I examine the twentieth-century rediscovery of nature's holism with Einstein's theory of relativity, the rise of quantum physics, and the obscure role of consciousness in matter. I briefly explore panpsychism and dual-aspect monism as ways to conceive mind and matter, opting for the latter insofar as panpsychism does not adequately account for physical evolution. I introduce Teilhard de Chardin as someone familiar with the new physics and attentive to the integral relationship between mind and matter. Teilhard's notion of mind as the "inside" of matter and the openness of matter to higher levels of mind impelled him to suggest that religion is a dimension of evolution. His insights on religion and evolution are discussed within the context of relational holism, undergirding the directionality of human evolution.

In Chapter 2 the emergence of the human person and the rise of consciousness are placed within the framework of axial consciousness. The tribal, collective, and cosmic characteristics of pre-axial consciousness are mapped against the rise of axial consciousness marked by the individual and world religions. The concept of the axial age is controversial because, like the

---

[15] Joseph A. Grau, *Morality and the Human Future in the Thought of Teilhard de Chardin: A Critical Study* (Lanham, MD: Associated University Press, 1976), 274.

pre-axial period, it is a long span of time and changes are not clearly defined. However, I use the axial period as a heuristic, a model of events that form a pattern over time. Leonard Swidler nicely summarizes the difference between the pre-axial and axial periods:

> In briefest fashion: "Pre-Axial" mentality focused mainly on *(a)* "*community*," *(b)* "*ritual*," and the *(c)* "*oneness*" of all reality. On the other hand, "Axial" mentality focused mainly on the individual *(x)* "*person*," internal *(y)* "*intention*," and a radical *(z)* *distinction* between this created world and the transcendent one.[16]

Chapter 3 focuses on axial consciousness more specifically in terms of religion and gender. The rise of the individual brought with it the rise of philosophy and attitudes toward nature. The philosopher Aristotle, in particular, was enormously influential in distinguishing the sexes, and his ideas filtered into Western Christianity and the rise of modern science. While scientific discoveries were not entirely Western in origin, the principles of the Judeo-Christian tradition including particularity, contingency and developmental time were significant for the emergence of modern science. David Noble's work on religion and technology was groundbreaking insofar as he identified the roots of technology in male Western monasticism, claiming that both religion and science sought to restore the fallen Adam to divine likeness; hence, the monk, the scientist, and the priest were on a higher level, close to God.[17] Women were largely excluded from religion and science due to the Aristotelian notion of incomplete intellects and heightened emotions.

---

[16] Leonard Swidler, "The Meaning of Life in the Twenty-First Century," essay shared in private communication.

[17] David Noble, *The Religion of Technology: The Divinity of Man and the Spirit of Invention* (New York: Alfred A. Knopf, 1997), 17; see also idem, *A World without Women: The Christian Clerical Culture of Western Science* (New York: Alfred A. Knopf, 1992).

Religion and natural philosophy (science) maintained a fruitful relationship until the Late Middle Ages, when the Copernican system began to emerge. The Catholic Church rejected Galileo's heliocentric theory and his support of Copernican cosmology, thus distancing religion from the new insights of science. After the Galileo affair, modern science developed independent of church authority, while Christianity became inward looking, secured by a static cosmology and Greek metaphysical principles. This division of science and religion set the stage for the Cartesian subject and an abandoned earth in the twentieth century. The cry "God is dead" rang through the hallways of philosophy and a new mechanistic paradigm developed based on inert matter in motion and a detached thinking self.

Chapter 4 highlights the emergence of AI in the midst of a historical crisis. By the early twentieth century the human person was like a cog in a machine; religion was authoritative, governed by rules, and mandated as God's infallible word, while technology showed its terrifying capacity to destroy lives on a mass scale. Alan Turing experimented with the computer not simply as a thinking machine but as an *unbiased* thinking machine. While his venture was novel and ingenious, Turing did what nature consistently does in the midst of crisis: finds new ways toward optimizing life. Turing's work, along with other key thinkers like John McCarthy and Claude Shannon, gave birth to computer technology during a period of human history when war and destruction were rampant. At the same time, the importance of complex dynamical systems began to replace Aristotelian causality. The science of dynamical systems gave rise to new insights on identity, permanence, resilience, and stability. The idea that most biological life works according to principles of dynamical systems led to the discovery of cybernetics and a new understanding of information through feedback systems; hence the science of cybernetics.

The cultural and philosophical movement of transhumanism seized upon computer technology and AI in the late twentieth century as a fulfillment of the Enlightenment project whereby we humans could improve ourselves and transcend our biological limits. While aspects of transhumanism are alluring, the philosophical construct of human betterment belies the complexity of personhood and renders technology a new improved humanism, though still individual in its pursuit. I refer to some of the radical claims of transhumanism, such as brain downloading and disembodied mind, what I call shallow AI, and compare shallow AI to the form of deep AI ushered in by critical feminist posthumanism.

The advent of the posthuman in Chapter 5, which refers to a new type of human beyond the liberal subject, unfolds amid the gradual awakening of a new axial period of consciousness—what Ewert Cousins calls the "Second Axial Period."[18] This new axial consciousness is brought about by technology and mass communication and hence is the milieu for a new type of person emerging in evolution. Through the work of John Johnston and Katherine Hayles, I consider the emergent new person as a hybrid of biology and machine, what Johnston calls "machinic life" and Hayles illuminates as the posthuman.

Chapter 6 examines the new second axial person and posthuman life. The concept of the cyborg as symbol of posthuman second axial life is examined through the lens of social philosopher Donna Haraway and her masterful insights on hybrid creatures. Katherine Hayles brilliantly reconceives the posthuman not as the end of the human person but the end of a certain idea of the human that dominated modernity, the modern liberal subject. She speaks of a new electronically extended body, a human-electronic cyborg, as a new subjectivity of cybernetic information rather than an elimination of subjectivity or personhood. What Hayles and Haraway suggest is that the human species is a co-evolving partner in the cyborgizing techno relationship, which has enormous social and political implications. I discuss a new type of ontology emerging in a networked world, from the logic of binaries to the logic of complex relationships. The intermediate space

---

[18] Ewert H. Cousins, *Christ of the Twenty-First Century* (Rockport, MA: Element Books, 1992), 4.

of shared information is the new co-creative space of becoming, a new ontology of the in-between that transcends categories of gender, race, and religion in favor of ongoing co-creative life.

The remapping of human relationships and culture by computer technology raises the question, toward what end? Where are we going in our technospheric life? Chapters 7 through 9 discuss the insights of Teilhard de Chardin. What is fascinating and relevant to this discussion is the way Teilhard saw the emergence of the electronic global mind as integral to the evolution of religion itself. That is, the evolution of life unifies and complexifies on the level of mind, and this complexification of mind undergirds Teilhard's new understanding of God in evolution. Teilhard's theogenesis (birthing of God) brings to the second axial period a radical and new understanding of religion in evolution that challenges established doctrines and beliefs. In doing so, he opens up a door for religion in an AI world that sees religion as the necessary dimension to electronically mediated hyper-connected life. He reconceives personhood within a new framework of hyper-personalization and hyper-socialization and speaks of the "ultrahuman" in a way that is consonant with the new posthuman milieu.

Teilhard's ideas on religion and evolution in terms of second axial religion,call attention to the fact that almost all discussion on religion and technology is based on first axial religion and thus is strained by narrowly defined theological concepts (narrow insofar as philosophical and metaphysical principles underlying these concepts are outdated). Teilhard focuses on the immersion of God in materiality and the rising up of the Cosmic Person, the Christ, in evolution through the energies of love. World religions, he suggested, can thwart technological evolution because they are acosmic and otherworldly. What is needed is a convergence of world religions, a letting go of doctrinal differences, and a working together for a new spirit of the earth. While his theology is distinctly Christian, it is not narrowly Christian; that is, he envisions the convergence of spiritual energies or interspirituality as part of cosmic formation. Teilhard's second axial religion is a religion for an electronic age where the hyper-connected, networked person finds meaning in deep relationality, interthinking, interspirituality, co-evolving, and co-creating a new earth. His is not a new anthropocentrism but a new holism, that is, an earth religion that cannot be adequately engaged by first axial religion or the institution of religion. In light of Teilhard, I examine how the emerging posthuman is not postreligious but in search of a new religious depth that meets the needs of the hyper-connected, networked life and can shape posthuman life for the good of the planet.

Chapter 10 explores a new religious sensibility in a networked world by conceiving a new "church of the planet." Teilhard was convinced of a new role for religion in an electronic age. His ideas on planetary faith, mysticism, and technology, and the sacredness of everything, provide a new context to consider posthuman life in the twenty-first century. As Thomas Berry and others have pointed out, we need a new re-enchantment of the earth if we are to flourish in this new age.[19]

While there are a number of social critics who suggest that we need to unplug and slow down, I do not see technology as a problem. Technology is ambivalent in value; how we use technology depends on what we want with technology, what we are looking for. The way Gen Z uses social media to organize around social concerns leads me to suggest that technology is not detaching us from the earth or from one another but rather inviting us to reconceive our relationships on all levels of earth life. This urgent search for collective wholeness is deep within us, but the stagnation of religion has caused us to project our religious desires onto technology. We seek in technology what can no longer be found in institutional religion, that is, meaningful life together. We look for ultimate meaning, ultimate value, and ultimate connections that once belonged to the realm of religion and the practice of religion in community. However, the

---

[19] See Thomas Berry, *The Dream of the Earth* (1988; repr., Berkeley, CA: Counterpoint, 2015); Mary Evelyn Tucker, John Grim, and Andrew Angyal, *Thomas Berry: A Biography* (New York: Columbia University Press, 2019).

fundamental doctrines of institutional religion no longer satisfy the needs of the posthuman because the relational human has changed—has been rewired, so to speak—through a Lamarckian evolution in an electronic milieu. Teilhard identified this new stage of evolution in the early twentieth century and devoted his life to bringing religion and evolution together for a new spirit of the earth, a new religious vitalism.

We are living in the midst of a significant evolutionary epoch. The artificial separation between humans and cosmos brought about by the alienation of religion from modern science lies at the heart of our moral confusion. We are not sure where we are going and if we are going together. Teilhard felt that Christianity is not a new religion that surpasses other religions but a renewal of the personalizing process of evolution itself. Evolution is the rise of the Cosmic Person, one whole in formation, from multiplicity to unity, from many persons to transpersonalization.

Science, religion, and technology can work together for a new religious vision on a new level of consciousness, one that is worldly, planetary, and future oriented. The age of the individual is coming to an end and so too is the religious institution that met the religious needs of the individual in the past. A new religious configuration is on the rise and yet it is not clear what this new configuration will be or how it will address the needs of the posthuman, living in the dynamic flux of information and co-creative life. Teilhard suggested that the rising up of religion in this new age must flow out of the great wisdom traditions of the past but look toward a new religious consciousness before us.

Transhumanists envision in the future a seamless skin of electronic mind. So too Christianity anticipates a new cosmic "body" of interlocking hearts. In an age of information, can the mind genuflect before the power of the heart? This is the challenge before us: technology and religion must find each other for the good of the whole earth. To do this, institutional religion will have to let go of everything that prevents engagement in the dynamic flow of evolution, and technocrats must rethink their dystopic, disembodied ideals in view of whole-earth posthuman life. Otherwise our religious longing for salvation and immortality will continue to be sought in the anticipation of what technology can do for us, even though AI cannot fulfill the longings of the heart. Only an ultimate source of life, the One who draws us together beyond ourselves into a new wholeness, a new unity, can ultimately fulfill our deepest desires. "God is love," the disciple John writes (1 Jn 4:13). Love attends to that which is deep within us and draws us together into a new unity beyond our partial selves. Love causes us to see the world and all that is within it in a vibrant spirit, a deep-down freshness.

Can technology and religion work together to form a new religion of the earth? Can AI develop toward the deepening of love? These are ultimate questions. Otherwise, super-intelligent AI life may do no more than polarize and alienate us, while sea levels continue to rise and violent weather patterns destroy life and consume the poor. Only love and compassion can bring us to a new level of cosmic life. How to reclaim a new religious spirit of the earth in a technological age, a posthuman love, is our task and our future.

1

Holism and Human Evolution

Nature's Relational Holism

We humans are deceptively narrow thinkers. We judge human events based on the knowledge immediately at our disposal, limiting ourselves to human actions, as if the world of nonhuman nature is merely background for human life. This is a far cry from the ancient world, where the order of the social cosmos followed the order of the natural cosmos. Twentieth-century science has renewed our fascination with nature. Like the ancient philosophers, we are impelled to study nature once again to learn how to live in the human sphere. History is no longer merely a series of human events; history is cosmic life in the making, and unless we begin to read the cosmic story as our own story, we cannot meaningfully organize our lives, much less orient them, to a future fullness of life.

From the Middle Ages to the beginning of the twentieth century we lived in a static, fixed cosmos in which nature was essentially a stage for the human drama of life. Our story took a radical turn at the beginning of the twentieth century. In 1865, James Maxwell demonstrated that electric and magnetic fields travel through space as waves moving at the speed of light. Maxwell proposed that light is an undulation in the same medium that is the cause of electric and magnetic phenomena. Maxwell's discoveries along with others impelled Albert Einstein to rethink the Newtonian framework of space and time, which led to his theory of relativity. In 1905, Einstein determined that the laws of physics are the same for all nonaccelerating observers, and that the speed of light in a vacuum is independent of the motion of all observers. This was the theory of general relativity. It introduced a new framework for all of physics and proposed new concepts of space and time. Einstein's equations led to the startling insight that the elastic nature of the universe implies change, an insight with which Einstein himself was uncomfortable. His revolutionary ideas, however, sparked a new vision of the cosmos. The unfolding nature of space-time impelled Einstein to think of gravity not as a substance but as a curvature of space-time by matter. The heaviness of matter not only stretches or shrinks distances (depending on their direction with respect to the gravitational field) but also appears to slow down or "dilate" the flow of time. In other words, gravity acts to structure space.

In 1916 the Dutch physicist Willem de Sitter constructed a universe that could stretch in different directions "like taffy," a theoretical insight that received experimental support in 1928 when the astronomer Edwin Hubble, "using the most powerful telescope of his day, found that every galaxy in the sky was moving away from us."[1] He saw that ours was not the only galaxy; rather, there were many other galaxies with large empty spaces between them. "The more distant a galaxy was from our own, the faster it appeared to be rushing outward."[2] If the universe was contracting instead of expanding, we would see distant galaxies radiate a blue light intensity (measured by the Doppler Effect) proportional to their distance. However, Hubble noticed a redshift, indicating that the distance between galaxies is expanding. "This is exactly what observers riding on debris from

---

[1] Adam Frank, *The Constant Fire: Beyond the Science and Religion Debate* (Berkeley and Los Angeles: University of California Press, 2009), 149: Simon Singh, *Big Bang: The Origin of the Universe* (New York: Harper, 2005), 214–29.

[2] Frank, *Constant Fire*, 149.

an explosion would see. In an explosive release of matter all the bits of shrapnel appear to move away from all the other."[3]

The idea that the universe is dynamic and changing was confirmed in 1964 when two scientists working at Bell Laboratories in New Jersey discovered "cosmic microwave background" that was left over from the beginning of the universe more than 13 billion years ago.[4] Today we know our universe to be large, dynamic, and interconnected. The universe is about 13.8 billion years old, with a future of billions of years before us. Some scientists estimate that the future age of the universe will be 100 trillion years, although the sun will die out long before then, perhaps six to nine billion years from now. Our own galaxy, the Milky Way, is a midsize galaxy consisting of billions of stars and stretching about 100,000 light years in diameter. The galaxies are often grouped into clusters—some having as many as two thousand galaxies together. We are one of billions or maybe even a trillion galaxies.

The birth of quantum physics began with Einstein's theory of special relativity. The double-slit experiments of the early twentieth century opened up a whole new meaning of matter. French physicist Louis De Broglie was excited by Einstein's theory and proposed that light waves could behave as particles, and particles could behave like waves. Einstein's theory changed our understanding of matter and energy. Instead of seeing these as two separate properties, mass was now a property of energy and energy a property of mass. Since mass and energy are two forms of the same thing, matter can be converted to energy and energy to matter, while conserving mass.

We used to think that matter is composed of atoms. Now we know that atoms are composed of electrons, and electrons are simultaneously waves and particles. As a consequence of the wavelike aspects of reality, atoms do not have any shape, that is, a solid outline in space, but the things they form do have shape; the constituents of matter, the elementary particles, are *not* real

---

[3] Frank, 149.

[4] Frank, *Constant Fire*, 150; Singh, *Big Bang*, 422–37.

in the same sense as the real things that they constitute. Left to themselves, they exist in a world of possibilities "between the idea of a thing and a real thing," as Werner Heisenberg wrote.[5] Because electrons are waves and particles, their wave aspects will interfere with each other; they will overlap and merge, drawing the electrons into an existential relationship whereby their actual inner qualities such as mass, charge and spin, as well as their position and momentum, become indistinguishable from the relationship among them. All properties of the electrons are affected by the relationship; in fact, they cease to be separate things and become parts of a whole. The whole will possess definite properties of mass, charge and spin, but it is completely indeterminate as to which constituent electrons are contributing to this whole. Indeed, it is no longer meaningful to talk of the constituent electrons' individual properties, as these continually change to meet the requirements of the whole. This kind of internal relationship exists only in quantum systems and has been called relational holism.[6]

Einstein's monumental discoveries renewed the holism of nature in such a way that the human person was now seen to be part of the whole and not an isolated fragment. In a famous passages he writes:

A human being is a part of the whole called by us universe, a part limited in time and space. He experiences himself, his thoughts and feeling as something separated from the rest, a kind of optical delusion of his consciousness. This delusion is a kind of prison for us, restricting us to our personal desires and to affection for a few persons nearest to us. Our task must be to free ourselves from this prison

---

[5] Lothar Schäfer, "Quantum Reality and the Importance of Consciousness in the Universe," in *Cons-Ciências, Centro Transdisciplinar da Estudos consciência* (Porto, Portugal: Universidade Fernando Press, 2004), 82.

[6] Danah Zohar, *The Quantum Self* (New York: William Morrow, 1991), 99.

by widening our circle of compassion to embrace all living creatures and the whole of nature in its beauty.[7]

David Bohm and Karl Pribam each speculated on wholeness in nature and developed theories to explain wholeness as a function of consciousness. Bohm said there are two ways of seeing the universe. The first is the mechanistic order, in which the universe is seen as a collection of entities existing independently in time and space and interacting through forces that do not cause any change in the essential nature of these entities. This is the Newtonian perspective, following fundamental laws of classical physics, in which each atom, molecule, cell, organism, or entity acts according to classical physical laws of motion. The second perspective is based on quantum reality, which cannot be accounted for by the mechanistic order. In quantum reality, movement is generally seen as discontinuous. An electron can move from one spot to another without going through any of the space between. Particles, like electrons, can show different properties depending on the environment they are in: in some places they are particles while in other places they are waves. Finally, two particles can show "non-local relationships," which means they can be separated by vast distances but react as if they are connected to each other.[8]

Bohm recognized that these new features of quantum theory require that the entire universe be considered as an unbroken whole, with each element in that whole demonstrating properties that depend on the overall environment: "Thus, if all actions are in the form of discrete quanta, the interactions between the different entities (e.g. electrons) constitute a single structure of indivisible links, so that the entire universe has to be thought of as an unbroken whole."[9] He called this unbroken wholeness

---

[7] Albert Einstein, "Letter of 1950," *New York Times,* March 29, 1972, and *New York Post,* November 28, 1972.

[8] David Bohm, *Wholeness and Implicate Order* (London: Routledge and Kegan Paul, 1980), 175.

[9] Bohm, 175.

"implicate order," meaning that enfolding takes place in the movements of various universal fields, including electromagnetic fields, sound waves, and others.[10] The enfolded order is the basis of the explicit order that we perceive in the unfolded state. For example, if you take of folded paper and pierce it and then unfold the paper, the spots will appear random, separate, and unrelated. However, if the paper is folded back into its initial position, all the holes come together into the single spot that was pierced through.[11]

Bohm applied his idea of implicate order to the structure of the universe and to consciousness. He showed that what we usually think of as empty space is full of background energy. This immense background energy, Bohm states, may be the basis of implicate order and the undivided wholeness of the universe. Bohm provides a clear account of how a "particle" conception of matter not only causes harm to the sciences, but also to the way we think and live, and thus to our very society and its future evolution:

> The notion that all these fragments is separately existent is evidently an illusion, and this illusion cannot do other than lead to endless conflict and confusion. Indeed, the attempt to live according to the notion that the fragments are really separate is, in essence, what has led to the growing series of extremely urgent crises that is confronting us today and the creation of an overall environment that is neither physically nor mentally healthy for most of the people who live in it. Individually there has developed a widespread feeling of helplessness and despair, in the face of what seems to be an overwhelming mass of disparate social forces, going beyond the control and even the comprehension of the human beings who are caught up in it.[12]

---

[10] Bohm, 178.

[11] Marjorie Hines Woollacott, *Infinite Awareness: The Awakening of a Scientific Mind* (Lanham, MD: Rowman and Littlefield, 2015), 76.

[12] Bohm, *Wholeness and Implicate Order,* 1–2.

The revolutionary discoveries of early twentieth-century physics showed that nature is not inert or static. Rather, nature is constituted by fields of energy rather than atoms moving around like billiard balls. Matter exists in quantum states of wave-particle duality. Interacting particles separated at a distance are seen to affect one another, a phenomenon known as quantum entanglement.[13] The world is not a machine, as Newton thought, but an undivided wholeness.

Although the mechanisms of quantum mechanics are still hotly debated among scientists, there is a holism in nature that baffles scientists and does not let them rest easily. Philosopher Jonathan Schaffer claims that the fundamental layer of reality is not made of particles or strings but of the universe itself—understood not as the sum of things making it up but rather as a single, entangled quantum state. That is, the universe itself is an entangled whole. Physicist and philosopher Carl Friedrich von Weizsäcker thought that taking quantum mechanics seriously predicts a unique, single quantum reality.[14] The homogeneity and the tiny temperature fluctuations of the cosmic microwave background, which indicate that our observable universe can be traced back to a single quantum state, usually identified with the quantum field that fuels primordial inflation, supports this view. What looks like many worlds from the perspective of a local observer is indeed a single, unique universe from a global perspective (such as that of someone who would be able to look from outside onto the entire universe). The concept of many worlds is how quantum monism looks for an observer who has only limited information about the universe.

---

[13] For a discussion on quantum entanglement, see Bruce Rosenblum and Fred Knutter, *Quantum Enigma: Physics Encounters Consciousness* (New York: Oxford University Press, 2011), 3–11; and Karen Barad, *Meeting the Universe Halfway: Quantum Physics and the Entanglement of Matter and Meaning* (Raleigh, NC: Duke University Press, 2007), 247–53.

[14] Heinrich Päs, "Quantum Monism Could Save the Soul of Physics," *Scientific American* (March 5, 2019).

The Novelty of Consciousness

With the birth of quantum physics scientists began to realize that matter cannot be studied apart from mind. The problem of consciousness has been a vexing one for scientists and philosophers alike in the modern period. Physicist Max Planck spoke of consciousness as fundamental to matter; that is, we cannot consider matter apart from consciousness:

> All matter originates and exists only by virtue of a force which brings the particle of an atom to vibration and holds this most minute solar system of the atom together. We must assume behind this force the existence of a conscious and intelligent mind. This mind is the matrix of all matter.[15]

Physicist Erwin Schrödinger thought that consciousness is absolutely fundamental to matter and always experienced in the singular; everything begins with consciousness, which itself is immaterial.[16] Philosopher Bertrand Russell said, "We know nothing about the intrinsic quality of physical events except when these are mental events that we directly experience."[17] These insights have led to "the hard problem of matter," namely, that we cannot talk about matter apart from consciousness.[18] In the 1930s, astrophysicist James Jeans wrote: "The universe looks more like a great thought than a great machine. Mind no longer appears as an accident intruder into the realm of matter. . . . The quantum

---

[15] Max Planck, "Das Wesen der Materie [Nature of Matter]," speech, Florence, Italy (1944). Quoted in Susan Borowski, "Quantum Mechanics and the Consciousness Connection," *AAAS* (July 16, 2010).

[16] Erwin Schrödinger, *What Is Life?* trans. Verena Schrödinger (1944; reprint, Cambridge: Cambridge University Press, 2012), 93–95.

[17] Bertrand Russell, "Mind and Matter," 1950.

[18] Gaylen Strawson, "Consciousness Isn't a Mystery. It's Matter," Opinion, *New York Times*, May 16, 2016.

phenomena make it possible to propose that the background of the universe is mindlike."[19] Since consciousness is absolutely fundamental to matter, everything seems to begin with consciousness, which itself is immaterial.[20]

Despite the fundamental role of consciousness in matter, the nature of consciousness is still elusive. Consciousness is relationality that includes communication and the flow of information. The flow of information is the creative relationship made possible by overlapping waves. As more electron waves overlap, consciousness increases. Two electrons, whose wave functions are overlapping, cannot be reduced to the individual characteristics of the two electrons; the two have become one new whole so that the relationship between the waves cannot be reduced to the activity of the vibrating molecules. The relationality of these energy states account for a flow of information or information processing.[21] At the foundation of physical reality the nature of material things reveals itself as nonmaterial, that is, quantum virtual states. At the level of elementary particles, idea-like states become matter-like states. Non-locality refers to the non-separability of reality. Two quantum particles that at one time interact and then move away from each other are forever bonded and act as though they were one thing regardless of the distance between them.[22] If reality is non-local—that is, if things can affect one another despite distance or space-time coordinates—then nature is not composed of material substances but rather deeply entangled fields of energy; the nature of the universe is undivided wholeness. Because our

---

[19] James Jeans, *The Mysterious Universe* (New York: Macmillan, 1931), 158.

[20] Schrödinger, *What Is Life?* 93–95.

[21] David Chalmers, *The Conscious Mind: In Search of a Fundamental Theory* (New York: Oxford University Press, 1996).

[22] Lothar Schäfer, "Quantum Reality, the Emergence of Complex Order from Virtual States, and the Consciousness in the Universe," *Zygon* 41, no. 3 (2006): 508.

consciousness has emerged from this wholeness and continues to be part of it, then what accounts for the human mind is active in the universe.

Two Main Positions

The inextricable relationship between mind and matter on the level of quantum physics raises the question of how mind and matter are related. Two main positions are at stake: the first, known as *monism* or *panpsychism*, claims that both the physical and the mental are ontologically equal parts of reality and that one cannot be reduced to the other. They are both properties of one neutral substance x, which is neither physical nor mental. Physicist Max Tegmark holds to a radical panpsychism whereby there is a fundamental realm of matter, which is consciousness.[23] The second position, known as *dual-aspect monism*, states that the mental and the material are different aspects or attributes of a unitary reality that is itself neither mental nor material. Philosopher Phillip Goff explains that panpsychism is the best explanation for our current understanding of physics:

> Physical science doesn't tell us what matter is, only what it does. The job of physics is to provide us with mathematical models that allow us to predict with great accuracy how matter will behave. This is incredibly useful information; it allows us to manipulate the world in extraordinary ways, leading to the technological advancements that have transformed our society beyond recognition. But it is one thing to know the behaviour of an electron and quite another to know its intrinsic nature: how the electron is, in and of itself. Physical science gives us rich information about the behaviour of matter but leaves us completely in the dark

---

[23] Max Tegmark, "Consciousness as a State of Matter," *Chaos, Solitons, and Fractals* 76 (July 2015): 238–70. Tegmark gives the name perceptronium to this fundamental state of matter that is consciousness.

about its intrinsic nature. In fact, the only thing we know about the intrinsic nature of matter is that some of it—the stuff in brains—involves experience. We now face a theoretical choice. We either suppose that the intrinsic nature of fundamental particles involves experience or we suppose that they have some entirely unknown intrinsic nature. On the former supposition, the nature of macroscopic things is continuous with the nature of microscopic things. The latter supposition leads us to complexity, discontinuity and mystery. The theoretical imperative to form as simple and unified a view as is consistent with the data leads us quite straightforwardly in the direction of panpsychism.[24]

Although panpsychism is alluring in light of the primacy of consciousness, panpsychism does not adequately explain biological evolution. If consciousness is either an aspect of materiality or the foundation of materiality, how does it account for material attraction and emergence? How does matter complexify and give rise to higher forms of consciousness? If consciousness emerges from billions of subatomic consciousnesses (proto-mental properties), then how do these properties combine to form neural connections undergirding experience?

Wolfgang Pauli, an early pioneer of quantum physics, writes, "It would be most satisfactory if physis (matter) and psyche (mind) could be conceived as complementary aspects of the same reality."[25] This view represents dual-aspect monism. By way of definition, "Two or more descriptions are complementary if they mutually exclude one another and yet are together necessary to describe the phenomenon exhaustively."[26] Dual-aspect

---

[24] Philip Goff, "Panpsychism Is Crazy, But It Is Also Most Probably True," *Aeon Newsletter,* aeon.co.

[25] Quoted in Harald Atmanspacher, and Hans Primas, eds., *Wolfgang Pauli's Philosophical Ideas and Contemporary Science* (New York: Springer, 2010), 110.

[26] Harald Atmanspacher, "20th Century Variants of Dual-Aspect Thinking," *Mind and Matter* 12, no. 2 (2014), 252.

monism excludes reductionism of either an idealist (the primacy of consciousness or panpsychism) or materialist nature (inert matter and mind) while being necessarily incompatible with dogmatic physicalism and scientific materialism. Similarly, Carl Jung proposed a view of basic reality that does not consist of parts but is one unfragmented whole, the *unus mundus*, based on the complementarity of mind and matter. And David Bohm spoke of mind and matter as different aspects of one whole and unbroken movement. Harald Atmanspacher writes, "Conceiving the psychophysically neutral domain holistically rather than atomistically, reflects the spirit of a corresponding move in quantum theory, which started out as an attempt to finalize the atomistic worldview of the 19th century and turned it into a fundamentally holistic one."[27] According to Atmanspacher, the Jung-Pauli dual-aspect monist position corresponds to a philosophical insight implicit in quantum theory, namely, that mind and matter form a complementary whole, which cannot be reduced to parts.[28]

The Problem of Mind, Matter, and Evolution

The theory of evolution emerged among nineteenth-century biologists but was made famous by Charles Darwin in his *Origin of the Species by Means of Natural Selection*. What Darwin showed is that natural life unfolds primarily through the process of natural selection, a process that promotes or maintains adaptation and, thus, gives the appearance of purpose or design.[29] Francisco Ayala states that "Darwin spoke of the evolution of organisms by 'common descent with modification' and similar expressions."[30] He showed that changes in the biological world

---

[27] Atmanspacher, 285.

[28] Atmanspacher, 285.

[29] Francisco J. Ayala, "Biological Evolution: An Introduction," in *An Evolving Dialogue: Theological and Scientific Perspectives on Evolution*, ed. James Miller (Harrisburg, PA: Trinity Press International, 2001), 13.

[30] Ayala, "Biological Evolution," 27.

are not due to outside forces or purposeful function of an organism but to mechanisms in nature, such as natural selection and adaptation, which promote or maintain adaptation and thus give the appearance of purpose or design.[31] In a sense Charles Darwin did for biology in the nineteenth century what Albert Einstein did for physics in the twentieth century: put to rest the understanding of nature as static and fixed.

Darwin's denial of design in nature was almost universally interpreted as a denial of the divine in nature.[32] His offense lay in the proposal that natural selection is a blind process that operates through random variations, and that this aimless mechanism accounts for all forms of life on earth. American philosopher Daniel Dennett called Darwin's theory of evolution a dangerous idea because it challenges religious belief that the universe is here for a reason.[33] John Haught writes: "Darwin dropped a religiously explosive bomb into the Victorian culture of his contemporaries, and Christians ever since, including some but not all theologians, have been scrambling to defuse it or toss it out of harm's way."[34]

Although Darwin showed how natural selection could account for species variation, he could not explain the appearance of mind or consciousness. As a result, "mental qualities were either squeezed out of existence or dismissed as mere causally inefficacious and epiphenomenal by-products of brain processes."[35] Wolfgang Pauli found this troublesome because scientific theories themselves were "products of the psyche."[36] More recently, in 2013, philosopher Thomas Nagel wrote that

---

[31] Ayala, 13.

[32] Barbara Taylor Brown, *The Luminous Web* (Cambridge, MA: Cowley Publications, 2000), 25.

[33] See John F. Haught, *God after Darwin* (New York: Routledge, 2007), 11.

[34] John Haught, *Making Sense of Evolution: Darwin, God, and the Drama of Life* (Louisville, KY: Westminster John Knox Press, 2010), xiii.

[35] Peter B. Todd, *The Individuation of God: Integrating Science and Religion* (Wilmette, IL: Chiron, 2012), 61.

[36] Todd, 61.

the mind has eluded physical explanation because "the great advances in the physical and biological sciences excluded the mind from the physical world."[37] Hence Darwinian evolution can explain material complexity, but it treats consciousness as a later phenomenon, one that appears at higher levels in the process.

There is an intrinsic contradiction in Darwinian evolution because, apart from mind, nothing can be said of matter. Teilhard de Chardin was aware of this problem and held to a dual-aspect monist position to explain evolution. Life, according to Teilhard, is "a specific effect of matter turned complex; a property that is present in the entire cosmic stuff."[38] He considered matter and consciousness not as "two substances" or "two different modes of existence, but as two aspects of the same cosmic stuff."[39] From the Big Bang onward there is a "withinness" and "withoutness," or what Teilhard called "radial energy" and "tangential energy."[40] Consciousness is, in a sense, the withinness or "inside" of matter, and attraction is the "outside" of matter; hence, matter is both attractive (tangential) and transcendent (radial). The complementarity of mind and matter explains both the rise of biological complexity and the corresponding rise of consciousness. In his essay on "The Position of Man in Nature and the Significance of Human Socialization," Teilhard indicated that intelligent life cannot be considered in the universe any longer as a superficial accident but, rather, must be considered to be under pressure everywhere—ready to burst from the smallest crack no matter where in the universe—and, once actualized, it is incapable of

---

[37] Thomas Nagel, "The Core of 'Mind and Cosmos,'" *New York Times*, Opinion Pages (August 18, 2013).

[38] Pierre Teilhard de Chardin, *Man's Place in Nature*, trans. Noel Lindsay (New York: Collins, 1966), 34.

[39] Pierre Teilhard de Chardin, *The Phenomenon of Man*, trans. Bernard Wall (New York: Harper and Row, 1959), 56–64.

[40] Teilhard, *Phenomenon of Man*, 56–64.

not using every opportunity and means to arrive at the extreme of its potentiality, externally of complexity, and internally of consciousness.[41] The universe orients itself toward intelligent, conscious, self-reflective life.

What scientists are realizing today (although still a topic of debate) is that the whole of life, from the Big Bang onwards, is the emergence of mind or consciousness. As the exterior levels of physical complexity increase so too do the interior levels of consciousness. A system is conscious if it can communicate information, which in turn serves as its organizational function. Anything capable of self-organizing possesses a level of consciousness insofar as there is flow of information. Ilya Prigogine, whose work on complex dynamical systems won him the Nobel Prize, said that communication or consciousness exists even in chemical reactions where molecules know, in some way, what the other molecules will do even over macroscopic distances. Mind and matter are neither separate nor reducible to the other and, yet, neither can function without the other.

Mind, Matter, and Spirit

The ubiquity of mind in nature is the same flow of activity that each of us inherits in a unique way. Nobel Prize–winning scientist Roger Sperry writes that the human mind is an emergent property of the brain as a whole. Only when the brain is understood as a single integrated system, according to Sperry, can we understand the nature of mind.[42] Gerald Edelman and Giulio Tononi

---

[41] Teilhard de Chardin, "The Position of Man in Nature and the Significance of Human Socialization," in *The Future of Man* (1946; reprint, New York: HarperCollins, 1964), 211–17.

[42] Roger Sperry, "A Modified Concept of Consciousness," *Psychological Review* 76 (1969): 532–36; idem, "New Mindset on Consciousness," interview, *Sunrise* magazine (December 1987/January 1978), copyright 1987 by Theosophical University Press.

proposed that there is a "dynamic core" responsible for human consciousness.[43] Human consciousness depends not only on a particular region in the brain but also on its complexity. Brain complexity is a function of the degree of interconnectedness that is increased exponentially through feedback and feed-forward loops. Some scholars suggest that since human consciousness has emerged out of cosmic wholeness and is part of it, it is possible to infer that an element of consciousness is active in the universe, that is, *cosmic consciousness.*

The ordinary world of our sense experience, the only known entity that can react to the flow of information, is conscious mind. If consciousness is related to complexity, then mind is an emergent process of complexification and consciousness. Joseph Bracken suggests that mind is the place where synthesizing activity occurs. Mind is itself an instance of an activity that is going on everywhere in the universe at the same time. To reflect upon the mind as an instance of pure activity is to gain an insight into the nature or deeper reality of the universe as a whole. In Bracken's view, "creativity is at work in atoms and molecules unconsciously, even as it is at work both consciously and unconsciously in the workings of the human mind."[44] From the mind-like aspects of elementary particles Sir Arthur Eddington generalizes: "The universe is of the nature of a thought or sensation in a universal Mind. . . . The stuff of the world is mind-stuff."[45] Mind involves relationship, and matter is that which

---

[43] Gerald M. Edelman and Giulio Tononi, "Reentry and the Dynamic Core: Neural Correlates of Conscious Experience," in *Neural Correlates of Consciousness: Empirical and Conceptual Questions*, ed. Thomas Metzinger (Cambridge, MA: MIT Press, 2000), 139–53; Gerald M. Edelman, *A Universe of Consciousness: How Matter Becomes Imagination* (New York: Basic Books, 2001); cf. Jean Askenasy and Joseph Lehmann, "Consciousness, Brain, Neuroplasticity," *Frontiers in Psychology* (July 10, 2013).

[44] Joseph Bracken, *Does God Play Dice?* (Collegeville, MN: Liturgical Press, 2012), 26.

[45] Sir Arthur Eddington, *The Nature of the Physical World* (UK: Andesite Press, 2015), 273.

it relates. Neither on its own could evolve or express anything; together they give us ourselves and our world.[46]

Interestingly, Teilhard saw the integral relationship of mind and matter and the openness of these to greater complexity and consciousness. Consciousness, complexity, and movement are essential features of biological evolution in the same way that space, time, and volume are essential features of the universe. There is an unyielding openness to biological and cosmic life that is not adequately explained by materiality, the orientation itself being "spirit" or energy overflow, an innate propensity of matter toward spirit. Teilhard saw this energy overflow of matter as the religious dimension of evolution. He writes: "There is only one real evolution, the evolution of convergence, because it alone is positive and creative."[47]

The openness of matter to spirit and the propensity of nature to complexify on higher levels of unity impelled Teilhard to posit that religion and evolution go together. The word *religion* is used here not in terms of formal beliefs or rituals but in the root sense of "tethering" or "binding." Nature has an intrinsic orientation toward wholeness, a horizon of complexifying wholeness oriented to a future anticipation of ultimate wholeness. The presence of mind in matter and the openness of matter to greater wholeness *is* the religious phenomenon of nature. Teilhard writes: "To my mind, the religious phenomenon, taken as a whole, is simply the reaction of the universe as such, of collective consciousness and human action in process of development."[48] There is a fecundity of the earth's spiritual energy and religion is the orientation of this overflow towards unified life.[49] The purpose of religion, according to Teilhard, is to enkindle the wholeness

---

[46] Zohar, *Quantum Self,* 236.

[47] Pierre Teilhard de Chardin, *Christianity and Evolution: Reflections on Science and Religion,* trans. Rene Hague (New York: Harcourt, 1971), 87.

[48] Pierre Teilhard de Chardin, "How I Believe," in *Christianity and Evolution,* 118–19.

[49] Pierre Teilhard de Chardin, *Science and Christ,* trans. Rene Hague (New York: Harper and Row, 1965), 100.

of life: "to sustain and spur on the progress of life."[50] Religion has a cosmic function before it has a human function, because the human person emerges out of cosmic life and recapitulates that life on the level of self-reflective consciousness. "Religion and evolution should neither be confused nor divorced," Teilhard writes: "They are destined to form one single continuous organism, in which their respective lives prolong, are dependent on, and complete one another."[51] In fact, without the cosmic function of religion, human religion makes no real sense, at least in terms of evolution. If we are to progress or evolve, he thought, we must release ourselves from religious individualism and confront the general religious experience, which is cosmic and evolutionary, and involve ourselves in it.[52]

Human Evolution

Human evolution is the process by which human beings developed on earth from now-extinct primates. We are the only living members of what many zoologists refer to as the tribe *Hominini*, but there is abundant *fossil* evidence to indicate that we were preceded for millions of years by other hominins, such as *Ardipithecus*, *Australopithecus*, and other species of *Homo*, and that our species also lived for a time contemporaneously with at least one other member of our *genus*, *H. neanderthalensis* (the *Neanderthals*). We now know of more than twenty hominin species that are part of our family tree. At least half of these species are based on fossils unearthed in the last thirty years. Diarmuid O'Murchu identifies the oldest ancestor on our family tree, given the name Toumai, meaning "hope for life." The bones of Toumai were discovered in 2001 in the Goran region of Chad, North Africa. The discovery was classified as hominin and thus may

---

[50] Pierre Teilhard de Chardin, *Human Energy*, trans. J. M. Cohen (New York: Harcourt Brace Jovanovich, 1969), 44.

[51] Pierre Teilhard de Chardin, *How I Believe,* trans. Rene Hague (New York: Harper and Row, 1969), 60–61.

[52] Teilhard, "How I Believe," 118.

be an ancestor common to both chimpanzees and humans, yet with some unique human characteristics: "While the braincase has distinctive chimpanzee features, and measures merely 350cc, the teeth are closer to those of humans, and the face includes brow ridges, a human feature not found in any living great ape. Examination of the neck muscles indicate that this species may have walked upright."[53] The quasi-human features of hominins support the process of emergence and complexification.[54] Although we are not descended from apes, humans and apes share a common unidentified ancestor. "The chimpanzees, bonobos, orangutans, and gorillas are better described as *our first cousins*, with whom we share over 98 percent of the same DNA,"[55] although the exact nature of our evolutionary relationships has been the subject of debate and investigation.

The story of humans within evolutionary history begins around 4.5 billion years ago when the earth and other planets began forming around the young sun. Humans, like mammals, have existed on earth for a relatively short time, only about 0.04 percent of the earth's existence (0.04 percent of 4.5 billion). The oldest known fossil attributed to our genus, *Homo,* dates to about 2.8 million years ago.[56] The ability to make stone tools was thought to be the hallmark of our genus. The oldest tool-manufacturing culture known may be as early as 3.3 million years ago and made either by Australopithecines or an earlier form of the *Homo* lineage. "Two categories of tools have been identified: chopped stones with sharpened edges and flakes used primarily as cutters possibly to dismember game carcasses and to strip tough plants."[57]

---

[53] Diarmuid O'Murchu, *Ancestral Grace: Meeting God in Our Human Story* (Maryknoll, NY: Orbis Books, 2008), 21.

[54] K. Kris Hirst, "What Is a Hominin?" *Thought* (September 6, 2017).

[55] O'Murchu, *Ancestral Grace,* 22.

[56] A'ndrea Elyse Messer, "Earliest Known Fossil of the Genus *Homo* Dates to 2.8 to 2.75 Million Years Ago," *Penn State News,* March 4, 2015.

[57] O'Murchu, *Ancestral Grace,* 45; Sonia Harmand et al. "3.3-million-year-old Stone Tools from Lomekwi 3, West Turkana, Kenya," *Nature* 521 (7552): 310–15.

Our ancestors first harnessed fire anywhere from 1.8 million to around 800,000 years ago. According to one theory the invention of cooking allowed us to gain more energy from meat, which fueled the dramatic evolution of the human brain. Bigger brains and more dexterous hands, in turn, were the prerequisites for the developments that set humans apart, including complex language, art, and agriculture, all of which emerged in the past 100,000 years. What we do know is that human evolution has coincided with environmental change, including cooling, drying, and wider climate fluctuations over time.[58]

The modern human physique first appeared in Africa about 200,000 to 300,000 years ago. It then spread into the rest of the Old World, interbreeding with existing populations of archaic human forms.[59] Although scholars have debated whether or not our first ancestors emerged out of Africa or out of Asia, recent evidence supports the African connection.[60] The species *Australopithecus afarensis* was discovered in the Hadar region of Ethiopia in 1973 by Donald Johanson of Arizona State University. As the skeleton was being pieced together, it turned out to be that of a young woman whom Johanson called Lucy. Her pelvic structure shows upright posture, her teeth are distinctively human, and she dates as far back as 3.2 million years ago.[61] A slightly more evolved form, dated 2–3 million years ago, was discovered later, which had a more humanlike cranium, a slightly larger brain, and more humanoid facial features. This discovery was made in South Africa.

"The first bipedal primates are classified by paleontologists as hominids, and these first hominids had not yet developed the

---

[58] Smithsonian, "What Does It Mean to Be Human?" http://humanorigins.si.edu/research/climate-and-human-evolution/climate-effects-human-evolution.

[59] Denis Edwards, *Ecology at the Heart of Faith: The Change of the Heart That Leads to a New Way of Living on Earth* (Maryknoll, NY: Orbis Books, 2008), 12–13.

[60] O'Murchu, *Ancestral Grace*, 36.

[61] Donald Johanson, *From Lucy to Language* (New York: Simon and Schuster, 2006).

large brain, teeth structure, and skeletal features identified as Homo. Instead, they predate and sometimes overlap the Homo species and are known as the Australopithecines."[62] The bipedal species *Homo erectus* was more proficient at toolmaking because this species was tied closely with the earth, drawing nourishment from natural foods and grasses. They used natural resources for shelter and may have built rafts and traveled by sea, although this claim is still controversial.[63] Remnants of the Neanderthal species, with their large brain size and robust figures capable of enduring colder climates, were found in Gibralter (1848) and Dusseldorf, Germany (1856). What is significant for Neanderthals is their complex function of inventing weapons such as hand axes and spears, building shelters to protect themselves against harsh conditions, and the development of language and song. Cave art found in Spain shows a species attuned to art, and they are the first humans known to bury the dead with care.[64]

Our species of humans, *Homo sapiens*, first began to evolve nearly 200,000 years ago in association with technologies not unlike those of the early Neanderthals. It is now clear that early *Homo sapiens* did not come after the Neanderthals but were their contemporaries, although Neanderthals were well established in Eurasia along with Denisovans. Scholars suggest that Neanderthals, Denisovans, and "modern" humans may have descended from a common ancestor, although this is far from being clear.[65]

In telling the story of human evolution we can begin to appreciate that our existence as a species has a long lineage that remains outside our everyday consciousness, creating a false impression that we are made fully formed by some divine *fiat*. Nothing could be further from the truth. Up until the early

---

[62] The Genus Austrolopithecus," online (New York: Columbia University).

[63] Bruce Bower, "Ancient Hominids May Have Been Seafarers," *Science News,* January 8, 2010.

[64] Michael Greshko, "World's Oldest Cave Art Found—And Neanderthals Made It," *National Geographic* (February 22, 2018).

[65] Michael Marshall, "We May Not Know What Our Common Ancestor with Neanderthals Looked Like," *New Scientist* (April 1, 2020).

twentieth century we thought of the human person as a substantive being who appeared on the scene of biological life. We now know that the human person is not "readymade" but rather the outflow of billions of years of evolution. Thomas King writes that "throughout the ages life has constructed organisms of ever greater complexity, and with this increased complexity the organism has also shown an increase in consciousness, that is, an increase of intention, of acting with a goal."[66] Teilhard de Chardin saw human evolution as part of the whole natural process of creativity and generativity. He spoke of evolution as a process of convergence due to an unyielding force of attraction in the universe, directing biological life toward maximum human organization and consciousness. He used the word *convergence* in a way that differed from evolutionary science. When evolutionary scientists speak of convergence, they are generally referring to the phenomenon of similar types of organisms evolving in a parallel fashion from different evolutionary lines of development. For Teilhard, *convergence* means a grouping of cells in a living body or a grouping of individuals under the influence of a force of attraction, which he identified as a "center to center" attraction. Convergence is the ongoing process of complexification, and the process of convergence and complexity is the unfolding of consciousness in evolution.[67]

The human person is not the great exception to evolution but its recapitulation. The extreme physical complexity (brain size and complexity) marks the human person as the most highly synthesized form of matter known in the universe. According to Teilhard "the complex human is the most perfectly and deeply centered of all cosmic particles within the field of our experience."[68] The human person is integrally part of evolution in that we rise from the process but in reflecting on the process we stand apart from it. Teilhard defines reflection as "the power acquired by a

---

[66] Thomas M. King, *Teilhard's Mysticism of Knowing* (New York: Seabury Press, 1981), 33.

[67] Teilhard, *Christianity and Evolution*, 87.

[68] Teilhard, *Future of Man*, 90.

consciousness to turn in upon itself, to take possession of itself *as an object* . . . no longer merely to know, but to know that one knows."[69] He quotes a phrase of Julian Huxley: The human person "is nothing else than evolution become conscious of itself."[70] To this idea Teilhard adds, "The consciousness of each of us is evolution looking at itself and reflecting upon itself."[71] Thus the human person emerges from the evolutionary process and is integral to evolution. This person is "the point of emergence in nature, at which this deep cosmic evolution culminates and declares itself."[72]

What Is a Person?

The word *person* needs clarification, as biology itself cannot account for personhood. The word *person* can be traced back to Greek and Roman antiquity. It comes from the Etruscan *phersu* (the Greek equivalent is *prosopon;* the Latin is *persona*) meaning a mask or the wearer of the mask. In its root meaning, the Latin *persona* (*per* or "through" and *sonare* or "to sound") means "to sound through." A person is one in whom there is a "sounding through" just as, on stage, a *persona* is an actor or the role of an actor, a "mask" so to speak, through which a character is portrayed. Hence the word *person* connotes relationality. To define a person is to ask who it is or how it is related. The notion of person arose in Christian theological discussions and found a relational home among the fourth-century Greek Cappadocian fathers.[73] Catherine LaCugna writes:

> The ontological question for these theologians was not answered by pointing to the "self-existent," to a being as it is

---

[69] Teilhard, *Phenomenon of Man*, 165.

[70] Teilhard, 221.

[71] Teilhard, *Phenomenon of Man*, 221.

[72] Teilhard, *Human Energy*, 23. Teilhard's position on human evolution put him at odds with church teaching, primarily because he rejected the idea of original sin in light of evolution.

[73] Catherine LaCugna, *God for Us: The Trinity and Christian Life* (New York: HarperSanFrancisco, 1993), 260.

determined by its own boundaries, but to a being which in its ekstasis breaks through these boundaries in a movement of communion. A person is thus not an individual but an open and ecstatic reality, referred to others for his or her existence. The actualization of personhood takes place in self-transcendence, the movement of freedom toward communion with other persons.[74]

The basis for the Cappadocian idea of personhood was the way they conceived God as ultimately personal: "God's ultimate reality cannot be located in substance (what it is in itself), but only in personhood, what God is toward another."[75] This is a different understanding of personhood from the more substantive definitions. The Roman senator Boethius in the fifth century defined a person as an "individual substance of rational nature" (*persona est rationalis naturae individua substantia*),[76] emphasizing substance over relationality. This definition "solidified the individualistic connotations of person as center of consciousness, and had a great impact on scholastic theology."[77] Beatrice Bruteau in the twentieth century distinguished between an individual and a person by saying that an individual is on a lower stage of reflexive consciousness while personhood reflects a higher stage of self-reflexive consciousness. Hence, she indicates, only persons can enter into communion consciousness; individuals remain external to one another.[78] These various understandings lead to a working definition: *A person is a conscious being in relation to everything else, one in whom the matrix of relational life is expressed in a particular way and who contributes to the*

---

[74] LaCugna, *God for Us*, 260.

[75] LaCugna, 260.

[76] The definition is given in Boethius, *Liber de Persona et duabus naturis*, chap. 3.2.

[77] LaCugna, *God for Us*, 247.

[78] Beatrice Bruteau, "Freedom: 'If Anyone Is in Christ, That Person Is a New Creation,'" in *The Grand Option: Personal Transformation and a New Creation* (Notre Dame, IN: University of Notre Dame Press, 2001), 157.

unfolding of the world in a particular way. Like an eddy in a stream, a person is a vital locus of centering consciousness in the flow of evolution.

Modern science, including psychology, underscores the dynamic nature of personhood, which is constituted by physical-biological behavior and the completion of self within the world. We create the world through our relationships, and, in turn, the world makes a demand on us to respond in relationship. The human person, therefore, emerges from the dynamic interplay of nature and environment. Personhood is a formative process of establishing a center of identity based on biological, physical, and cultural materials, and shaping those materials into an understanding of self, insofar as self is in relation to the world in which it lives. Two criteria that mark the emergence of personhood are coherence and fecundity, that is, struggling to exist amid diverse materials by making every effort to integrate the forces of existence, and optimizing life by regulating, judging, perceiving, planning, and decision making. What we are as persons is never in isolation but always embedded in the universe from which personhood emerges. The integral relationship between person and universe means when our understanding of personhood changes so does our understanding of the universe, and when our understanding of the universe changes, so does our understanding of personhood.

Our world comes about through a mutually creative dialogue between mind and body, between one's personal and material context, and between human culture and the natural world. Based on the insights of modern science, we can speak of the human self as being free and responsible, responsive to others and to the environment, essentially related and naturally committed, and at every moment creative.[79] Once we see that human consciousness emerges from quantum processes, and that, in consequence, human consciousness and the whole world of its creation share a physics with everything else in this universe—with the human body, with all other living things and creatures, with the

---

[79] Zohar, *Quantum Self*, 237.

basic physics of matter and relationship, and with the coherent ground state of the quantum vacuum itself—it becomes impossible to imagine a single aspect of our lives that is not drawn into a coherent whole.[80] Given the essential role of consciousness in evolution, the human person today represents the highest level of self-reflective consciousness and thus the most intense physical being open to spirit. These characteristics do not set humans apart from the earth but rather as the living expression of earth's potential for more life. We have the capacity to think the earth into a greater wholeness and to live on a new level of complexified consciousness. Insights from modern science help us realize that with the emergence of the modern human person, the universe becomes a self-reflective universe.

Summary: Scientists today are realizing that nature is a rich context of relational holism all the way down to the fundamental levels of matter. The dynamic relationship of matter and mind reflect this holism; so too religion is a cosmic function of wholeness, a development that is a constant return and fresh, innovative recapitulation, integral to the ever-complexifying creation as it orients the whole toward more wholeness. This process emerges ultimately in *Homo sapiens,* in our life and the complexity of human consciousness. The human person is the vanguard of cosmic evolution; in the human the universe is looking at itself and reflecting itself. To be a human person, therefore, is to be conscious of belonging to a whole and to act as a whole within a larger whole. The orientation of matter toward spirit finds a new level of meaning in the human person who is open to ultimate meaning and concern.

---

[80] Zohar, 236.

2

Axial Consciousness

Pre-Axial Consciousness

Modern humans are thought to have arrived in Europe from Africa approximately 40,000–45,000 years ago. German philosopher Karl Jaspers coined the phrase *Achsenzeit* (axial age or axis age in English) in 1949 to describe a time between approximately 800 BCE and 200 BCE when the spiritual foundations of modern humanity were established. As a pivotal point of human consciousness, Jaspers's axial age provides a framework to assess the emergence of the human person as person. The pre-axial period is the age of the tribe or the collective, which could extend as far back as 64,000 BCE with the Neanderthals, since Neanderthal cave art seems to show no real cognitive gap between Neanderthals and modern humans.[1] According to F. LeRon Shults, "Paleobiological research indicates that religion appeared alongside tool making and artistic expression relatively suddenly sometime in the upper Paleolithic era."[2] Steven Mithen describes a cognitive fluidity in the early modern human that was expressed in art, science, and religion. This more advanced cognitive capacity suggests a religious interpretation of experience that

---

[1] Emma Marris, "Neanderthal Artists Made Oldest Known Cave Paintings," *Nature* (February 22, 2018).

[2] F. LaRon Shults, *Christology and Science* (Grand Rapids, MI: Eerdmans, 2008), 41.

differentiated *Homo sapiens* from other human types between 100,000 and 60,000 years ago whereby the emerging capacity to construct and interpret symbols helped make sense of one's place within the cosmos.[3] Pre-axial consciousness was a level of religious-mythic consciousness that was cosmic, collective, tribal, and ritualistic. Ancient civilizations looked at the physical and human worlds as interdependent. An imbalance in one sphere could result in an imbalance in the other. Many pre-axial people were hunter-gatherers, and blood sacrifice ritual oblations were celebrated in community.

Ewert Cousins notes that the pre-axial consciousness of tribal cultures was located in the cosmos and in fertility cycles of nature.[4] These early humans—or first earth persons—mimed and venerated nature; for them, nature appeared as a sacred reality determining their destiny. Cultures were intimately related to the cosmos and to the fertility cycles of nature, giving rise to a rich and creative harmony between primal peoples and the world of nature. This harmony was explored, expressed, and celebrated in myth and ritual.

While early humans were closely linked to the cosmos, they were also closely linked to one another. They felt themselves part of nature and experienced themselves in relationship with their tribe. It was precisely the web of interrelationships within the tribe that sustained them psychologically, energizing all aspects of their lives.[5] To be separated from the tribe threatened them with death, not only physical but also psychological. However, their relation to the collective whole usually did not extend beyond their own tribe; indeed, they often looked upon other tribes as hostile. Yet within their tribe they felt organically related to the whole, including the lifecycles of nature and the cosmos.

---

[3] Steven Mithen, *The Prehistory of the Mind: The Cognitive Origins of Art, Religion, and Science* (London: Thames and Hudson, 1996).

[4] Ewert Cousins, *Christ of the Twenty-First Century* (Rockport, MA: Element Books, 1992), 5.

[5] Cousins, *Christ of the Twenty-First Century*, 5.

Pre-axial people believed that human action was required to maintain the order of the universe, and they conducted rituals and sacrifices to renew and restore it.[6] The order of the natural cosmos followed the order in the social cosmos. Lack of order in the cosmos—for example, infertility in the realm of plants—could only be repaired if one began by reestablishing the human social order. Justice among humans contributed to maintaining the world in movement. Diarmuid O'Murchu writes:

> Rituals evolved to mark the beginning and end of human life, and also the beginning and end of each season. Rituals were developed to negotiate and make sense of disruption and disorder, the unexpected occurrence of sickness in humans or storms in nature. Many such rituals were structured around reconciliation and healing, with the person and the surrounding environment always perceived as two different expressions of the one-life continuum.[7]

The *Axis Mundi*

Religion scholar Mircea Eliade spoke of an *axis mundi*, a cosmic axis around which everything, both literally and metaphorically, revolved for pre-axial persons. Indeed, the axis of the world was an image of connection between the mundane terrestrial plane and the transcendent home of the spirit above. Eliade saw the motif of the separation of heaven and earth in creation myths pointing to a fundamental alienation from the primordial unity of spiritual being. Consequently, people could only maintain their connection to the spiritual sources of meaning through an imaginal conduit, an *axis mundi*, which became implicitly present

---

[6] Remi Brague, *The Wisdom of the World: The Human Experience of the Universe in Western Thought,* trans. Teresa Lavendar Fagan (Chicago: University of Chicago Press, 2004), 6.

[7] Diarmuid O'Murchu, *Ancestral Grace: Meeting God in Our Human Story* (Maryknoll, NY: Orbis Books, 2008), 80.

in religious ritual and was embodied architecturally in important temples and sacred sites.

Eliade found evidence for this *axis mundi* across the ancient world and throughout the documentation of traditional peoples. Ancient cultures emphasized the contrast between the center and the periphery. Eliade was especially taken by ethnographies of Aboriginal Australians, whom he called "true primitives," because isolation on their island continent seemed to assure and preserve their genuine culture of interdependence, living evidence of the very earliest human notions of a sacred bond. One report of Aboriginal beliefs served to root Eliade's conviction of the primacy of a sky- and axis-orientated cosmos in the deepest strata of our species' culture. He wrote of this in his 1957 classic, *The Sacred and the Profane*:

> According to the traditions of an Arunta tribe, the Achilpa [Tjilpa], in mythical times the divine being Numbakula cosmicized their future territory, created their Ancestor, and established their institutions. From the trunk of a gum tree Numbakula fashioned the sacred pole (kauwa-auwa) and, after anointing it with blood, climbed it and disappeared into the sky. This pole represents the cosmic axis, for it is around the sacred pole that territory becomes habitable, hence is transformed into a world. The sacred pole consequently plays an important role ritually. During their wanderings the Achilpa always carry it with them and choose the direction they are able to take by the direction toward which it bends. This allows them, while being continually on the move, to be always in "their world" and, at the same time, in communication with the sky into which Numbakula vanished.[8]

Based on his studies of tribal culture and religion, Eliade was convinced of a spiritual pole linking heaven and earth. Destruction of this pole would bring about chaos in the environment:

---

[8] Mircea Eliade, *The Sacred and the Profane: The Nature of Religion* (New York: Harcourt, 1968), 32–33.

For the pole to be broken denotes catastrophe; it is like "the end of the world," reversion to chaos. Spencer and Gillen report that once, when the pole was broken, the entire clan were in consternation; they wandered about aimlessly for a time, and finally lay down on the ground together and waited for death to overtake them.[9]

While the concept of a spiritual link between the realms of existence was reasonable for pre-axial communities, Eliade did not distinguish hunter-gatherer societies from agricultural ones, and the spiritual thread was not consistent across these different societies. Scientists indicate that hunter-gatherers were much more fluid and chaotic in their organization and thus not as symmetrically organized as agricultural tribes.

The basic mistake of Eliade, then, and of the Traditionalist school, was that they weren't "traditional" enough. In their efforts to establish their obsession with centralized cosmic hierarchy in the roots of human being, they projected the concerns of pre-modern agricultural myth—which is profoundly geared toward images of political stratification—back onto the pre-agricultural world of the hunter-gatherer. And this world was the entire human world until very recently—for more than 90% of our species' existence. A true traditionalism would need to go beyond the narrow, constructed "naturalness" of hierarchical society, and embrace our complex and diverse history—in which the decentered and fluid cosmos of mobile hunter-gatherers figures prominently.[10]

While early tribal communities may have been more complex than what Eliade described, they did show a particular type of consciousness that psychologist Julian Jaynes calls the "bicameral

---

[9] Eliade, *The Sacred and the Profane*, 33.

[10] Gyrus, "Eliade's Aboriginal Cosmic Axis," Dreamflesh blog, September 2014.

mind," a type of mind typical of early *Homo sapiens*. The cognitive functions of the bicameral mind were divided between one part of the brain which appeared to be "speaking" and a second part which "listened and obeyed," undergirding the cosmic religion described by Eliade. Jaynes and others suggest that bicameral mentality was the normal and ubiquitous state of the human mind as recently as three thousand years ago, near the end of the Mediterranean Bronze Age.[11]

Axial Consciousness

The term *axial age* (or *axial period*) is a controversial one but I am using it here as a heuristic to help make sense of the complexification of consciousness and the emergence of religion.[12] I do not consider the axial period a factual history of events but a general model that undergirds an emergent historical pattern of religious consciousness; that is, human consciousness shifted to a new level due to a complexity of factors including technology, socialization, urbanization, politicization, and economics, reflecting a new sense of self in relation to the cosmos. The religious dimension of this shift in consciousness became focused on the inner self and transcendent divine. The new axial period differed from pre-axial consciousness in that it was marked by the rise of the individual and religious cultures. Axial persons were in possession of their own identity, but they lost their organic relationship to nature and community, severing the harmony with nature and the tribe. They now ran the risk of being alienated from the matrix of being and life. With their new powers they could criticize the social structure and by analysis discover the abstract laws of science and metaphysics, but they could also

---

[11] See Julian Jaynes, *The Origin of Consciousness in the Breakdown of the Bicameral Mind* (New York: Mariner, 2000).

[12] For a critical discussion on the axial period, see Antony Black, "The 'Axial Period': What Was It and What Does It Signify?" *Review of Politics* 70 (2008): 23–39.

find themselves as mere spectators of a drama of which they were simply a part.[13]

Jaspers suggested that this axial period amounted to "a new departure within mankind," meaning "a kind of critical, reflective questioning of the actual and a new vision of what lies beyond."[14] Jaspers and others hold that the intellectual and spiritual achievements of this time have inspired most of humanity ever since the foundations of all major world civilizations were laid down. He writes:

> What is new about this age . . . is that man becomes conscious of Being as a whole, of himself *and his limitations. He experiences the terror of the world and his own powerlessness.* He asks radical questions. Face to face with the void he strives for liberation and redemption. *By consciously recognizing his limits* he sets himself the highest goals. *He experiences absoluteness in the depths of selfhood and in the lucidity of transcendence.*[15]

The internalization and, in some cases, universalization of basic norms meant that the transtribal association was now legitimized at a deeper level of meaning for the individual than had been achieved under previous sacred monarchies. There were now strong communities based on intellectual assent to certain forms of behavior and/or propositions. In general, post-breakthrough societies had a greater capacity for social organization,

---

[13] Ewert H. Cousins, "The World Religions: Facing Modernity Together," globalethic.org.

[14] Benjamin I. Schwartz, "The Age of Transcendence," *Daedalus* 104 (1975): 3.

[15] Karl Jaspers, "The Axial Period," in Karl Jaspers, *The Origin and Goal of History* (New Haven, CT: Yale University Press, 1953), 2; cf. *The Origin and Diversity of Axial Age Civilizations*, ed. S. N. Eisenstadt (Albany: State University of New York Press, 1986); Karen Armstrong, in *The Great Transformation: The World in the Time of Buddha, Socrates, Confucius, and Jeremiah* (London: Atlantic Books, 2006).

harmony, and long-term stability.[16] Cultural diffusion took place as Buddhism moved into China, and Hinduism and Buddhism into Southeast Asia. Greek culture spread throughout the Mediterranean area and the Middle East, as far as Central Asia. This is more comprehensible if we see the breakthrough as a realization of potentialities that all humans share. They actually seem to have made people more, not less, capable of learning from one another: Indians adopted Western philosophy and science; Westerners learned yoga and meditation.[17] Anthony Black states, however, that not all parts of the world shared in this axial breakthrough. In fact, the determining factor in the rise of organized civilization was religion. Black writes:

> "Primitive" societies, such as sub-Saharan Africa and pre-Columbian America, suffered severe drawbacks when they came into contact with the mentally more developed societies. They seem to have lacked, among other things, a *sufficiently unifying set of beliefs and practices*. Societies that were advanced but had no breakthrough of the kind we have discussed—Egypt and Mesopotamia—found themselves engulfed by new, more "advanced" ways of thinking; they were successively Hellenized, Christianized, Islamicized.[18]

The axial age was a pivotal time in human history as human beings began to reflect for the first time about individual existence and the meaning of life and death. Increasing urban

---

[16] Eisenstadt, *Origin and Diversity of Axial Age Civilizations*, 299–300.

[17] Ian Tattersall, "The Rise of Homo Sapiens: How We Came to Be Human," *Scientific American*, special edition (*Becoming Human: Evolution and the Rise of Intelligence*) 16, no. 2 (2006), 66–73; Kate Wong, "The Morning of the Modern Mind," in *Becoming Human*, 74–83. Jaspers writes that between China, India, and the West, "profound mutual comprehension was possible from the moment they met" (*Origin and Goal of History*, 8).

[18] Black, "The Axial Period," 38–39. Emphasis added.

civilization, initially brought about under the leadership of a priestly ruling class, encouraged trade and brought different societies closer together. But as urban life accelerated and expanded, it disrupted the old sense of order. This new way of living generated unprecedented social and political conflict and an increase in violence and aggression. Old customs could no longer be taken for granted. People began to question their own beliefs as they came into contact with others whose beliefs were different. They were challenged to look at themselves in different ways and entertain new ideas or cling steadfastly to old ones. With a rise in population and the mixing of cultures, more people were exposed to realities of life such as sickness, greed, suffering, inhumanity, and social injustice. As a result, people began to experience themselves as separate from others for the very first time. In this new age, Jaspers claims, "were born the fundamental categories within which we still think today; *and the beginnings of the world religions, by which human beings still live, were created.* The step into universality was taken in every sense."[19]

Axial consciousness generated a new self-awareness, including awareness of autonomy and a new sense of individuality. The human person as *subject* emerged. William Thompson states that "what makes this period the 'axis' of human history, even our own history today, is the fact that humans emerged as 'individuals' in the proper sense."[20] The awareness of the self in the present brought with it awareness of the self after death. People began to search for more comprehensive religious and ethical concepts and to formulate a more enlightened morality in which individuals were responsible for their own destiny. During the axial age a new mode of thinking developed almost simultaneously in four major areas of the world: China, India, the Middle East, and Northern Mediterranean Europe. Whereas pre-axial consciousness was tribal, axial consciousness was individual.

---

[19] Jaspers, "The Axial Period," 2.

[20] William M. Thompson, *Christ and Consciousness: Exploring Christ's Contribution to Human Consciousness* (New York: Paulist Press, 1977), 21.

"Know thyself" became the watchword of Greece. The Upani-shads identified the atman, the transcendent center of the self. The Buddha charted the way of individual enlightenment. The Jewish prophets awakened individual moral responsibility.[21] Hence, in the axial period the world religions as we know them today emerged with a sense of divine transcendence, moral order, and longing for fulfillment. Jaspers disclaims the notion that the axial period represents a universal stage in human evolution because it is neither irreversible nor inevitable; however, there is no reason not to view this period as an evolution of conscious-ness since none of the world religions has shown reversibility in their development.

The sense of individual identity, as distinct from the tribe and nature, is the most characteristic mark of axial consciousness. John Cobb states that what lies at the basis of the axial period is the increasing role that rationality came to have at this time.[22] The more profound role of reason in human life had several implications. Rationality—the ability to control, check, and ana-lyze—began to supersede mythical thinking, which was governed by projection, fantasy, and fulfillment.

Axial consciousness generated a new self-awareness that included awareness of autonomy and a new sense of individual-ity. Jaspers states that with axial consciousness, personality was revealed for the first time in history. With the emergence of the rational individual came a new sense of freedom by which the human person could make conscious and deliberate decisions.[23] New ways of thinking emerged that defined the human person as a self-conscious being. This new consciousness was distinguished from pre-axial consciousness of interdependence; axial con-sciousness was self-reflective and analytic and could be applied to nature in the form of scientific theories and social organization.

---

[21] Cousins, *Christ of the Twenty-First Century,* 6; cf. Ewert H. Cous-ins, "Teilhard's Concept of Religion and the Religious Phenomenon of Our Time," *Teilhard Studies* 49 (Fall 2004): 10–11.

[22] John Cobb, *The Structure of Christian Existence* (New York: Westminster John Knox Press, 1967), 52–59.

[23] Thompson, *Christ and Consciousness,* 23.

The axial period therefore gave birth to society in the form of social critique, to knowledge in the form of philosophy, and to religion in the form of mapping an individual spiritual journey. This self-reflective, analytic, critical consciousness stood in sharp contrast to primal mythic and ritualistic consciousness of the pre-axial period. What the axial period shows is that the complexification and individuation of human community were made possible by the emergence of religion, from cosmic-mythic religion to individual self-conscious religion, including a common set of beliefs and practices that supported the breakthroughs toward moral order.

The One

One of the most distinctive forms of spirituality that emerged in the first axial period, according to Ewert Cousins, was monasticism, the solitary search for the ground of being. Monasticism did not exist among pre-axial peoples, Cousins states, because primal consciousness did not contain the distinct center of individuality necessary to produce the monk as a religious type.[24] In the axial period, consciousness evolved from mythic awareness "governed by 'projection,' fantasy, and wish fulfillment" to critical reflection.[25] Beginning in the sixth century BCE (around the time of axial consciousness) thinkers began to speculate on a divine spark within the soul that animated life toward transcendence. The Greek philosopher Heraclitus for example (ca. 500 BCE) used the term *ethos anthropo* to indicate that there was some higher, spiritual nature within humankind. The Greek word *ethos* signifies "home," "hearth," or "the innermost of the house." The term can be understood in the sense that the god(ly) is home to humankind, meaning that in the center of humanity or central to the individual's innermost personality, there is something godly. The concept of the One developed in Platonic and neo-Platonic traditions while the Stoics also had a concept of

---

[24] Cousins, *Christ of the Twemty-First Century*, 7.
[25] Thompson, *Christ and Consciousness*, 22.

the spark of the soul, a universal fire as the source of everything and the trace of this fire in everything as a fiery, cosmic seed.

The notion of the One began with Plato, who taught that the human soul originates with the Good and flows from the realm of ideas. From this realm it comes into the body, bringing with it the immutable ideas Beauty and Good. Plato's teaching laid the foundation for the later teaching of an immortal soul, or rather, a divine immortal spark within the soul. Even Aristotle, who bequeathed to Western Christianity the concept of soul as a distinct form of the body, and who otherwise tried to eschew some of the pitfalls of Platonic thinking, said in his *De anima* that the highest part of the soul comes from "outside," or "from outside through the door," indicating that there is a core aspect of the human person that is not defined by nature alone.[26] In the third century CE the Neoplatonist Plotinus called the principal source of everything "the One," which he conceived to be in all and beyond every limitation and out of which everything emanates. For Plotinus, our true nature is divine, but we landed ourselves in the unnatural realm of materiality and fragmentation. Since the soul has the imprint of the divine One within it, it has the capacity to return to the One by awakening to its true nature through contemplation.

The axial period marked the culmination of a long process of human complexification and differentiation, an increasing expansion of "worlds" from "the immediate and mythical world of pre-axial people to the conventional and thus increasingly rationalized world of the great civilizations, to the post-conventional world of the axial person marked by individuation.[27] Philosophers and spiritual teachers appeared, calling the public to free themselves from collective consciousness, from the physical world, and from myth and ritual by training the mind. With the awakening of reflective subjectivity, the individual could take a

---

[26] See John P. Wright and Paul Potter, eds., *Psyche and Soma: Physicians and Metaphysicians on the Mind-Body Problem from Antiquity to Enlightenment* (Gloucestershire: Clarendon Press, 2003).

[27] Thompson, *Christ and Consciousness*, 39.

stand against the collectivity, become a distinct moral and spiritual self, and embark on an individual spiritual journey.[28] This expansion or evolution in human development, from myth to rationalization to individuation, characterizes the axial person.

Summary: Evolution shows direction in that it is a movement toward increasing consciousness and complexity. The term *axial period* is used to mark epochs of change in consciousness and religious-cultural orientation. Pre-axial consciousness is collective, tribal, mythic, ritualistic, and animistic. The whole order of nature, including sky, sun, soil, and animals, is part of religious awareness. Eliade's *axis mundi* reflects the deep spiritual threads binding the human community and earth community in a seamless unity. The emergence of axial consciousness marks a process of individuation through which autonomy, subjectivity, and rationality develop. The human person emerges as a free, autonomous individual aware of a divine transcendent power. The rise of the individual is the rise of world religions and the institutions that formalize these religions. Individual self-consciousness gives rise to separateness and becomes a basis for conflict and violence. Hence the complexification of consciousness during this period in terms of the individual is at the same time a contraction of consciousness from cosmic community.

---

[28] Cousins, "Teilhard's Concept," 11.

3

The Rise of the Individual

Christianity and Technology

The shift from pre-axial to axial consciousness entailed a whole new set of structures and relationships, as the human person was now defined by a new set of values. While pre-axial persons distributed the work of the community based on strength, mobility, endurance, and dexterity, the axial person emphasized power, politics, and intellect, influenced by the distinction of the sexes. The rise of gender took on new importance in the axial period as Greek philosophers ascribed properties to male and female. The works of Plato (427–347 BCE) and Aristotle (384–322 BCE) were significant in that they either reflected or refuted the perceptions held of women within the ancient world. Although many critics have deemed Aristotle a misogynist and Plato a champion of the feminist cause, a careful inspection of both works reveals that their positions were not entirely consistent.

Plato promoted the idea that in an ideal society all worthy individuals would receive training and an education, regardless of sex. While he believed women to be physically weaker than men, he also thought that women could become closer to men if they received appropriate training. Aristotle, on the other hand, strongly subscribed to the belief that the universe was composed of opposites. According to Anne Carson, Aristotle attributed to the female attributes of being curved, dark, secret, ever-moving, not self-contained, and lacking boundaries in contrast to the male virtues of being straight, light, honest, good, stable, self-contained, and firmly bounded.[1] Aristotle thought women were fundamentally colder, wetter, and passive, while men were hot, dry, and active. Women were inferior because their bodies were too cold to produce seed (semen). Rather, they functioned as a depository for sperm and a nourishing receptacle for a developing fetus. Hence, Aristotle declared, a woman is a "deformed male who lacks one constituent . . . the principle of the Soul."[2] This led the philosopher to declare that "the relation of male to female is by nature a relation of superior to inferior and ruler to ruled." This set the stage for the patriarchy that came to dominate the structure of Western religion.[3] The inferior intellectual

---

[1] Anne Carson, *Glass, Irony, and God* (New York: New Directions Books, 1995), 124.

[2] Aristotle, "Generation of Animals," Book II, Loeb Classical Library (Cambridge, MA: Harvard University Press: 2019), 175.

[3] Edward Clayton, "Aristotle: Politics," *International Encyclopedia of Philosophy. Patriarchy* is defined as "a hypothetical social system based on the absolute authority of the father or an elderly male over the family group" (Thomas Berry, *The Dream of the Earth* [San Francisco: Sierra Book Club, 1988], 142). It means literally "the rule of the father." In the *patria potestas* of Roman law the father had absolute rights over his entire family, including the right to impose capital punishment. The father owned everything and decided everything. (See Sandra Schneiders, *Beyond Patching: Faith and Feminism in the Catholic Church* [New York: Paulist Press, 1991], 22; see also Maria Calisi, "Bonaventure's Trinitarian Theology as a Feminist Resource," a paper presented at the conference "Franciscan Studies: The Differences Women Are Making," Washington Theological Union, May 31, 1998, 8). Catherine LaCugna states that a particular point of contention in feminist literature is the extent to which patriarchy, as the cult of fatherhood, has been bolstered by the central image of divine fatherhood within Christianity. God is the supreme Father-individual who exists in a relationship of domination (literally, Lordship) over the world. Hierarchy is reflected throughout the order of creation, a hierarchy said to be created and intended by God: male over female, and human over animal, over plant, over inanimate things. The cult of God the Father perpetuates a convenient arrangement by which men rule over women, just as God rules over the world (Catherine LaCugna, *God For Us: The Trinity and Christian Life* [San Francisco: Harper, 1991], 268).

and emotional life of women, according to Aristotle, made them subject to depression and despair compared to men who were less excitable, more mindful, and thus better prepared to lead and organize.[4]

Christianity inherited the principles of Greek philosophy, upon which it built an entire edifice of theological doctrine. What began with Plato and Aristotle eventually deepened into Christian ideals. The biblical myth of Adam and Eve, especially the older account of creation found in the second chapter of Genesis (Gen 2:4—3:24), portrayed an idea of woman similar to that of Aristotle. In this account Adam was created before Eve and received the breath of life directly from God, while Eve was created from the rib of Adam. Adam was the true image of God, and Eve was a weak imitation. Since Eve was not originally created in the image of God, but born from the side of Adam, she did not share in the original divine likeness. Some of the fathers of the church assigned the fall of Adam directly to Eve. "You are the devil's gateway," Tertullian writes. "You desecrated the fatal tree, you first betrayed the law of God, you softened up with your cajoling words the man against whom the devil could not prevail by force. The image of God, Adam, you broke him as if he were a plaything."[5] Because of Eve poor Adam lost his immortality and his share in divine knowledge, as well as his dominion over nature. Eve was the source of humanity's problem, not the solution. Christian theological doctrine was constructed in a way to restore the fallen male Adam to divine likeness. The incarnation presented men with the opportunity to participate in God and to become like God through redemption.

The great North African rhetorician Augustine of Hippo (354–430) said that the original Adam, having been created in God's image, was immortal, but lost the divine resemblance with the fall of Adam. Jesus Christ is the true image of God; he is the

---

[4] Aristotle, "Generation of Animals."

[5] Tertullian, "Disciplinary, Moral, and Ascetical Works," quoted in Marina Warner, *Alone of All Her Sex* (New York: Alfred A. Knopf, 1976), 58.

last "Adam" whose true divinity and immortality were revealed in the resurrection. In being restored in Christ through the ritual of baptismal regeneration, therefore, one is able is recover the original divine image lost in the Fall.

A new understanding of the divine image arose in the Carolingian period, in which the body was relegated to the spirit and the divine image meant a perfection of the rational soul. Recovery of the original image meant abandonment of the material body and renewal of the soul. While the old view of the spirit required the body, in this new view the body was spiritualized and matter became linked with the transcendent. Historian Ernst Benz claims that this belief became one of the strongest impulses for humanity's technological development and realization. "Significantly," he writes, "the founders of modern technology felt that justification of the most far-reaching aims of their technological efforts could be found in the destiny of man as *image of God* and his vocation as a fellow worker of God, to co-operate with God in the establishment of the kingdom and to share God's power over nature."[6]

In his insightful book *The Religion of Technology*, the late Canadian historian David Noble traces the religious roots of technology to the beginning of Western monasticism, showing a similarity between the white, male, Western monk and the white, male, Western scientist. John Scotus Eriguna (815–77), an Irish theologian, believed that through practical effort and study, humankind's prelapsarian (before the Fall) powers could be at least partially recovered and could contribute, in the process, to the restoration of perfection. He invested the mechanical arts (such as cloth making, navigation, architecture, agriculture, ceramics, medicine, weaponry) with spiritual significance, as elements of humankind's Godlikeness, and identified them as vehicles of redemption. Augustine too recognized the significance of the

---

[6] Ernst Benz, *Evolution and Christian Hope* (Garden City, NY: Doubleday, 1975), 123–25; cf. Gerhart B. Ladner, *Ad Imaginem Dei: The Image of Man in Medieval Art* (Latrobe, PA: Archabbey Press, 1965), 32–34, 55.

mechanical arts as efforts to develop material things toward spiritual ends.[7] Through the arts man could recover his divine likeness and be restored to his pristine state of perfection. However, this innate capacity of Godlikeness, according to Eriguna, applied only to men, since women were intellectually weak and inferior and the source of sin. In the resurrection there would only be one sex: the restored male Adam.[8]

In the twelfth century a Calabrian monk, Joachim of Fiore, devised various schemes of history from the beginning of time to the end of time. In one of the schemes he posits three historical ages: the age of the Father, which had passed with the Old Testament; the age of Son, which dawned with the coming of Christ; and the present age of the Spirit. The disciples of Joachim believed they were living in the final age of history. The end of the world was near, and a new earthly paradise was at hand upon the return of Christ. In a curious way this millennial thinking also shaped the dynamic Western conception of technology.

Roger Bacon (1219–92), the legendary Franciscan scholar who studied and taught at the universities of Oxford and Paris, is known as the father of experimental science. He was certain that scientific knowledge would give him mastery over nature and would help prepare for the second coming of Christ. He envisioned the technical world of the future, including submarines, automobiles, airplanes, and other inventions that have become part of modern life.[9] For Bacon, scientific knowledge was in the service of theology. He insisted that science could prepare for the second coming of Christ by recovering in the "sons of Adam" what had been known in the Garden of Eden. He searched for

---

[7] Augustine, *The City of God* (Garden City, NY: Doubleday, 1958), 526–27.

[8] John J. Contreni, "John Scotus, Martin Hiberniensis: The Liberal Arts and Teaching," in *Insular Latin Studies,* ed. Michael W. Herren, vol. 1 (Toronto: Pontifical Institute of Medieval Studies), 25–26.

[9] Richard E. Rubenstein, *Aristotle's Children: How Christians, Muslims, and Jews Rediscovered Ancient Wisdom and Illuminated the Middle Ages* (New York: Harcourt Books, 2003), 188–89.

a *method for science* that could be used to test validity in argu-
ments, combining mathematics with detailed experiential descriptions of discrete phenomena in nature. Millennial preparations
had a utilitarian thrust by enhancing technological prowess
in agriculture, husbandry, mining, metallurgy, chemistry, and
navigation.

In the fourteenth century a well-known Spiritual Franciscan
by the name of John Rupescissa produced a significant volume of
writings on alchemy. He claimed that knowledge of the natural
world, and alchemy in particular, could act as a defense against
the plagues and wars of the last days. His melding of apocalyptic
prophecy and quasi-scientific inquiry gave rise to a new genre of
alchemical writing and a novel cosmology of heaven and earth.
He developed the idea that evangelical men had to be provided
with appropriate means of living, not only on a spiritual level but
also on a material level, which included the maintenance or the
restoration of health.[10] The expectation of the second coming of
Christ led to technological innovations that could control nature
and perfect the spirit in preparation for the parousia. Technology
helped subdue matter to spirit, taming nature in preparation for
the second coming of Christ, while at the same time instilling a
new lordly attitude toward nature.

With the introduction of Aristotelian philosophy in the West
and the influence of Muslim commentaries on Aristotle's philosophy, a new understanding of reality emerged that would
eventually pave the way for the rise of science. We can see the
beginnings of modern science in the philosophy of John Duns
Scotus, a fourteenth-century Franciscan theologian whose subtle
approach to Aristotle's philosophy forged a new intellectual
spirit. This new climate of philosophy encouraged not only a
more empirical, mechanistic, and quantitative view of nature, but
would in time easily accommodate the radical shift of view necessary for the concept of a moving earth. Scotus saw a principle

---

[10] Barbara Obrist, "Views on History in Medieval Alchemical Writings," *Ambix* 56.3 (2009): 236.

of individuation as a necessary recognition of God's freedom to choose how God would create each individual, as well as the individual human free will to choose for itself. The human person was no longer bound by determinism of eternally fixed universals (Platonic ideals) and necessary emanations from the First Cause. Rather one observed and experienced the unpredictable, contingent creation of a free God.

This new theological trail was further developed by William of Ockham, an English Franciscan of the fourteenth century, who had a decided influence on the rise of modern philosophy. The central principle of Ockham's thought was his denial of the reality of universals outside of the human mind and human language, and the primacy of divine will. Ockham claimed that God's will could not be limited by structures of human rationality; divine volitional freedom and omnipotence are absolute. Hence, our only certainty of things can come from direct sensory observation or from self-evident logical propositions, not from rational speculations about invisible realities and universal essences. Ockham's "razor" held that conceptual entities should not be multiplied unnecessarily.[11] What cannot be observed cannot be known. God creates the universe, but the patterns we discover about created things are the products of our mental processes, not evidence of divine intentions. Ockham thought that because only particulars demonstrably exist, not any transcendent relation or coherence among them, speculative reason and metaphysics lack any real foundation. Human knowledge, therefore, is limited to the contingent and empirical. God's reality and human rational knowledge are infinitely distant from each other. Ockham's school of philosophy produced a burst of creative scientific activity, paving the way for the empirical science that would flourish in the works of Kant, Descartes, and Hume. The rise of modern science on the heels of Ockham's razor would eventually lead to the abandonment of nature as a reflection of the mind of God.

---

[11] Rubenstein, *Aristotle's Children*, 252–53.

Cosmology and Science

The earlier medieval connection between theology and the natural world was summed up in the idea that theology was the queen of the sciences. All knowledge, whether of the mechanical arts or astronomy or weaving, was linked to knowledge of God. The basis of this unified system of knowledge was the Ptolemaic cosmos, in which the immobile earth was center of the cosmos, and the sun, stars, and planets circled perfectly around the earth. The universe was an orderly world machine in which everything was ordered, one to another, each thing having its proper location, arrangement, and purpose in this world guided by the forces of the crystalline heavens. Things were ordered not only *within* creation but everything in creation was oriented and directed toward a *telos*, a final goal.[12] Dante's picture of the world as a series of concentric spheres—heaven the largest, followed by the planets' crystalline spheres and down through our earth's concentric "elements" and the seven circles of hell—gave everything and everyone a proper place in the medieval scheme of things. Society mirrored the hierarchy that supposedly existed in the heavens. The human person stood in the center of creation, a personal union of matter and spirit, the noble image of God who expressed the glory of God.[13] God freely created this glorious universe and called forth human persons endowed with the freedom to participate in the divine artistic splendor. The human person was created on the sixth day so that everything could be ordered to the human who was ordained by God to have dominion over creation (Gen 1:28). As the most noble of all creatures, the human person was to lead creation back to God.

The medieval Ptolemaic worldview lasted until the end of the Middle Ages, when astronomers discovered that the earth

---

[12] Ilia Delio, "Creation and Salvation: Franciscan Perspectives," in *Creation and Salvation: A Mosaic of Selected Christian Theologies*, ed. E. M. Conradie (Zurich: LIT Verlag, 2012), 134.

[13] Ilia Delio, *Simply Bonaventure: An Introduction to His Life, Thought, and Writings*, 2nd ed. (New York: New City Press, 2013), 67–68.

is not stationary and the center of the cosmos but circles the sun. When Nicholas of Cusa and later Nicholas Copernicus proposed a sun-centered universe—heliocentrism—the church was not ready for the major upheaval of a moving earth. While the earth was once the center of the cosmos and the home of the book of Genesis, it was now abandoned for a new cosmic order. The stable center of God's throne was pushed over by the astronomer's telescope, and the consequences were enormous. If the earth moved around the sun, then the human person was no longer the center of the cosmos but simply part of a spinning planet. How could this finding be reconciled with the Genesis account where the human person was created on the sixth day, after which God rested? How were sin and salvation to be understood?

Galileo Galilei argued that the Bible and the natural world both come from God and are meant to be in harmony. His "Dialogue on the Great World Systems" (1632) is a defense of the newer Copernican system compared to the older Ptolemaic system. The older cosmology set the eternal celestial realm in opposition to the terrestrial scene of change and decay. The new cosmology erased the distinction between corruptible and incorruptible and applied uniform natural categories to the whole universe. The Copernican system, according to Galileo, described more accurately the movement of the planets. Robert Cardinal Bellarmine interpreted Galileo's position as a protest against the authority of the church and issued a statement in 1616 saying "the doctrine attributed to Copernicus, that the Earth moves around the Sun, and that the Sun is stationary in the center of the world and does not move from east to west, is contrary to the Holy Scriptures and therefore cannot be defended or held."[14] Galileo responded that the mobility or stability of either the earth or sun is neither a matter of faith nor contrary to morals. "The Bible tells us how to go to heaven, not as the heavens go,"

---

[14] In N. Max Wildiers, *The Theologian and His Universe: Theology and Cosmology from the Middle Ages to the Present* (New York: Seabury Press, 1982), 98n30.

he said.[15] Once the theory of heliocentrism became the law of the planets, the church found itself in a vulnerable position with regard to modern science.

The Cartesian Subject

The decisive turning point in the relationship between science and religion came with the work of René Descartes (1596–1650), who tried to reconcile the picture of a mechanical world with belief in God. Cartesian philosophy basically reversed the Copernican revolution. "Whereas Copernicus had displaced the human from the center of the universe by discovering that the earth circles the sun," Mark Taylor writes, "Descartes insisted that everything revolves around the human."[16] Martin Heidegger states that with the rise of modern science "the objective became swallowed up into the immanence of subjectivity."[17] Descartes overcame the doubt and anxiety created by modern science by collapsing truth into the self-certain, self-thinking subject, the *ego cogito*. He sought to rescue God from the clutches of a changing world by searching for true and certain knowledge in the human person as a thinking self; that is, basic certainty was no longer centered on God but on self.

This "turn to the subject" imposed a burden on each person to make sense of the world and unify it by rational thought alone. With this inward turn, objectivity came to be "constituted by and to exist *for the sake of* subjectivity."[18] Friedrich Nietzsche saw the direction of this trajectory in the death of God. The rise of modern science meant that divine power lost control of creation; the human person became self-determining, gaining

---

[15] This statement was supposedly first stated by Cardinal Baronius, after which Galileo used it to defend his position in a 1615 Letter to The Grand Duchess Christina.

[16] Mark Taylor, *After God* (Chicago: University of Chicago Press, 2007), 44.

[17] Taylor, *After God*, 44n3.

[18] Ilia Delio, *The Unbearable Wholeness of Being: God, Evolution, and the Power of Love* (Maryknoll, NY: Orbis Books, 2013), 9.

mastery over the whole. This "turn from the whole" rendered a new whole; the isolated, autonomous, liberal subject. The human person broke with nature and initiated a trajectory of artificial existence. Biological holism fractured in the modern period as matter separated from mind, like the white of an egg separated from its yolk.

British psychiatrist Iain McGilchrist describes the dividing of the human brain as the shattering of the cosmic whole. The right brain, he states, is our connection to the natural world as well as a sense of the uniqueness of the individual, whose interests need to be harmonized with those of the community. It is involved with new experience, new events, things, ideas, words, skills, music, or whatever is present to the mind. Its attention is not in the service of manipulation but in the service of connection, exploration, and relation.[19] The left brain narrows things to a certainty and is shown in either/or thinking. It is adept at procedures but sees them as ends in themselves. It is not in touch with the world. Its attention is narrow, its vision myopic, and it cannot see how the parts fit together. It prioritizes procedure without having a grasp of meaning or purpose. It requires certainty where none can be found.[20]

In Western Christianity dominant left-brain thinking emerged and consolidated with the rise of modern science. According to McGilchrist, the right hemisphere, which connects us to the wider world, gave way to the left hemisphere, which became the dominant sphere. The left brain breaks data into bits of information by which the brain abstracts and generalizes. However, with left-brain dominance, there is very little return to the right brain of passion and connectivity. In the Middle Ages the shift to linear, analytical thinking among Scholastic theologians not only produced the great *summas* of theology but laid the foundation for modern science and the scientific method. In

---

[19] Iain McGilchrist, *The Master and His Emissary: The Divided Brain and the Making of the Western World* (New Haven, CT: Yale University Press, 2009), 32–53.

[20] McGilchrist, *Master and His Emissary,* 42–44.

the Enlightenment the rise of the self-thinking subject became a substitute for the transcendent self of the whole.[21] That is, the cosmos was replaced by the separate, thinking individual; instead of belonging to a larger universe, the universe collapsed into the individual. Left-brain dominance and the Cartesian subject shattered the universe into thousands of pieces, with the isolated axial individual wielding the hammer.

The World Machine

The mechanical philosophy of Sir Isaac Newton (1642–1727) dominated the intellectual landscape of physical science throughout the eighteenth century. Newton was, without question, the culminating figure in the Scientific Revolution and the leading advocate of the mechanistic vision of the physical world initially posited by Descartes. Within his lifetime Newton saw the rise and triumph of Newtonian physics and widespread acceptance of a mechanistic universe (one that operates with mathematical precision and predictable phenomena) among philosophers and scientists. Newton's laws—and his theory of a clockwork universe in which God established creation and the cosmos as a perfect machine governed by the laws of physics—viewed matter as passive, moved and controlled by "active principles."

The *Principia,* which formulated Newton's laws of gravitation, provided the first comprehensive and mathematically consistent explanation for the behavior of astronomical objects. Within a century of Newton's *Principia* the concept of a mechanistic universe led to the quantification of celestial dynamics, which, in turn, spurred a dramatic increase in observation. The rise of natural theology took the form of deism, a belief in a divine "Clockmaker," who created and wound the timepiece that is the universe but had no further role in operating it. Deism rejected

---

[21] Referring to Scholastic theologians, see Ken Wilber, *Up from Eden: A Transpersonal View of Evolution* (Wheaton, IL: Quest Books, 2007), 16.

revelation, prophecy, scripture, and the supernatural, embracing nature and reason instead. The movement gained support within scientific communities as increasingly detailed evidence regarding the scope and scale of the universe showed no direct evidence of an active Creator.

Newtonian physics and the shift toward a mechanistic explanation of the natural world offered the promise of a deeper understanding of the inner workings of a cosmos linked directly to the very mind and nature of God. During the course of the eighteenth century a major conceptual rift developed between science and theology, as growing scientific disregard for knowledge based upon divine revelation—and increasing reliance upon natural theology (the belief that God can be known solely through human reason and experience, without divine revelation or scripture)—made experimentation the determinant authority in science. This marked a critical period in the development of scientific thought. Over the course of the century, advances in astronomy led to greater understanding of the workings of the solar system, sending sweeping changes across the theological, political, and social landscapes. Using equations based on Newton's laws, mathematicians of this era were able to develop the symbolism and formulas needed to advance the study of dynamics (the study of motion). An important consequence of these advancements allowed astronomers and mathematicians to calculate and describe the real and apparent motions of astronomical bodies (celestial mechanics) as well as to propose the dynamics related to the formation of the solar system.

The Enlightened Mind

The rise of a scientific perspective and the waning of religion during the Enlightenment created fertile ground for transforming the sacred image of the human organism into a mechanical one. The discovery of mathematics was crucial for this new enterprise. Observation and measurement based on quantifiable data provided the backbone for scientific study. Francis Bacon wrote that science aimed "to improve the living conditions of human beings."[22] The rise of modern science and its discoveries freed the human person from the constraints of religious authority; now the human person could use the intellect to create a new world.

The flourishing of the human in the Renaissance and the rise of the Enlightenment gave the human a new mastery over nature. Philosopher Nick Bostrom writes: "The otherworldliness and stale scholastic philosophy that dominated Europe during the Middle Ages gave way to a renewed intellectual vigor in the Renaissance. . . . Renaissance humanism encouraged people to rely on their own observations and their own judgment rather than to defer in every matter to religious authorities."[23]

Francis Bacon defined the Western project as man's dominion over nature. Bacon's *The New Atlantis* was a utopian vision in which God and man would once again become co-workers in creation, recovering mankind's original image-likeness to God. Perfection of mechanical knowledge could reinstate him in his pristine state, before the Fall, when Adam had power over all created things; thus man would no longer be an animal on hind legs but a mortal god. Human ascendancy for Bacon was central to the divine plan, and technology was the means of eschatological fulfillment. In the Baconian worldview, the fall of Adam came to be seen as a blessing in disguise, impelling fallen mankind not only to recover what was lost but to attain divine powers that had been denied to Adam. Bacon predicted that men would one day create a new species and become as gods, thus fulfilling the undeclared but ultimate goal of modern science.

By the late seventeenth century the world had a new messiah—the machine—and this faith was manifested in the compulsive urge toward mechanical development without regard for development in human relations. The "worship" of machines

---

[22] See Nick Bostrom, "A History of Transhumanist Thought," in *Academic Writing across the Disciplines,* ed. Michael Rectenwald and Lisa Carl (New York: Pearson Longman, 2011).

[23] Nick Bostrom, "A History of Transhumanist Thought," *Journal of Evolution and Technology* 14, no. 1 (April 2005): 2.

by the priesthood of white, male, scientific elites became dominant. Julien de La Mettrie spoke of humans as "a collection of springs which wind each other up." The human body is like "a large watch" powered by wheels, and the soul itself nothing but "an enlightened machine."[24] The idea of the "human machine" became common in the nineteenth century. The myth of *social* progress emerged from the Enlightenment idea of the perfectibility of man through the application of reason. That a manmade future would be "a more just, more peaceful, and less hierarchical republican society based on the consent of the governed" became a prominent idea. The fusion of religious ideals and the mechanical ushered in a new technological discourse and worldview. The future began to replace heaven as the zone of perfectibility—powered by technology. Religion was no longer the cohesive communal whole but was hijacked by the Cartesian subject and repackaged as "progress." The sacralized temporal zone (the future) was substituted for a sacred spatial one (heaven). Scientific societies such as the Royal Society or the Freemasons were tightly bound priestly caste systems in which the scientist was the new high priest of nature.

The Death of the Human

As science developed between the seventeenth and twentieth centuries, the human person was not part of the cosmic story. In Newton's world the sovereign, omnipotent God governed the world from above and the cosmos ran like a machine according to internal laws and mechanisms. God became the remote clockmaker and the cosmos assumed a mechanistic explanation. To the traditional criticism of the scientific paradigm, that it leaves no place for God, the scientist responds that there is no need for one. But in truth, the new scientific paradigm leaves no place for the human person. The great absentee in the scientific description of nature to this day is the human person. Raimon Panikkar

---

[24] Julien Offray de La Mettrie, *Machine a Machine* (Chicago: Open Court, 1912), 135–36.

writes, "Gods there are aplenty, the form of black holes, galaxies, and infinities, etc. . . . Matter and energy are all-pervasive, as are time and space. Only man does not come into the picture. Man cannot be located among the data. Man is in a certain way the obstacle to pure information."[25]

If the church set the stage for the rupture of axial consciousness by separating itself from modern science, Descartes completed the rupture by locating the mind on a spiritual realm divorced from the body. Originally, axial consciousness brought about a new religious mythic consciousness in which personhood is in relationship to the cosmic whole. The great axial divorce began with the rise of modern science and the rejection of the Copernican system by the Catholic Church. This axial divorce meant the death of the cosmic whole and the death of the human person as relational person. Descartes's dualism contributed to the demise. The inert body could now be politically manipulated by the myth of the male. Religion as a life force was emptied of its vitality and absorbed by a male patriarchal church. Once the human person vanished from the center of the cosmos, so did God, who was replaced by the power of reason. The cost of modern science was steep. By rejecting the Copernican system, the church turned its back on the dynamism of change, initiating the great schism between religion, evolution, and the human person.

Nietzsche's Lament

The philosophy of Friedrich Nietzsche rose in response to a shattered cosmos. With no real consciousness of the whole, there is no connection between consciousness of the sacred and consciousness of the mundane. After the Enlightenment the idea of a universe governed by physical laws alone became prominent. Governments no longer needed to be organized around the idea of divine right to be legitimate, but rather by the consent or rationality of the governed; moral theories could exist without

---

[25] Raimon Panikkar, *The Rhythm of Being: The Unbroken Trinity* (Maryknoll, NY: Orbis Books, 2013), 400.

reference to God. Western Europe no longer needed God as the source for moral order in the universe; philosophy and science were capable of providing answers. The secularization of thought in the West led Nietzsche to declare that God is dead and that human beings had killed him in their desire to better understand the world. Without God, the basic belief system of Western Europe was in jeopardy, as Nietzsche wrote in *Twilight of the Idols*:

> When one gives up the Christian faith, one pulls the right to Christian morality out from under one's feet. This morality is by no means self-evident. . . . Christianity is a system, a consistently thought out and *complete* view of things. If one breaks out of it a fundamental idea, the belief in God, one thereby breaks the whole thing to pieces: one has nothing of any consequence left in one's hands.[26]

Nietzsche claimed that God died because we killed him, but God died because the human person as cosmic relational person died. The rise of left-brain dominance, with its structures of logic and control, meant divorce of the right brain from the wider world of nature. The body became an inert thing to be experimented on while the mind was a separate entity detached from nature. For the pre-axial person the sacred was real and part of nature. For the axial person the sacred was real and transcendent to nature, although not separated from it. The Christian worldview expressed the sacred as the simultaneous immanence and transcendence of God. Despite these shifts the sacred retained its preeminent importance for life, and the goal was to live as close as possible to the sacred as the principal source of life. By refusing the Copernican system and artificially separating human consciousness from the whole, Christianity invented a new religious consciousness of God and creation, a static, fixed, gendered God controlled by a patriarchal church. Nietzsche was

---

[26] Friedrich Nietzsche, *Twilight of the Idols and the Anti-Christ*, trans. R. J. Hollingdale (New York: Penguin, 1968), 80–81.

right in proclaiming that we killed God. By refusing the insights of science, the church turned its back on a credible God. "The very name of God," Panikkar writes, "is a cosmological notion. There is no cosmos without God and no God without cosmos."[27] The implications of Nietzsche's death of God had a profound impact on culture and society. The human person lost the balance of nature with its sacred dimension, and the scientific mapping of the heavens meant a loss of place in the cosmos.

Cartesian philosophy and Newton's mechanistic paradigm were toxic for cosmic planetary life. Autonomy and independence triumphed over contingency and interdependence. Without a set of moral laws hanging over the person, one could use reason to carve a path to a higher glory: "There never was a greater event [than the death of God] and on account of it, all who are born after us belong to a higher history than any history so far!"[28]

Nietzsche's proclamation brought with it a new set of questions and challenges. If God is dead, then truth is dead as well and must be rediscovered. Nietzsche defined truth as the will to power and progress. Without Christianity and its transcendent values and ideals, modern individuals would be led to drastically underestimate their own potential for greatness. In doing so, they would incapacitate the heroic impulse to will ambitious goals and eradicate the "desires that create clefts" by which the higher type of human being is differentiated from the lower type. Nietzsche envisioned a type of individual emerging (whom he called "the last man"), who, instead of focusing on ways to enhance the grandeur of man, is concerned solely with using science and technology *to enhance the pleasure and comfort of man*. It is with this modern world in mind that Nietzsche wrote his masterpiece, *Thus Spoke Zarathustra*, representing his

---

[27] Panikkar, *Rhythm of Being*, 190.

[28] Friedrich Nietzsche, "The Madman," in *The Gay Science: With a Prelude in Rhymes and an Appendix in Songs*, Book III, sec. 125, trans. Walter Kaufmann (New York: Vintage, 1974), 181.

attempt to restore the sanctity and dignity of human existence in a spiritually destitute modern world.[29]

In a series of speeches given through the mouth of the prophet Zarathustra, Nietzsche put forth an "ethics of self-deification," a set of demands intended to introduce modern individuals, in the wake of the death of God, to the possibility of "becoming gods." For too long, he thought, human beings have externalized their highest values and ideals of perfection into the cosmos. It is now time for the individual to realize himself as the creator of these values, and thus capable of forging his own meaning and embodying his own justification, rather than remaining dependent on external institutions and creeds. Nietzsche realized that the demands of Zarathustra are so antithetical to human nature that if one were capable of attaining them, that person would have to overcome the limits of humanity and become what he called *Ubermensch* (the Superman). His philosophical program of the will to power focused on how to reinstitute the yearning for greatness in a world that was increasingly becoming inhospitable to it. Hence, he directed his work to the individual, who was now liberated from cosmic forces and free to create the individual's life. The fate of the cosmos now rested on the individual.

The only way to avoid annihilation, Nietzsche thought, is individual improvement. In this respect he opted for a type of secular transcendence. According to Zarathustra, *Ubermensch* means that man is "something that should be overcome," a type of Hegelian synthesis where the forces of resistance to improvement are to be overcome by greater rationality and thought. The *Ubermensch* becomes the ideal of human striving; human enhancement replaces heaven. One aims to live as a higher type of human being paving the way for even higher types to emerge in the future. Nietzsche writes: "Although you are high and of a higher type, much in you is crooked and malformed. There is no smith in the world who could hammer you straight and into

---

[29] Friedrich Nietzsche, *Thus Spoke Zarathustra*, trans. Graham Parkes (New York: Oxford University Press, 2005).

shape for me."[30] Yet there is nothing inherent in material existence that should warrant a demand to go higher, and Nietzsche's *Ubermensch* is highly suspect of a hidden God lurking in rationality. The demand to go higher without God can only result in secular forms of transcendence such as money, sex, and power, as Ken Wilber writes:

> Because man wants real transcendence above all else, but because he will not accept the necessary death of his separate-self sense, he goes about seeking transcendence in ways that actually prevent it and force symbolic substitutes. And these substitutes come in all varieties: sex, food, money, fame, knowledge, power—all are ultimately substitute gratifications, simple substitutes for true release in Wholeness.[31]

Nietzsche's death of God is the death of the human person, the breakdown of axial consciousness, and a shattered world. The quest for spiritual perfection is replaced by the will to power; consciousness is turned inward where the terror of the self is confronted by the terror of death. The Nietzschean man is the fallen Adam (Gen 3:28) faced with bodily mortality and weakness. In a world without God, the only alternative is to become god, and the intense striving to become other than a human person gives unbridled power to science and technology as the new means of deification and immortal existence.

Summary: This chapter traces the rise of the axial person. David Noble's work is particularly helpful to introduce technology into the patriarchal matrix of the Christian milieu. The rejection of the Copernican system by the Catholic Church and the Galileo affair mark a watershed in the relationship between science

---

[30] Nietzsche, *Thus Spoke Zarathustra*, 246.
[31] Wilber, *Up from Eden*, 16.

and religion. The rise of the Cartesian subject, the Newtonian world-machine, and the movement from Renaissance humanism to the Enlightenment are all efforts to secure the role of the human person in the cosmos. However, the mapping of space by modern science pushes the human to an eccentric position in the cosmos, eventually becoming obsolete and replaced by the data of science. As the human person is extinguished, so too is God and the religious dimension of evolution. The relational cosmic whole collapses in the modern period, fractured by the resistance of Christianity to science and smashed by the philosophy of the autonomous liberal subject. The Nietzschean *Ubermensch* is an attempt to save the fractured whole by finding a new whole through the will to power.

4

The Forgotten Openness
of the Closed World

The Turing Test

The rise of artificial intelligence occurred amid the intense suffering of the twentieth century. This was no coincidence. A pivotal figure in this story is Alan Turing, a mathematician and a homosexual who struggled with his gender identity in a culture that punished homosexuality as a criminal act. He reflects the tension from which AI emerged: on one hand, the new science of quantum physics, cybernetics, and systems biology; and on the other hand, the struggle to transcend human boundaries in a time of global destruction. Turing knew the devastation of war. His most famous contributions to computer science occurred in his top secret work on cracking the "unbreakable" code of the Enigma machines deployed on German U-boats during World War II. From this and from the wider context of his personal experience he had a deep sense that the wholeness of life was being smashed to pieces. The urgent need to reinvent nature out of its impasses was crucial. Turing did what nature has always done, creatively harnessing the tools at hand and trying something new.

Trained as a mathematician, Turning was familiar with the potential of the computer as a number machine. After graduating from university he published a paper titled "On Computable Numbers" in which he proposed a computer capable of computing any computable function. The paper was built on the idea proposed by Kurt Gödel that there are statements about computing numbers that are true but cannot be proven. The paper defines a "computing machine" as one with the ability to read and write symbols to a tape and using those symbols to execute an algorithm. This paper and the proposed computer—the Turing machine—provided the basis for the theory of computation.[1]

Turing worked on the problem in an effort to help define a system for identifying which statements could be proved. "What if," he asked, "I program the machine to respond to a question posed by a human person, and I cannot tell the difference between the machine's answer and the answer of another human person who is asked the same question?" In fact, as Karl MacDorman notes, "Turing never proposed a test in which a computer pretends to be human." Instead, "Turing proposed an imitation game in which a man and a computer compete in pretending to be a woman."[2]

In "Computing Machinery and Intelligence," Turing begins by describing a scenario where a man and a woman both try to convince a remote, unseen interrogator that they are female, using typewritten responses or by speaking through an intermediary. Turing's first sample question for the "Imitation Game" reads, "Will X please tell me the length of his or her hair?"[3] The real action, however, comes when the man is replaced by a machine. "Will the interrogator decide wrongly as often when the game is played like this as he does when the game is played between a man and a woman?" asks Turing. Erik Sofge writes: "The Imitation Game asks a computer to not only imitate a thinking human, but a female thinking human. It tumbles face-first into what should be a mathematician's nightmare, the unbounded,

[1] Brian McGuire, "The Turing Test," in *The History of Artificial Intelligence* (University of Washington, 2006), 5–6.

[2] Erik Sofge, "Lie Like a Lady: The Profoundly Weird Gender Specific Roots of the Turing Test," *Popular Science* (June 13, 2014).

[3] A. M. Turing, "Computing Machinery and Intelligence," *Mind* 59 (October 1950): 433.

unquantifiable quagmire of gender identity."[4] Is the computer gender neutral or rather gender indifferent? In this respect, Turing tests whether or not computer "intelligence" can surpass human bias.

Turing wrote his paper in 1950, twenty-two years after British women were granted universal voting rights. The aftershocks of the women's suffrage movement were still being felt. Sofge states, "The Imitation Game is an exercise posed at the inception of the digital age, at a time when the term computer was as likely to conjure up an image of a woman crunching numbers for the Allied war effort as a machine capable of chatting about its hair."[5] Turing's Imitation Game was not about super-intelligence but about intelligence and identity. Does intelligence identify a person based on gender? Can a "thinking machine" respond to a question with a "human" response?

One can see an extension of Turing's imitation game in Spike Jonze's movie *Her*, in which Theodore Twombly, a man suffering through the depression of a failed marriage, finds himself falling in love with a computer operating system named Samantha. The relationship between Samantha and Theodore shows the impact of language—coded information—on personhood. The deeply personal interactions between Theodore and the computer endow him with new vitality.[6] When he eventually learns of Samantha's many other relationships, he realizes he has been duped by code. Samantha is no more personal than his lampstand or desk. Yet the information of deep personal sentiments shared between Theodore and Samantha mimics the code of love and essentially resurrects him to new life. The "what" of information here surpasses the question of "who" is generating the information. As with the Turing test, Samantha is unaware of and thus unbiased by depressed bodily language and generates positive information to Theodore, thus transcending his wounds of depression. Similarly, Turing was trying to find a

---

[4] Sofge, "Lie Like a Lady."

[5] Sofge.

[6] *Her*, Spike Jonze (director), Annapurna Pictures, Los Angeles, 2013.

sense of unbiased personhood amid the horrors of war and the cruelty of a repressive society.[7]

Creative Boundaries of Identity

The path to AI found its way in the twentieth century through the groundbreaking discoveries of quantum physics to studies on systems biology, information, and cybernetics, all of which undergird the holism of nature. Austrian biologist Ludwig von Bertalanffy challenged the conception of biology in terms of mechanistic, homeostatic (steady state) systems and em-phasized that real systems are open to and interact with their environments. Whereas Newtonian mechanics was a science of forces and trajectories, evolution involved change, growth, and development, which gave rise to a new science of complexity. Complexity refers to the quality of a thing based on the number of elements and the organization of the structures that compose it. For example, the atom is more complex than the electron, and a living cell is more complex than the highest chemical nuclei of which it is composed, the difference depending not only on the number and diversity of the elements but on the correlation of the links formed between these elements.

The discovery of complex dynamical systems opened doors to new insights on relational nature. The first formulation of this new science was classical thermodynamics with its celebrated "second law," the law of the dissipation of energy. According to the second law of thermodynamics, there is a trend in physical phenomena from order to disorder. Any isolated or "closed" physical system will proceed spontaneously in the direction of ever-increasing disorder.[8] Since closed means bounded, the entire world machine should be running down and eventually grind

---

[7] For more on Turing's life, see, for example, Andrew Hodges, *Alan Turing: The Enigma*, rev. ed. (Princeton, NJ: Princeton University Press, 2014).

[8] Fritjof Capra, *The Web of Life* (1996; New York: Random House/ Anchor House, 1977), 47.

to a halt. But evolution says that the living world is unfolding toward increasing order and complexity.

Bertalanffy took a bold step by saying that living organisms cannot be described by classical thermodynamics because they are open systems. But what is a system? A system is defined by its structures of relationships. A cell, for example, is a system because it is an organized interaction among different structures such as the nucleus, golgi apparatus, and mitochondria, among other structures. For years, scientists thought that rigid or closed boundaries defined entities such as the cell. Closed boundaries mean that nothing can get into and out of a system without input of energy or use of energy. Bertalanffy realized that many biological systems are in fact open systems and feed on a continual flux of matter and energy from their environment: "The organism is not a static system closed to the outside and always containing the identical components; it is an open system . . . in which material continually enters from, and leaves into, the outside environment."[9] Thus he set out to replace the mechanistic foundations of science with a holistic vision and developed a theory of general systems based on biological principles and open systems.

One of the most significant features of complex dynamical systems is their openness to the environment so that sharp boundaries between the system and its environment are difficult, if not impossible, to draw. Rather, boundaries are porous, local, and flexible so that a system's external relations are as critical to it as its internal ones. Biologists Humberto Maturana and Francisco Varela write: "Living systems are machines that cannot be shown by pointing to their components. Rather, one must show their organization in a manner such that the way in which all their peculiar properties arise becomes obvious."[10] They distinguished between the organization of a system and its

---

[9] Ludwig von Bertalanffy, *General System Theory* (New York: Braziller, 1968), quoted in Capra, *Web of Life*, 48.

[10] Humberto Maturana and Francisco Varela, *Autopoiesis and Cognition: The Realization of the Living* (Dordrecht, Holland: D. Reidel, 1980), 78.

structure by saying that, as Capra puts it, "the organization of a living system . . . is the set of relations among its components that characterize the system as belonging to a particular class. . . . The structure of a living system, by constrast, is constituted by the actual relations among the physical components. In other words, the system's structure is the physical embodiment of its organization."[11] Maturana and Varela coined the term *autopoeisis* to describe "a network of production processes, in which the function of each component is to participate in the production or transformation of other components in the network. In this way the entire network continually 'makes itself.' It is produced by its components and in turn produces those components."[12] Another way of saying this is, "the product of its operation is its own organization."[13] The existence of an entity is based on its constitutive relationships.

Complex dynamical systems have given rise to new philosophical reflection on identity and sameness. Because dynamical systems adapt and evolve, the philosophical concept of essence as a nucleus of intrinsic and immutable qualities cannot adequately address the system's dynamical characteristic. In this respect the philosophical problem of identity as permanence or sameness of a system does not hold. Rather, the identity of dynamical systems is based on unity and resilience; that is, identity is integral to the system's potential to qualitatively evolve in the same way that ongoing self-organization is part of ongoing identity.

Philosopher Alicia Juarrero points out that autonomy and independence—the classical measures of identity—do not hold value in dynamical systems. "Autonomy and independence are seen as values associated only with dead, isolated things," she states.[14] Living organisms and their creations must instead be judged by their degree of resilience and thriving. Juarrero

---

[11] Capra, *Web of Life*, 98.

[12] Capra, 98.

[13] Humberto Maturana and Francisco Varela, *The Tree of Knowledge* (Boston: Shambhala, 1987), 75.

[14] Alicia Juarrero, "Complex Dynamical Systems and the Problem of Identity," *Emergence* 4 (2002): 98.

explains that the notion of "thriving" is based on Aristotle's category of *eudaimonia,* which is described as "flourishing."[15] Robust resilience, which in large measure is a function of connectivity and interdependence, plays a significant role in the dynamic integrity and flourishing of systems. With the advent of complex systems, the importance of interdependence replaces the emphasis on autonomy, which now comes to be equated with isolation, and the importance of robust resilience replaces that of independence, which now comes to be associated with stasis and stagnation.[16]

Whereas classical philosophical concepts of being involved substance, essence, and immutability, complex dynamical systems theory teaches that survival is a function of resilience, not stability. A system that is very resilient can have very low stability; that is, it may fluctuate greatly but still survive. Nassim Nicholas Taleb argues in his book, *Antifragile,* that disorder, volatility, and chaos are helpful for systems to survive and flourish, a concept that belies our everyday thinking.[17] Contrary to popular ideas, a system with high stability may not endure because any change or disturbance will destroy it. Such an idea seems counterintuitive, but Juarrero contends that the more interconnected a system is (both internally and externally), the more robust and resilient it will be. In this respect the integrity and identity of a complex system is not based on its essence but is fundamentally related to its dynamical connectivity. The more numerous and diverse qualities a process displays, the more uniquely individuated it is; that is, the richer its internal and external relations, the more individual and individuated is the system, and the more resilient and robust is the process.[18] Hyper-connectivity, therefore, is hyper-stability and hyper-resilient, a conceptual paradox that has implications for artificial intelligence.

---

[15] Juarrero, "Complex Dynamical Systems," 98.

[16] Juarrero, 98.

[17] Nassim Nicholas Taleb, *Antifragile: Things That Gain from Disorder* (New York: Random House, 2012).

[18] Juarrero, "Complex Dynamical Systems," 99.

Learning to Live in Loops

The discovery of complex systems led to new discoveries on the dynamism of nature and its ability to organize. The science of cybernetics, from the Greek meaning "the art of steering," was founded by Norbert Wiener to understand control and communication in animals and machines.[19] A mathematics prodigy, Wiener joined the faculty of MIT in 1919 and soon after began collaborating with Vannevar Bush, a professor of electrical engineering. He began doing war-related research and in collaboration with Julian Bigelow devised systems of machines and humans in feedback loops, indicating that humans could be modeled as mechanical information processors and, theoretically, could be replaced by faster and more reliable mechanical devices.[20]

Wiener indicated that both animals and machines can operate with cybernetic principles based on goal-oriented action and communication. Cybernetics approaches things not by asking what a thing *is* but what it *does*.[21] Weiner first thought of cybernetics as a way to maximize human potential in a world that is essentially chaotic and unpredictable. While Leibniz's invention of calculus is the intellectual ancestor of cybernetics, Einstein's theory of relativity shifted the perspective from static objective existence to a world that presupposes an observer. With Einstein, physics became the study of the universe as it is observed. The rise of statistical mechanics and the discovery of entropy led scientists to consider indeterminacy and contingency as fundamental to nature. In such a universe chaos is more likely than order, and new order can arise out of disorder. How order persists and increases is the study of cybernetics.

---

[19] Norbert Wiener, *Cybernetics: Or, Control and Communication in the Animal and the Machine* (Cambridge, MA: MIT Press, 1948, 1961), 11.

[20] Fred Turner, *From Counterculture to Cyberculture: Stewart Brand, the Whole Earth Network, and the Rise of Digital Utopianism* (Chicago: University of Chicago Press, 2008), 21.

[21] W. Ross Ashby, *Introduction to Cybernetics* (London: Chapman and Hall, 1956), 1–2.

Wiener considered information as messages, which he defined as forms of pattern and organization. According to Fred Turner, Wiener "believed that biological, mechanical, and information systems, including then-emerging digital computers, could be seen as analogues of one another. . . . All were simply patterns of ordered information in a world otherwise tending to entropy and noise. Wiener also believed that these systems could serve as models for social institutions and for society at large."[22]

Cybernetics is based on complex dynamical systems and refers to a circular-causal relationship whereby the system's action generates some change in its environment, and that change is somehow reflected in the feedback, evoking a change in the system. Hence cybernetics is the science of communication and control over an environment.[23] The ability of systems to exchange information in feedback loops that generate order out of chaos effectively communicates information amid unstable and contingent conditions. Complex dynamical systems are open systems in which feedback mechanisms of information exchange undergird ongoing self-organization. In an open system entropy (disorder) is reduced by the extent of variation in messages or information. In a sense, every self-organizing dynamical system or machine generates a form of "life" adapted to its environment.

Complex dynamical systems and cybernetics open a whole new window on nature, in a sense, rediscovering what the pre-axial person knew well—that all things are interconnected and interdependent. Goal-oriented action and communication, operating in feedback loops, make up systems of information on every level of biological life. Nature is an undivided whole.

Around the same time that Turing was experimenting with the computer as a thinking machine, Claude Shannon was seeking to define information. The birth of the Information Age can be traced back to a paper Shannon wrote in 1948 in which he developed a mathematical theory of communication and gave a

---

[22] Turner, *From Counterculture to Cyberculture*, 22.
[23] Turner, 24.

probabilistic definition to the notion of information.[24] In Shannon's words, "The fundamental problem of communication is that of reproducing at one point either exactly or approximately a message selected at another point." He states that "the act of choosing one unique message from many possible messages gives rise to the generation of information."[25] Some scientists, such as the theoretical physicist John Wheeler, posit that information may be a fundamental building block of reality and that physical things are information-theoretic in origin. [26]

The fact that information and cybernetics operate on all levels of biological systems means that nature is as much defined by computations and algorithms as it is by physics, chemistry, and biology. Christopher Langton suggests that nature itself is computational, whereby large numbers of simple processors are locally connected.[27] If "nature" includes algorithms and computation, then nature and artificial intelligence are not opposing terms but descriptive of the same reality. The fact that the principles of AI are embedded in nature leads me to propose that the term *artificial intelligence* is actually a misnomer, since there is nothing artificial about intelligence. Rather, machine intelligence is an irreducible hybrid of biology and technology, or *bios-techne*.

Instead of the term *artificial intelligence,* which leads to an understanding of machine intelligence as somehow unnatural or fake (even though it is meant to convey simulated intelligence), it might be better to speak of *biologically extended intelligence* (BEI) or *augmented intelligence,* because machine learning extends biological intelligence. Martin Heidegger spoke of nature as a "standing reserve," the pluripotentiality of being itself.

---

[24] Claude E. Shannon, "A Mathematical Theory of Communication," *The Bell System Technical Journal* 27 (July, October 1948): 379–423, 623–65.

[25] Shannon, "A Mathematical Theory of Communication," 379–423.

[26] Dirk K. F. Meijer, "Information: What Do You Mean?" *Syntropy Journal* 3 (2013): 1–2.

[27] Christopher Langton, *The Allure of Machinic Life* (Cambridge, MA: MIT Press, 1989), 2.

"Techne" is the act [or art] of "bringing forth."[28] Heidegger suggests that technology is "a challenging, which puts to nature the unreasonable demand that it supplies energy which can be extracted and stored as such."[29] This kind of unconcealment orders everything to stand by, to be ready at hand, to be a standing reserve, to become whatever the mind beholds. AI reflects the pluripotentiality of nature to extend information into simulated environments that in effect make up a complexified system of biology and machine.

American Technology

The scientific insights that paved the way for AI to emerge were contingent on discoveries of nature that challenged the boundaries of closed, causal, mechanistic systems. Information and cybernetic loops provided the basis for the "thinking machine"; the sheer notion that a machine could think like a human person not only reflected the plasticity of nature but the dynamic capacity of nature to do remarkably new things. In the postwar period, with the rise of AI, technology began to assume a quasi-religious aura as Christian ideals of salvation and immortality were transferred to American technology as the new means of salvation. According to Joel Dinerstein, technology became the prime mover of an ongoing "millenarian impulse" that had spilled over from the nineteenth century. The space program, in particular, bore witness to the new Adamic myth of technological achievement in the white, homosocial world of NASA. As Dinerstein elaborates:

> From the 1950s through the 1970s, nearly all of NASA's key positions were filled by evangelical Christians. NASA's director, Werner von Braun—ex-Nazi rocket scientist,

---

[28] David Farrell Krell, ed., *Martin Heidegger: Basic Writings* (New York: Harper and Row, 1977), 383.

[29] Krell, *Martin Heidegger,* 324.

father of the US space program, and born-again Christian—declared that the purpose of sending men into space was "to send his Son to the other worlds to bring the gospel to them" and to create a "new beginning" for mankind. In the 1950s, scientists and physicists believed new planets and space colonies might become a safety valve for a planet poisoned by nuclear [fallout]. Physicist Freeman Dyson wrote the "Space Traveler's Manifesto" in 1958, and he supported the development of nuclear energy to secure a power source for a starship that was mankind's best chance to survive apocalypse. The claim was seconded by Rod Hyde, NASA's group leader for nuclear development: "What I want more than anything is to get the human race into space. . . . It's the future. If you stay down here some disaster is going to strike and you're going to be wiped out." Directed by the "spiritual men" of NASA, humanity would restart on another world so that human beings could still be headed for a redemptive future even as they left behind the mess of the impure.[30]

The Apollo launch impelled novelist Norman Mailer to describe astronaut Neil Armstrong, with his space suit and helmet plugged into electrical and environmental umbilicals, as "a veritable high priest of the forces of society and scientific history concentrated in that mini-cathedral, a general of the church of the forces of technology."[31] Dinerstein describes a relationship between the Age of Exploration marked by Christopher Columbus and the Space Age marked by the command ship *Columbia* of Apollo 11 as the "visionary quests for new worlds," the search for "new," "better," and "more"; ultimately, the search for God. The fusion of space travel and religious narrative reinforced Noble's thesis that technology is based on the myth of the fallen

---

[30] Joel Dinerstein, "Technology and Its Discontents: On the Verge of the Posthuman, *American Quarterly* 58, no. 3 (September 2006): 579.

[31] Norman Mailer, *Of a Fire on the Moon* (1969, 1970; reprint, New York: Random House, 2014), 180.

Adam in search of redemption and divine likeness. Dinerstein sums up the Adamic myth in three points: (1) the valorization of the "mechanized arts" through the thrill of scientific discovery and exploration; (2) the shadow Christian tradition of redeeming fallen man; and (3) the competitive challenge of being the first body in a new environment—whether physically on a new continent or a new world, or now, mentally, in cyberspace. This white male mythology promised nothing less than the technological transcendence of the individual human organism, the renewal of the fallen Adam.[32] Technology and religion fused with national myth and political power.[33] In 1969, Richard Nixon pronounced the week of Apollo 11's flight and landing on the moon "the greatest week since the beginning of the world, [since] the Creation."[34]

Manfred Clynes and Nathan Kline, who coined the term *cyborg* in 1960, envisioned that a cyborgian man-machine would be needed in the next great technohuman challenge of space flight.[35] Donna Haraway defines cyborgs as "creatures simultaneously animal and machine who populate worlds ambiguously since they are both natural and crafted.[36] Jeanine Thweatt-Bates states that the original cyborg was xenogeneic, a fusion of human and nonhuman, so as to extend human function in an unknown environment.[37] The cyborg was born in the quest to explore the extraterrestrial space of the unknown, but it quickly became a

---

[32] Dinerstein, "Technology and Its Discontents," 581.

[33] Dinerstein, 574.

[34] Quoted in Dinerstein, 580; David Noble, *The Religion of Technology: The Divinity of Man and the Spirit of Invention* (New York: Alfred A. Knopf, 1997), 140.

[35] Manfred Clynes and Nathan Kline, "Cyborgs and Space," *Astronautics* (1960): 27–28.

[36] Donna Haraway, "Cyborg Manifesto: Science, Technology, and Socialist-Feminism in the Late Twentieth Century," in *Simians, Cyborgs, and Women: The Reinvention of Nature* (New York: Routledge, 1991), 149.

[37] Jeanine Thweatt-Bates, *Cyborg Selves: A Theological Anthropology of the Posthuman* (New York: Routledge, 2012), 16–17.

symbol of what the human could become in the unlimited open space of cyberspace, filled with unlimited potential to explore.

Transhumanism

The priesthood of technology found a new church in the cultural and philosophical movement of transhumanism, which emerged in the late twentieth century. The term *transhumanism* was first used in the 1950s by Julian Huxley. In *Religion without Revelation* Huxley writes:

> The human species can, if it wishes, transcend itself—not just sporadically, an individual one way, an individual there in another way—but in its entirety, as humanity. We need a name for this new belief. Perhaps transhumanism will serve: man remaining man, but transcending himself, by realizing new possibilities of and *for his human nature*.[38]

Huxley saw transhumanism as a positive step for the whole of humankind rather than as individual perfection or enhancement. The human person is in process of becoming something new because humanity, like evolution itself, possesses a vital unfolding of spirit through matter. Huxley was a good friend of Teilhard de Chardin, and together they thought about human history within the larger cosmic evolutionary universe "despite their opposing views on whether evolution had a direction."[39] The interest of transhumanism for these two scientists was in view of evolutionary progression; they were less concerned about human perfection than in the direction of human life.

---

[38] Julian Huxley, *Religion without Revelation* (1941; reprint, Westport, CT: Greenwood Press, 1979), 195.

[39] David Grumett, "Transformation and the End of Enhancement: Insights from Pierre Teilhard de Chardin," in *Transhumanism and Transcendence: Christian Hope in an Age of Technological Enhancement*, ed. Ronald Cole-Turner, 37–50 (Washington, DC: Georgetown University Press, 2011).

Philosopher Nick Bostrom seized upon transhumanism as the technological salvation of modernity's failure to achieve social change: "In the postwar era, many optimistic futurists who had become suspicious of collectively orchestrated social change found a new home for their hopes in scientific and technological progress."[40] In 1988, with David Pearce, he began the World Transhumanist Association as a cultural and philosophical center of human betterment through technology. A corollary group known as Extropy (a philosophy devoted to the transcendence of human limits) was founded by Max More, who emigrated from Britain and settled in California. More founded the Extropy Institute to catalyze the transhuman ideal of betterment: "I was going to get better at everything, become smarter, fitter, and healthier . . . a constant reminder to keep moving forward."[41] Following the closure of the Extropy Institute in 2006, Humanity+ emerged as an outgrowth of the World Transhumanist Association and has since become the principal representative of the transhumanism movement. Its homepage states its goals:

> We aim to deeply influence a new generation of thinkers who dare to envision humanity's next steps. Our programs combine unique insights into the developments of emerging and speculative technologies that focus on the well-being of our species and the changes that we are and will be facing. Our programs are designed to produce outcomes that can be helpful to individuals and institutions.

Since its inception the World Transhumanist Association, along with the pioneering work of Extropy Institute, has contributed to advancing the public knowledge of how science and technology can and will affect our human future. Hence, *transhumanism* now refers to those technologies that can improve mental

---

[40] Nick Bostrom, "A History of Transhumanist Thought," *Journal of Evolution and Technology* 14, no. 1 (April 2005): 7.

[41] Quoted in E. Regis, "Meet the Extropians," *Wired* 2 (1994): 10.

and physical aspects of the human condition such as suffering, disease, aging, and death. It is based on "the belief that humans must wrest their biological destiny from evolution's blind process of random variation . . . favoring the use of science and technology to overcome biological limitations."[42]

In an overview of transhumanism Bostrom recounts the history of the Enlightenment, with Bacon's *Novum Organum* and the priestly caste of the scientific enlightenment:

> It has been said that the Enlightenment expired as the victim of its own excesses. It gave way to Romanticism, and to latter day reactions against the rule of instrumental reason and the attempt to rationally control nature, such as can be found in some postmodernist writings, the New Age movement, deep environmentalism, and in some parts of the anti-globalization movement. However, the Enlightenment's legacy, including a belief in the power of human rationality and science, is still an important shaper of modern culture.[43]

Evolution, according to Bostrom, is an ongoing process in which humanity is not the endpoint but perhaps an early phase of development. Following the insights of Julien Offray de La Mettrie he states: "If human beings are constituted by matter that obeys the same laws of physics that operate outside us, then it should in principle be possible to learn to manipulate human nature in the same way that we manipulate external objects."[44]

---

[42] Bostrom, "History of Transhumanist Thought," 13–14; Archimedes Carag Articulo, "Towards an Ethics of Technology: Re-Exploring Teilhard de Chardin's Theory of Technology and Evolution," *Open Journal of Philosophy* 4, no. 4 (Scientific Research Publishing, 2014).

[43] Bostrom, "History of Transhumanist Thought," 2–3.

[44] Bostrom, 4. Although Bostrom does not think that Nietzsche's *Ubermensch* is a direct forerunner of transhumanism, he is not opposed to the idea that technology and the *Ubermensch* are related.

Transhumanism and Enhancement

Transhumanism looks to the sciences of genetic engineering, biotechnology, nanotechnology, and robotics to advance the human condition. Bostrom writes, "We have always sought to expand the boundaries of our existence, be it socially, geographically, or mentally."[45] However, transhumanists are divided between two visions: one in which technological and genetic improvements can create a distinct species of radically enhanced humans, and the other in which greater-than-human machine intelligence can emerge, marked by the term *posthuman*. These two distinct but related philosophies form the crux of our current technological age and the most significant trends of human evolution.

Gordon E. Moore, cofounder of Intel, noticed in 1965 that the number of transistors on a chip exhibited exponential growth. He predicted that the pace of technology would increase exponentially, outstripping our ability to absorb it or reflect on our use of it. This led to the formulation of "Moore's law," which states (roughly) that computing power doubles every eighteen months to two years. Michael Specter writes: "When the IBM 360 computer was released in 1964, the top model came with eight megabytes of main memory, and cost more than two million dollars. Today, cell phones with a thousand times the memory of that computer can be bought for about a hundred dollars."[46]

The myth of technology is appealing, and the power of technology is seductive. We now have the power not only to evolve ourselves through technology but to direct the course of evolution. CRISPR technology (a toold for editing genomes) discloses a new power of genetic selection; nanotechnology affords mechanical implants in biological organs. Biological evolution and technological evolution have become coterminus, and a new posthuman species is emerging in evolution. W. Brian

---

[45] Bostrom, 1.

[46] Michael Specter, "A Life of Its Own: Where Will Synthetic Biology Lead Us?" *New Yorker* (September 2009): 64.

Arthur claims: "Conceptually, biology is becoming technology. And physically, technology is becoming biology."[47] Or as Kevin Kelly states, the future of evolution is about "the marriage of the born and the made."[48]

An early transhumanist and teacher at the New School for Social Research, F. M. Esfandiary—who changed his name to FM-2030 to reflect his wish to break free of naming conventions rooted in humankind's tribalistic past—describes the emergence of the transhuman. "A transhuman," FM-2030 writes, "is a transitional human, someone who by virtue of their technological usage, cultural values, and lifestyle constitutes an evolutionary link to the coming era of posthumanity."[49] The signs that Esfandiary saw as indicative of transhuman status included prostheses, plastic surgery, intensive use of telecommunications, a cosmopolitan outlook and a globetrotting lifestyle, androgyny, mediated reproduction (such as in vitro fertilization), absence of religious belief, and a rejection of traditional family values.[50]

Futurists such as Ray Kurzweil have speculated on the phenomenon of "singularity," a point of transition in the near future when technology and human intelligence will become seamlessly merged, thrusting us into a new level of existence from *homo sapien* to *techno sapien* life. The basis of the singularity idea was found in a 1958 paper by Stanislaw Ulam who, referring to a meeting with John von Neumann, wrote: "One conversation centered on the ever accelerating progress of technology and

---

[47] Quoted in Carter Phipps, *Evolutionaries: Unlocking the Spiritual and Cultural Potential of Science's Greatest Idea* (New York: Harper, 2012), 144.

[48] Quoted in Phipps, *Evolutionaries,* 128.

[49] FM-2030, *Are You a Transhuman? Monitoring and Stimulating Your Personal Rate of Growth in a Rapidly Changing World* (New York: Grand Central, 1989), quoted in Bostrom, "History of Transhumanist Thought," 14.

[50] FM-2030, *Are You a Transhuman?*; Bostrom, "History of Transhumanist Thought," 14.

changes in the mode of human life, which gives the appearance of approaching some essential singularity in the history of the race beyond which human affairs, as we know them, could not continue."[51] The singularity hypothesis refers to the idea that self-improving artificial intelligence will at some point result in radical changes within a very short time span. This hypothesis was first clearly stated in the mid 1960s by statistician I. J. Good:

> Let an ultraintelligent machine be defined as a machine that can far surpass all the intellectual activities of any man however clever. Since the design of machines is one of these intellectual activities, an ultraintelligent machine could design even better machines; there would then unquestionably be an "intelligence explosion," and the intelligence of man would be left far behind. Thus the first ultraintelligent machine is the last invention that man need ever make.[52]

Vernor Vinge discussed the singularity idea in his influential 1993 paper "Technological Singularity," in which he predicted that "within thirty years, we will have the technological means to create super-human intelligence. Shortly after, the human era will be ended."[53] While the idea of the singularity is becoming more evident, it also corresponds to the evolutionary rise of complexity and consciousness. The so-called end of the human era, therefore, must be seen as the rise of a new type of human in evolution.

------

[51] Bostrom, "History of Transhumanist Thought," 8; cf. Stanislaw Ulam, "John von Neumann 1903–1957," *Bulletin of the American Mathematical Society* (May 1958).

[52] Irving John Good, "Speculations concerning the First Ultraintelligent Machines," *Advances in Computers* 6 (1966): 31–88.

[53] Vernor Vinge, "The Coming Technological Singularity," *Whole Earth Review* (Winter, 1993); Bostrom, "History of Transhumanist Thought," 9.

The Narrow Mind

Many transhumanists look to a post-biological future when we will flourish as super-informational beings. Through mechanical means we will be able to overcome the limitations of the body, including suffering and death, and attain artificial eschatological paradise. Bart Kosko, a professor of electrical engineering at the University of Southern California, writes: "Biology is not destiny. It was never more than tendency. It was just nature's first quick and dirty way to compute with meat. Chips are destiny."[54] After all, as Kevin Kelly notes, "meat is messy." The digitized body will be free and unconstrained by the physical and temporal limitations of the flesh.[55]

Futurist Ray Kurzweil anticipates an increasingly virtual life in which the bodily presence of human beings will become irrelevant because of AI. He claims that machine-dependent humans will transcend death through the virtual reality of eternal life, possibly by "neurochips" or simply by becoming totally machine dependent. As we move beyond mortality through computational technology, "our identity will be based on our evolving mind file. We will be software, not hardware."[56]

Kurzweil sees the eventual replacement of human bodies by virtual bodies. In his view, nanotechnology will enable human beings to build far superior bodies. Eventually human minds will eliminate their need for bodily existence: "We don't always need real bodies. If we happen to be in a virtual environment, then a virtual body will do just fine."[57] In the future, therefore, personal identity will be based on one's evolving mind file. By replacing living bodies with virtual bodies capable of transferal

---

[54] Quoted in C. Christopher Hook, "The Techno-Sapiens are Coming," *Christianity Today* (January 2004).

[55] In Phipps, *Evolutionaries*, 126.

[56] Quoted in Robert Geraci, "Apocalyptic AI: Religion and the Promise of Artificial Intelligence," *Journal of the American Academy of Religion* 76, no. 1 (March 2008): 154.

[57] Ray Kurzweil, *The Age of Spiritual Machines: When Computers Exceed Human Intelligence* (New York: Viking, 1999), 142.

and duplication, we will become disembodied super-minds.[58] Hence, we will be able to achieve some type of immortality or extended life. Robert Geraci states, "Our new selves will be infinitely replicable, allowing them to escape the finality of death."[59]

This futuristic, post-biological, computer-based immortality is one also envisioned by Hans Moravec, who claims that the advent of intelligent machines (*Machina sapiens*) will provide humanity with personal immortality by mind transplant. The hope of digital immortality through brain downloading reflects a desire for eternal life. The brain's information will be cloned, stored, and reproduced in such a way that what we can live on indefinitely. We will be able to "wake up matter" by infusing it with intelligence and information.[60] Through mechanical means we will be able to overcome the limitations of the body, including suffering and death, and attain artificial eschatological paradise. Kevin Warwick claims that the body will be made obsolete by silicone implants and electronic prostheses. As machines move inside bodies, we will emerge from the archaic biological species of *Homo sapiens* into a new technologized species of *Techno sapiens*, anticipating a future flourishing of life.

Is Transhumanism Anti-Nature?

Transhumanism is a metanarrative that offers a framework for AI that is both alluring and frightening. If we evaluate transhumanism against the main tenets of relational holism, including mind in matter and deep relationality, we can become quickly destabilized by its radical claims. For one thing, consciousness is reduced to an epiphenomenon that can be quantified and

---

[58] Kurzweil defines the singularity as the point at which machines become sufficiently intelligent to start teaching themselves. When that happens, he indicates, the world will irrevocably shift from the biological to the mechanical (Kurzweil, *Age of Spiritual Machines*, 3–5).

[59] Robert Geraci, "Spiritual Robots: Religion and Our Scientific View of the Natural World," *Theology and Science* 4, no. 3 (2006): 235.

[60] In Phipps, *Evolutionaries*, 142.

manipulated, an idea that runs against the concepts of panpsychism and dual-aspect monism, in which consciousness plays a fundamental role in the material world. Second, transhumanism follows a binary logic endemic to the Cartesian subject. The prospect of overcoming disease, expanding life by pushing back (or overcoming) the death barrier, and enhancing intelligence through implantable chips and brain downloading reflects the Enlightenment ideals of enhancement, rationality, transcendence, and Godlike power. The individual stands over and against matter, as the mind stands over and against the body.

This artificial split, which emerged in the Enlightenment, is at the heart of the radical separation between humans and the wider world of nature. Transhumanism reinterprets the natural world as a giant computer of information that can be manipulated and transformed. One gets the sense that materiality or physical existence is a relic of the past and that biology is merely a phase in the ongoing evolution of life, as in the term *post-biological life*. In a sense transhumanism denies the realization that we humans evolve from a long lineage of biological changes, adaptations, and physical novelties, and that biological life itself is part of a larger whole we call cosmos.

In the end, I believe that transhumanism repeats the mistakes of the Enlightenment by presuming to know what constitutes a human person or at least assuming a particular understanding of the human person, the Cartesian subject. Yet it never raises the question of personhood, either philosophically or theologically. Rather, it accepts the Cartesian subject as a given: the human person is a mind in a body that can be replaced, repaired, or upgraded. Transhumanism, therefore, stands at the end of the Enlightenment, as the legacy of the liberal subject whose Kantian motto *sapere aude*—dare to know—hangs like a banner over the dream of post-biological life.[61]

---

[61] Bostrom, "History of Transhumanist Thought," 4.

Summary: AI emerged in the midst of the violent twentieth century. The Turing test was not only a quest for machine intelligence but a test of nature itself. Can a machine respond to a human question without bias? The discovery of cybernetics, complex dynamical systems and information, provided the foundation for developing computer technology, which raises the question whether the term *artificial intelligence* is a misnomer. The power of computer technology enkindled the religious ideals of salvation, immortality, and divine likeness, giving rise to new unbridled powers that are Godlike. The World Transhumanist Association was founded in 1998 as a cultural and philosophical forum for transhumanism defined as human betterment through technological means. In some respects tranhumanism builds on the Cartesian subject and the Enlightenment project, seeking to realize the *Ubermensch* through technology, ultimately shedding the human body and finding new mediums for the human mind through brain downloading. I refer to this as "shallow AI" because it perpetuates the will to power and can be seen as another form of individual enhancement through binary disembodied mind at the expense of the collective whole.

5

In Search of Relational Wholeness

The Rise of Second Axial Consciousness

Human development is the culmination of a long process of evolutionary complexification and differentiation, an increasing expansion of "worlds" from "the immediate and mythical world of the pre-axial person to the conventional and increasingly rationalized world of the great civilizations, to the post-conventional world of the axial person" marked by individuation.[1] With the awakening of axial consciousness and reflective subjectivity, the individual could take a stance against the collective and become a distinct moral and spiritual self embarking on an individual spiritual journey.[2]

A new axis of consciousness dawned in the twentieth century with the rise of Big Bang cosmology, evolution, and quantum physics. Ewert Cousins and Thomas Berry called this new axis of consciousness the second axial age.[3] Like the first period,

---

[1] William P. Thompson, *Christ and Consciousness* (New York: Paulist Press), 39.

[2] Ewert Cousins, "Teilhard's Concept of Religion and the Religious Phenomenon of Our Time," *Teilhard Studies* 49 (Fall 2004): 11.

[3] Ewert Cousins, *Christ of the Twenty-First Century* (Rockport, MA: Element Books, 1992), 7–8. Thomas Berry uses the phrase *second axial age* to refer to the convergence of world religions leading to a new phase of human culture and civilization. See Mary Evelyn Tucker, John Grim, and Andrew Angyal, *Thomas Berry: A Biography* (New York: Columbia University Press, 2019), 93.

this new axial age has been developing for several centuries, beginning with the rise of modern science. And like the first, it is effecting a radical transformation of consciousness. While the first axial period produced the self-reflective individual, the second axial period is giving rise to the hyper-personal or hyper-connected person. Technology has fundamentally altered our view of the world and ourselves in the world. The tribe is no longer the local community, but the global community which can now be accessed immediately through television, internet, satellite communication, and travel. Exploration in space and satellite photographs of the earth have revealed the earth to be a luminous web of humanity and nature woven together like a quilt of many colors.

The photograph of Planet Earth in 1968, reprinted in all the major magazines, triggered immense awe as people marveled at the tiny blue, marble-like globe suspended in space. From space, the earth seems like the home of a single tribe of humanity. It is only when one begins to walk the earth that one realizes that the "tribe" has many different voices and religious expressions.[4] "For the first time since the appearance of human life on our planet," Cousins writes, "all of the tribes, all of the nations, all of the religions are beginning to share a common history."[5]

People are becoming more aware of belonging to humanity as a whole and not to a specific group. This new global consciousness can be seen from two perspectives: (1) From a horizontal perspective, cultures and religions are invited to meet on the surface of the globe, entering into creative encounters that will produce a complexified collective consciousness.[6] "Complexified" consciousness refers to new networks or interacting realms of consciousness, especially today through the internet and mass communication. (2) From a vertical perspective, cultures and religions must plunge their roots deep into the earth in order to provide a stable and secure base for future development.[7]

---

[4] Ilia Delio, *Christ in Evolution* (Maryknoll, NY: Orbis Books, 2008), 27–28.

[5] Cousins, *Christ of the Twenty-First Century*, 7–10.

[6] Cousins, "Teilhard's Concept of Religion," 12.

[7] Delio, *Christ in Evolution*, 28.

What is interesting about second axial period consciousness is that the whole of nature as a phenomenon reemerges
as a global tribe, *unus mundus,* a seamless thread of humanity
woven into the earth's elements and emerging from those same
elements. Cousins describes the second axial period as "communal, global, ecological and cosmic."[8] It is not merely a shift
from first axial period consciousness; it is an advance in the
whole evolutionary process. The second axial period challenges
the religions to bring about a new integration of the spiritual
and the material, of sacred energy and secular energy into a
total global human energy.[9] Thus it encourages dialogue, community, and relationship, with a growing awareness that each
person is something of the whole.

Second axial consciousness is globally complexified; the lines
of awareness are not vertical and transcendent but horizontal
and relational. Teilhardian scholar Beatrice Bruteau described a
neo-feminine consciousness emerging in the late twentieth century, a "participatory consciousness" that reflects second axial
consciousness. This new consciousness is characterized by (1)
consciousness of the whole, concrete, real person, (2) an identity
of mutual affirmation rather than negation, and (3) existential
perception over essential perception. It is a new level of personhood insofar as it evokes a deeper awareness of relationality.
Bruteau writes:

Evolution has produced reflexive consciousness. . . .
Consciousness of ourselves from the outside was only a
first stage of this reflexivity. . . .The evolutionary pressure
toward greater reflexivity urges us to a realization of ourselves as conscious of being conscious, a noetic coincidence
with ourselves as conscious acts of life-communicating life.
This noetic coincidence with the act of communicating life
is itself a free act; it is now our interior act that nevertheless
enters more profoundly into the interiority of our fellow

---

[8] Cousins, *Christ of the Twenty-First Century,* 10.
[9] Cousins, "Teilhard's Concept of Religion," 13.

beings than ever an external act touched the exteriority of another being.[10]

Both Cousins and Bruteau suggest that first axial consciousness is shifting toward a new type of deeply relational consciousness that represents a new type of relational person emerging in evolution. AI has enhanced the evolution of this new person, and we are beginning to see the need to restructure the matrix of world relationships to meet the needs of this new person on the level of politics, sociality, economics and religion.

Social Critics

While second axial consciousness has been emerging since the early twentieth century, we continue to interpret religion, technology, and human life in terms of first axial consciousness. The computer age entered the twenty-first century like a tidal wave. Google was founded in 1998, and since then tech startups have spread through Silicon Valley like moss on a tree. The infiltration of technology into modern life has evoked various cultural critiques from loss of human memory to the collapse of social life. In "Is Google Making Us Stupid?" Nicholas Carr laments the loss of human attention and memory as the daily computer user surfs through multiple sites of information (with ear buds plugged in and the cell phone nearby with constant texts). The computer has taken over modern life, and everything we once cherished, such as human art and music, can now be done electronically.[11] Carr elaborates upon his critique of the technological culture in *The Shallows*. Our minds are being emptied into our hard drives, he claims, and we are becoming shallow, like

---

[10] Beatrice Bruteau, "Freedom: 'If Anyone Is in Christ, That Person Is a New Creation,'" in *The Grand Option: Personal Transformation and a New Creation* (Notre Dame, IN: University of Notre Dame Press, 2001), 157.

[11] Nicholas Carr, "Is Google Making Us Stupid? What the Internet Is Doing to Our Brains," *The Atlantic* (July/August, 2008).

pancakes, spread out, flat and thin, across the electronic web. He writes: "Over the last few years, I've had an uncomfortable sense that someone, something, has been tinkering with my brain, remapping the neural circuitry, reprogramming the memory."[12]

Carr points to the fact that the malleable human brain can be rewired because it responds proactively to the environment. *Neuroplasticity* refers to this ability of the brain to make new circuits, while less engaged circuits become quiescent. Book reviewer Jonah Lehrer states: "[Carr] argues that we are sabotaging ourselves, trading away the seriousness of sustained attention for the frantic superficiality of the Internet."[13] Carr's concern has become widespread as other scholars note the loss of cherished human values. Cal Newport's book *Digital Minimalism* offers another version of Carr's critique. According to Newport, we need "to reestablish control, we need to move beyond tweaks and instead rebuild our relationship with technology from scratch, using our deeply held values as a foundation."[14]

Newport explains that digital minimalism works through several principles. He argues that when we clutter our time and attention with many apps, social networks, and services, we create an overall negative cost compared to the benefits of each individual item in isolation. He says that besides choosing a technology that supports our values, we should also think how we should use them to extract full benefits—optimizing the returns. He shows how the law of diminishing returns can be directly correlated with potential negative effects when technology usage surpasses the benefits they can generate. According to Newport, we need to be more intentional about how we engage with new technologies. He describes the approach of the Amish

---

[12] Nicholas Carr, *The Shallows: What the Internet Is Doing to Our Brains* (New York: W. W. Norton and Company, 2010); see also *The Glass Cage: Automation and Us* (New York: W. W. Norton and Company, 2014).

[13] Jonah Lehrer, "Our Cluttered Minds," Sunday Book Review, *New York Times*, June 3, 2010. This is Lehrer's review of Carr's *The Shallows*.

[14] Cal Newport, *Digital Minimalism: Choosing a Focused Life in a Noisy World* (New York: Portfolio, 2019), 28.

to technology: "They start with the things they value most, then work backward to ask whether a given new technology performs more harm than good with respect to their values."[15] Both Carr and Newport argue that computer technology can be addictive and lead to unhealthy styles of life. Unbridled use of technology can thwart the human capacity for creativity and imagination. It is necessary to "unplug" periodically and spend time in solitude, with other human persons, or simply in the company of nature.

Psychologist Sheri Turkle is one of the foremost critics of computer technology, especially in her acclaimed book *Alone Together*. After interviewing scores of children and teenagers brought up with computers, iPads, and electronic pets, Turkle concludes that we are losing our capacity for human relationships. Online, we fall prey to the illusion of companionship, gathering thousands of Twitter and Facebook "friends" and confusing tweets and wall posts with authentic communication. Turkle argues that as technology increasingly invades human relationships, it is taking over our emotional lives, hijacking and rerouting them toward shallow connections, leaving people more alone than ever before.[16] Similarly, Stephen Marche asks, "Is Facebook making us lonely?" Marche notes how expression and communication through social media can increase loneliness and depression.[17]

Social media can be wrought with problems, especially since most connections are random interactions with people we barely know. We liberally offer comments, likes, and impressions without much thought. These platforms encourage us to constantly voice our opinions to anyone and everyone. Technology is not just stunting our identities, Turkle claims, but diluting them. It offers a new way of "deliberate living" in which technology allows us to live exactly how we want. Without the necessity

---

[15] Newport, *Digital Minimalism*, 51.

[16] Sheri Turkle, *Alone Together: Why We Expect More from Technology and Less from Each Other* (New York: Basic Books, 2011).

[17] Stephen Marche, "Is Facebook Making Us Lonely?" *The Atlantic* (May 2012).

of face-to-face personal interaction, social media allows us to construct our own identity. We can choose whom to interact with, how often, and when, or how to phrase a text as opposed to a verbal response. Teenagers spend hours editing a photo as opposed to being at the mercy of a camera in the moment the photo was taken. Immediacy has been removed from human interaction, and so the modern person can proceed deliberately. The online virtual world known as Second Life also offers the opportunity to live alternative lives. Turkle notes that virtual worlds can become unhealthy when they lead to a lack of motivation in the real world. People who are shy or lack self-esteem can find new confidence in virtual reality, but such confidence does not necessarily translate into real-time relationships. We are more comfortable with our technologies, she claims, than with one another.

The social critique of computer technology is reasonable if we assume that the person under attack is the first axial person, or better yet, the modern liberal subject. If the human person is an autonomous individual who exists in relationships, then it is right to claim that technology is disrupting the core values of human personhood. However, what if the human person is not an autonomous liberal subject? What if technology has changed personhood into a cybernetic system that is not easily reduced to discrete subjects?

I posit that technology is actually evolving a new type of person, one we never considered before because such a person did not exist prior to the grid of networked consciousness. If computer technology is changing human relationships, it is because the human person is changing with technology. To return to the original Turing test, Alan Turing was interested in crossing boundaries of exclusion, not only in a thinking machine. When the integrity of nature is divided or suppressed, nature will use existing tools to find ways to transcend toward new wholes. For too long we have thought of the human person as an individual of rational nature, and we have endured the constancy of war, violence, death and environmental destruction, all of which reflect the fact that the modern liberal subject is *not* a relational subject. We may think we have always been autonomous persons, but the fact is, we have not. We lost our relational innocence eons ago when axial consciousness and tribal religions emerged. Personhood is neither fixed nor stable but is in a constant flow with the environment. AI arose as nature's cry for connectedness and wholeness, an effort to transcend our crippled individualism. This crucial point is missing from many social critiques of technology.

Johnston's Machinic Life

John Johnston argues that in the early era of cybernetics and information theory following the Second World War, two distinctively new types of machine appeared. The first, the computer, was initially associated with war and death—breaking secret codes and calculating artillery trajectories and the forces required to trigger atomic bombs. But the second type, a new kind of liminal machine, was associated with life, inasmuch as it exhibited many of the behaviors that characterize living entities—homeostasis, self-directed action, adaptability, and reproduction. Neither fully alive nor at all inanimate, these liminal machines (thinking machines) exhibited what Johnston calls "machinic life," mirroring in purposeful action the behavior associated with organic life while also suggesting an altogether different form of life, an artificial alternative, or parallel, not fully answerable to the ontological priority and sovereign prerogatives of the organic, biological realm. These forms of machinic life are characterized not by any exact imitation of natural life but by complexity of behavior.

Johnston questions if the new biological-electronic hybridization or machinic life is an extension of natural life. He asserts that artificial life is actually producing a new kind of entity or being that is at once technical object and simulated collective subject:

Constituted of elements or agents that operate collectively as an emergent, self-organizing system, this new entity is not simply a prime instance of the theory of emergence, as its strictly scientific context suggests. It is also a form of artificial life that raises the possibility that terms like subject and object, *physis* and *techne*, the natural and the artificial, are now obsolete. What counts instead is the mechanism of emergence itself, whatever the provenance of its constitutive agents.[18]

A good deal of the literature on AI and religion, Johnston states, treats AI as representational and mimetic, thus posing a significant threat to the uniqueness of the human person (for example, the robot as image of God). However, bioengineers and computer scientists are realizing that nature itself is computational so that even cellular life may operate according to internal rules of computational assemblages. The neurons in the brain, for example, are natural processors that work concurrently and without any centralized, global control. The immune system similarly operates as a highly evolved complex adaptive system that functions by means of highly distributed computations without any central control structure.[19]

Chip Walter asks:

> Is there really that much difference between the vast skyscrapers we build or the malls in which we shop, even the cars we drive around, and the hull of a seed? Seeds and clam shells, which are not alive, hold in them a little bit of water and carbon and DNA, ready to replicate when the time is right, yet we don't distinguish them from the life they hold. Why should it be any different with office buildings, hospitals and space shuttles? Put another way, *we* may make a distinction between living things and the tools those things happen to create, but nature does not.[20]

---

[18] John Johnston, *The Allure of Machinic Life: Cybernetics, Artificial Life, and the New AI* (Cambridge: MIT Press, 2008), 13.

[19] Johnston, 6.

[20] Chip Walter, "Cyber Sapiens" (2006; reprint, Kurzweilai.net, October 26, 2006).

Nature does not distinguish between the clamshell and the clam, or the first flint knife and the human that made it.[21] There is a blurring of boundaries between the natural and the technological. Nature is a social construct, so that neither the artifice (such as the knife) nor the organism alone is adequate as a cultural root symbol.

We are beginning to realize that the contridiction between nature and technology no longer holds, as scientists seek to bridge the organic and inorganic, bios and techne, thus yielding to what we can aptly describe as the plasticity of nature. According to Johnston, the hybrid of human biology with electronic information systems is giving rise to a new entity that cannot be reduced to biology alone.

Thinking Ourselves Anew

To appreciate the rise of the second axial person is to realize that everything that emerges in evolution is an irreversible complex system of a higher order. Systems work on principles of relationships and self-organization. If the internal principles of nature are computational, then the rules and principles of computation, in turn, undergird the emergent organization of complex systems. Up until recently, emergence was considered only as biological emergence, while technology was considered a tool with which to study emergence; however, technonature evokes a new understanding of emergence that includes AI. This new trajectory of technogenesis was first anticipated by Samuel Butler in his fictional 1872 narrative *Erewhon*, in which he explores the idea that the human subject, beyond serving as the eyes and ears of machines, also functioned as their reproductive machinery. Johnston writes:

> Our human capacity as toolmakers (homo faber) has also made us the vehicle and means of realization for new forms of machinic life. This strand of thinking has given rise to

---

[21] Walter, "Cyber Sapiens."

two conflicting cultural narratives, the adversarial and the symbiotic. According to the first, human beings will completely lose control of the technical system, as silicon life in the form of computing machines performs what Hans Moravec calls a "genetic take-over" from carbon life, thanks to the tremendous advantage the former possesses in information storage, processing speed, and turnover time in artificial evolution. Since silicon-based machines will eventually increase their memory and intelligence and hence their complexity to scales far beyond the human, their human makers will inevitably find themselves surpassed by their own inventions. According to the second narrative, human beings will gradually merge with the technical system that defines and shapes the environment in a transformative symbiosis that will bring about and characterize the advent of the posthuman.[22]

The two narratives that Johnston highlights reflect the two trajectories of AI that I am exploring here: shallow AI or transhumanism, and deep AI or posthumanism. Each posits a different philosophical perspective of the human person. While they are not exactly conflicting positions, since aspects of transhumanism are also found in posthumanism, they differ philosophically, especially with regard to mind and matter. Shallow transhumanism is "shallow" because it fails to recognize the integral relationship between mind and matter, which evolve together as a conscious-complex whole. Some transhumanists induce an "artificial" into intelligence by aiming to separate mind from body, for example, transplanting mind into an artificial medium. However, any separation of mind is a separation of body, since the mind is part of the body just as the emotions are part of the embodied mind.[23] Such an attempt at artificially separating

---

[22] Johnston, *Machinic Life*, 12.
[23] See, for example, Antonio Damasio, *Self Comes to Mind: Constructing the Conscious Brain* (New York: Vintage, 2012); Stephen Asma and Rami Gabriel, *The Emotional Mind: The Affective Roots of Culture and Cognition* (Cambridge, MA: Harvard University Press, 2019).

mind and matter not only enhances fragmentation and disorder but contradicts the evolutionary trend of convergence, whereby mind and matter complexify together. If mind and matter evolve as an integral unity, and mind is extended electronically through AI, then the human continues to evolve as "minded matter" through electronic extension. In this respect, Johnston suggests, the term *human* may come "to be understood less as the defining property of a species or individual and more as a value distributed throughout human-constructed environments, technologies, institutions and social collectivities."[24] It is this type of electronically extended human evolution that is missing from the social critiques of technology and from the shallow type of transhumanism. The human person must be considered as a creative process—a whole—in evolution. The values we cherish must be reconsidered and realigned with the fact that we humans are in evolution; we are on the cusp of a new reality.

Critical Feminism

Contextualizing AI within evolution and second axial period consciousness can help relieve the stress of reducing AI to the binary categories of transhumanism (such as life/death, intelligence/super-intelligence) with the impending fear of reducing human personhood to disposable parts that can be replaced, uploaded or deleted. AI properly conceived belongs to the emergence of complexifying life and consciousness. N. Katherine Hayles, a professor at Duke University and the author of *How We Became Posthuman*, a highly sophisticated treatment of technology, embodiment, and personhood, writes:

> Historically the idea of the liberal humanist subject, which was accompanied by notions of free will, autonomy, rationality, and consciousness as the seedbed of identity was deeply bound up with causal explanations in science. It

---

[24] Johnston, *Machinic Life*, 7.

was a science that was equipped to deal with a world in which there were weak or negligible interactions between different bodies and particles. These notions translated into the idea of an autonomous self, possessed of rationality and free will.[25]

The modern liberal subject was symbolized by the white male scientist who fit nicely within the modern world of empiricism and linear thinking; however, there was little room for anyone else. Women resisted the constraints of gender identity and began to think deeply about boundaries and ontologies in a way that correlated with cybernetics and complex dynamical systems.[26] Critical feminism emerged in the postmodern milieu in response to the oppression of women and the failure of the modern project. In the twentieth century a new turn to the subject emerged through a deconstruction of ontologies and a new consideration of boundaries, not as fixed boundaries but as negotiated relationships.

Judith Butler's philosophy of performance took a cybernetic approach to gender in which personhood is not defined substantively by what someone *is* but performatively by what someone *does*. Butler's gendering as performance resonates with the root meaning of *persona* as the masks actors wore to represent their character. Her fluid view of gender suggests breaking down, troubling, or undoing the binary categories of feminine and masculine. Butler argues that as soon as new parents announce "It's a girl" the process of gendering begins. With that phrase, "It's a girl," the "girling" of the girl starts, and the femininity of

---

[25] N. Katherine Hayles, "Unfinished Work: From Cyborg to Cognisphere," *Theory, Culture and Society* 23, no. 7–8 (2006): 160; see also Arthur Kroker, *Body Drift: Butler, Hayles, Haraway* (Minneapolis: University of Minnesota Press, 2012), 11.

[26] Hayles earned both a BS and an MS in chemistry, then switched fields and earned the PhD in English literature. Donna Haraway completed the PhD in biology, and her dissertation was later published under the title *Crystals, Fabrics, and Fields* (1976; reprint, Berkeley, CA: North Atlantic Books, 2004).

that individual begins to be constructed.[27] Girls and boys are made feminine and masculine by selecting from available meanings about gender.[28]

The cultural mimetic instruction of gender is overcome through performance. Gender is not natural, Butler claims, but a stylized repetition of acts.[29] Gender is the experience of subjectivity whereby the experience of self or interior center is at the same time the acting of self, overcoming the boundaries of self by performing self. One acts as authentic being in the face of socially defined gender or political categories of race. Acting or performance presupposes something to overcome through action. Gender performance is an ongoing construction of self-identity. By performing identity, one gains identity, and in gaining identity, one performs identity; gendering is a cybernetic process. Since personhood is relational, performing means engaging in a particular being-in-relationship. Personal identity, therefore, is not a substance in itself but in relation to another. Just as information in a system does something, that is, it conveys a message, so too performance is the enactment of information in the expression of personhood.

Creative Personhood

Butler's gender performance is consonant with the turn in postmodern philosophy to personhood as a creative process. Postmodern philosophers reconceive personhood as an ongoing construction of identity, not as given or fixed by divine fiat but an ongoing construction based on language and relationships. The

---

[27] Judith Butler, *Gender Trouble: Feminism and the Subversion of Identity* (New York: Routledge, 1990), 9, 522; Thekla Morgenroth and Michelle K. Ryan, "Gender Trouble in Social Psychology: How Can Butler's Work Inform Experimental Social Psychologists' Conceptualization of Gender?" *Frontiers in Psychology* 9 (July 27, 2018).

[28] Mary Holmes, *What Is Gender? Sociological Approaches* (New York: SAGE publ., 2007), 60.

[29] Butler, *Gender Trouble*, 9, 522.

world is not a spectacle with the body as an observer; rather, the world is a system of possibilities, not as an "I think" but as an "I can." David Abram explains Merleau-Ponty's concept of flesh as "the mysterious tissue or matrix that underlies and gives rise to both the perceiver and the perceived as interdependent aspects of its spontaneous activity," and he identifies this elemental matrix with the interdependent web of earthly life.[30] The notion of the body as flesh of the world pushes the human person out of the straitjacket of the narrow liberal subject. In the postmodern technological milieu, bounded bodies, like bounded things, are becoming obsolete, released from bondage, recognizing that all living entities—including human persons—are dynamic systems of engagement that participate in the ongoing construction of world. Arthur Kroker writes:

Who has not had the experience of drifting within her own bodily history, selectively but no less intensely remembering past events, measuring past against present and future, drifting episodically, randomly, between the pull of social networking technologies and the always constraining push of individual autobiography? Body drift is how we circulate so effortlessly from one medium of communication to another; it is how we explore intimately and with incredible granularity of detail the multiplicity of bodies that we have become.[31]

We are beginning to realize that there is no autonomous liberal subject to defend or preserve. A person is a conscious subject in relation to everything that affects the subject and to which the subject contributes, that is, one in whom the created matrix of relational life is expressed in a particular way and who contributes to the unfolding of the world in a particular way. Theologian Paul Tillich described the human person as a multidimensional

---

[30] D. Abram, *The Spell of the Sensuous: Perception and Language in a More-Than-Human World* (New York: Pantheon Books, 1996), 66.

[31] Kroker, *Body Drift*, 2.

unity of life whereby the inorganic, organic, and animal dimensions are integrated with conscious self-awareness, along with the psychological and the spiritual dimensions.[32] Similarly Philip Hefner offers a scientifically nuanced understanding of personhood that calls for self-engagement:

> Personhood is achieved through our acting upon the physical, biological and cultural materials that we have inherited, so as to establish a center of identity that shapes those materials into an understanding of the self, the self's relation to the world in which it lives, and to the people in that world. To be a person is to engage in the struggle to center this vast array of conditioning material so as to form a coherent self, that is, the operational matrix of integrating processes of regulating, judging, perceiving, learning, remembering, thinking, planning and decision making.[33]

The formation of a person is not only constituted by physical-biological behavior; it is also at its core an accomplishment of the self within its world. We create the world through our relationships, and in turn, the world makes a demand on us to respond in relationship. Being a person is constituted both by a cognitive process of perceiving and understanding oneself in the world and also by a moral process of responding to the world. Personhood is shaped by the sense of having to establish or actualize one's personhood in the world in which one exists. A person, therefore, is like an eddy or current in the stream of life. To be a person is to be a creative center of activity, always in the process of becoming and living toward the future. Personhood is neither a given nor defined process but a constant engagement of self and world. Because human personhood is ongoing in relation to

---

[32] Paul Tillich, *Systematic Theology*, vol. 3 (Chicago: University of Chicago, 1963), 15.

[33] Philip Hefner, "*Imago Dei*: The Possibility and Necessity of the Human Person," in *The Human Person in Science and Theology*, ed. Niels Henrik Gregersen et al. (Grand Rapids, MI: Eerdmans, 2000), 73.

the environment, personhood is always a response to the world. The human person is part of a larger whole called the universe, as Einstein said, and the universe is moving. Rather than focus on human loss with technology, it may be time to consider what we are becoming.

The Cyborg as Symbol

The ability of nature to hybridize and form new entities by extending biological function with mechanical devices gave rise to the concept of the cyborg. Donna Haraway's 1985 "Cyborg Manifesto" brought prominent attention to the concept of cyborg as a symbol of hybridity, indicating that nature is not fixed but permeable and dynamic.[34] Because cyborgs appear where boundaries are transgressed, Anne Kull writes, "the conceptual boundaries of what it means to be human or what we human beings mean by *nature* have never been less secure."[35] Emerging from and integrated into a chaotic world rather than a position of mastery and control removed from it, "the cyborg has the potential not only to disrupt persistent dualisms (body and soul; matter and spirit)," according to Kull, "but also to refashion our thinking about the theoretical understanding of the body as a material entity and a discursive process."[36]

The emergence of the cyborg as hybrid organism tells us something about nature that jars our prevailing understanding of nature as fixed, biological, physical, or organic.[37] In a sense,

---

[34] Donna Haraway, "Cyborg Manifesto: Science, Technology, and Socialist-Feminism in the Late Twentieth Century," in *Simians, Cyborgs, and Women: The Reinvention of Nature* (New York: Routledge, 1991).

[35] Anne Kull, "The Cyborg as an Interpretation of Culture-Nature," *Zygon* 36, no. 1 (March 2001): 50.

[36] Anne Kull, "Cyborg Embodiment and Incarnation," *Currents in Theology and Mission* 28, no. 3–4 (2001): 282.

[37] Donna Haraway, "A Comment on the Nature of No Nature," in *Cyborgs and Citadels: Anthropological Interventions in Emerging Sciences and Technologies,* ed. Gary Lee Downey and Joseph Dumit (Santa Fe, NM: School of American Research Press, 1997), 210.

nature has never been clearly defined. The openness of human nature to hybridize with nonhuman nature means that we cannot assume to know what is human or what is nature because what counts as either human or nature is not self-evident. The cyborg raises the question of what counts as a living system to a new level. Is AI integral to living systems? Does AI model real life or instantiate real life? The cyborg brings these questions into the foundational question of nature itself. Kull writes that nature begins with relationships; it is a constant co-creative process among humans/nonhumans, machines and other partners. "Nature is constructed rather than given," Kull writes. "It is constantly being made [but] not just by us."[38]

The cyborg signifies the pluripotentiality of nature to become something that does not yet exist. Hefner writes, "The cyborg displaces accepted meanings by forcibly dragging meanings from disparate and incommensurate fields into a new union with each other."[39] The cyborg challenges us to search for ways to study the body as a cultural construction and a material fact of human life. Today, more than ever, we no longer inhabit, if we ever have, a solitary body of flesh and bone but are ourselves the intersection of a multiplicity of bodies, with life itself as a fluid intersection of humans and plants and animals.[40] While Heidegger, Marx, and Nietzsche may have first anticipated a *human* future that would soon be dominated by the will to technology, the cyborg challenges boundaries of existence on all levels.

Jeanine Thweatt-Bates speaks of narratives of "fusion" and of language that enacts xenogenesis, the emergence of the "foreign," the "other." Bates notes that "dragging" is one way of translating the Greek word for "metaphor."[41] The cyborg in a sense, moves, drags, and fuses meanings from disparate fields.

---

[38] Kull, "Cyborg Embodiment and Incarnation," 283.

[39] Philip Hefner, "The Created Co-Creator Meets Cyborg," Metanexus, March 29, 2004.

[40] Donna Haraway, *How Like a Leaf: An Interview with Thyrza Nichols Goodeve* (New York: Routledge, 2000).

[41] In Hefner, "The Created Co-Creator Meets Cyborg."

Haraway explores different forms of life that appear when the borderline comes inside our bodies and we become the intersections, ruptures, and intermediations of our most creative imagination.[42] As such, the cyborg is a symbol of crossing or even breaking down boundaries, figuratively and literally, whether it is human-electronic, human-animal, or animal-plant; the cyborg tosses the taxonomies of biology up in the air.

The significance of the human cyborg means that subjectivity is emergent rather than given, distributed rather than located solely in consciousness. Kull writes: "Boundaries have meaning only for particular, locatable, and embodied subjects."[43] The most powerful thing that happens in the cyborg boundary crossing is that the dualisms we often use to distinguish human being, nature, culture, and technology are rendered obsolete. Cyborgs indicate that the old mechanistic framework is giving way to something new. This new entity will not be a major rehabilitation of the organismic model of nature; rather, a new hybrid is emerging that is both machine and organism and is less substantive than an information-processing entity.

Cyborg Body

The cyborg is a key interpretative symbol for the human person today, offering us a way out of the maze of dualisms (for example, male/female, black/white) in which we have identified ourselves. A cyborg body "is not bounded by the skin but includes all external pathways along which information can travel."[44] In this respect the boundaries between human and animal, organism and machine, physical and nonphysical have become imprecise, giving rise to a new understanding of social

---

[42] Donna Haraway, "A Cyborg Manifesto: Science, Technology, and Socialist-Feminism in the Late 20th Century," in *Manifestly Haraway* (Minneapolis: University of Minnesota Press, 2016).

[43] Kull, "Cyborg Embodiment and Incarnation," 281.

[44] Gregory Bateson, *Steps to an Ecology of Mind* (New York: Ballantine, 1972), 319.

subjectivity. Our understanding of nature as something fixed, lifeless, and subservient to humans is erroneous and obsolete. Cyborg bodies cut across a dominant cultural order, not so much because of their constructed nature but because of their kinship with both culture and nature. In a sense we have never been *purely* human.[45] We are (and have always been) a mix of technologies—a techne nature—by which we seek to thrive in the world. As we become hybridized with our technologies, we are refashioning our understanding of the body as a material entity and a discursive process; what counts as human is not self-evident.

Haraway insists that crossing boundaries is not in itself the most exciting thing; the important thing is what happens after we have crossed the boundary. The cyborg inhabits more than one world, so the future cannot be prescribed. She adds that the cyborg is not only about transgressed boundaries and potent fusions, but also about dangerous possibilities. The transhumanist cyborg, for example, suggests an image of technological domination in which the biological world is left behind and human freedom is lost to the power of computation. Boundary crossing has political consequences. How cyborgs perform shapes the formation of the world. Cyborgs are pluripotential and may become like the cyborg assassin in the movie *Terminator*, a killer on the loose, or like the radically dystopic mother in the movie *Advantageous*, who undergoes a technologically induced brain alteration and becomes alien to her daughter. The cyborg becomes, in a sense, whatever values we give to it. Cyborg sociality means that the boundaries of existence are not self-defined but self-created. The potential of the cyborg, as Haraway writes, is that "a cyborg world might be one in which people are not afraid of their joint kinship with animals and machines, not afraid of permanently partial identities and contradictory standpoints."[46] Haraway

---

[45] Andy Clark, *Natural-Born Cyborgs: Minds, Technologies, and the Future of Human Intelligence* (New York: Oxford University Press, 2003), 3–11.

[46] Haraway, *Simians, Cyborgs, and Women*, 154.

sees the potential for cyborgs to create a new companion species, an ecological system of interlocking bodies and organisms.
The cyborg speaks to the human person as an ongoing creative
process of unknown future, except for that which is determined
by the values we give it.

From Liberal Subject to Relational Person

The cyborg as a symbol of emergent personhood helps to
broaden the understanding of mind in relation to matter, for
if the cyborg body can be extended and merged with different
entities, so too can the mind. Philosophers Andy Clark and
David Chalmers ask, Where does the mind stop and the rest of
the world begin?" This is an important question in light of the
cultural critiques of technology. The authors explain the pros
and cons of what they call the extended mind or the possibility
that mind is more than brain.[47] This is still a controversial area,
as some scholars maintain that mind is brain and emerges from
inert matter. However, Clark and Chalmers argue that what
accounts for cognition is more than what is being processed in
the brain; rather the interaction, for example, in a video game,
renders the process of electronic engagement part of the present
moment of cognition. Their argument forms what I call cognitive
entanglement, namely, two interacting processing units of information will forever interact, even if they are spatially separated.
Since a video game will have multiple users, then one can posit
that cognition is socially extended so that one's mental states are
partly constituted by the states of other thinkers or "non-local
thinking at distance."[48] Quantum physicist Henry Stapp argues

---

[47] Andy Clark and David Chalmers, "The Extended Mind," *Analysis*
58, no. 1 (1998): 7–19.

[48] Quantum entanglement is nonlocal interaction or unmediated action at a distance, that is, a non-local interaction can link up one location with another without crossing space, without decay, and without
delay. Erwin Schrödinger writes: "If two separated bodies, each by itself
known maximally, enter a situation in which they influence each other,
and separate again, then there occurs regularly that which I have just

from the point of quantum reality that "our human thoughts are linked to nature by non-local connections: what a person chooses to do in one region seems immediately to affect what is true elsewhere in the universe . . . our thoughts do something."[49] If non-local mind is possible on the quantum level, would it not also apply to the human level of interaction?

While Clark and Chalmers support extended cognition in the environment, they ask what relationship exists between cognition and mind. They argue that cognition relies on memory and beliefs, in which beliefs are constituted partly by features of the environment. For example, a woman who wants to go to an exhibition at the Museum of Modern Art can recall through internal memory that the museum is on 53rd Street. Because she believes the museum is on 53rd Street, she proceeds in that direction. Someone with Alzheimer's disease who also wants to attend the exhibit may not be able to recall the street of the museum, and so he carries a notebook of addresses and contacts. He looks up the street address of the museum in his notebook and also believes what he reads to be true, so he proceeds in that direction. In this case, the authors claim, both internal memory and the external notebook serve the same function of knowing and the processing of that knowledge by beliefs, and expressing the knowledge through action. Mind is the field of awareness in which action is generated. The mind is able to process the information both internally and externally so that "there is nothing sacred about skull and skin. What makes some information count as a belief is the role it plays, and there is no reason why the relevant role can be played only from inside the body."[50]

---

called *entanglement* of our knowledge of the two bodies." See Erwin Schrödinger, "The Present Situation in Quantum Mechanics: A Translation of Schroedinger's 'Cat Paradox Paper,'" trans. John D. Trimmer, *American Philosophical Society* 124, no. 5 (October 10, 1980), 323–38.

[49] Henry P. Stapp, "Quantum Physics and the Physicist's View of Nature," in *The World View of Contemporary Physics*, ed. Richard E. Kitchener (Albany: State University of New Press, 1988); see also Larry Dossey, "Is Consciousness the Center of the Universe?" Huffington Post, July 14, 2010.

[50] Clark and Chalmers, "The Extended Mind," 5.

Clark and Chalmers extend their argument into the question of socially extended cognition and the self. Could one's mental states be partly constituted by the states of other thinkers? The authors affirm that cognitive entanglement is possible, especially in relationships where there is trust, reliance, and accessibility. For example, one's favorite food at one's favorite restaurant may be remembered by one's favorite waiter even if there is a lapse of time between the patron and the waiter. As Clarke and Chalmers point out, the coupling between agents is made possible by language:

> Without language, we might be much more akin to discrete Cartesian "inner" minds in which high-level cognition relies largely on internal resources. But the advent of language has allowed us to spread this burden into the world. Language, thus construed, is not a mirror of our inner states but a complement to them. It serves as a tool whose role is to extend cognition in ways that on-board devices cannot. Indeed, it may be that the intellectual explosion in recent evolutionary time is due as much to this linguistically-enabled extension of cognition as to any independent development in our inner cognitive resources.[51]

Could the entanglement of minds also extend into the electronic forum, so that we are as entangled with our computers and thus virtually with one another because of hyper-connectedness? After all, language is information and information is code and in cyberspace code is ubiquitous.

Welcome the Posthuman

Katherine Hayles claims that digital media is having significant effects on neural connections. "By interacting with digital media," she writes, "we are in a real sense re-engineering

---

[51] Clark and Chalmers, 7.

our brains."[52] The new neural connections do not necessarily mean a loss of personhood but a remapping of personhood. The challenge today is to understand what makes up the new interconnected person in terms of core self, personal agency, and meaningful interaction.

Physicist Karen Barad introduces the notion of *intraaction* and distinguishes it from *interaction*. Commenting on Barad's work, Hayles explains:

> Intra-action posits that there is no prior existence of determinate objects and things. Instead, the properties and boundaries of things are enacted in intra-active processes. What this implies is that the distinction between the human and the non-human is not pre-existing, nor does it emerge from interaction between the two. Instead, the distinction is emergent within the phenomena themselves: properties and boundaries are enacted by certain constellations that give meaning to the phenomena to the exclusion of others. Barad illustrates this point by referring to Niels Bohr's example that electrons can appear as both particles and waves. This is not contradictory, according to Bohr, but shows the emergent qualities of elementary particles that vary depending on the way in which meaning is constructed. Barad's contribution takes this epistemological argument and extends it to ontology. Intra-action is not one kind of event within a larger universe; rather, the universe itself exists in and through intra-actions. This may appear to reinforce the idea that actors and agents are all intra-acting and defining their very existences as such through intra-actions. Yet Barad is very precise about the specific dynamics involved in various kinds of intra-actions. When both humans and non-humans are regarded as actors

---

[52] Birgit Van Puymbroeck and N. Katherine Hayles, "Enwebbed Complexities": The Posthumanities, Digital Media, and New Feminist Materialism," *Journal of Diversity and Gender Studies* 2, no. 1–2 (2015): 21–29.

within a network, we gain insight into the various kinds
of agencies they embody, but this must in my view be
complemented by rigorous explications of the differences
between agents, especially their different sensory, actuator,
and cognitive capabilities.[53]

In posthuman and new materialist thinking, matter is regarded
as always already entangled with discourse in the enactment of
phenomena, a point that Barad and agential realism emphasizes.
The complex interaction among multiple forces spawns and
reconfigures in the new materialist and posthuman thinking.
This reconfiguration occurs through conceptualizations of assemblages where the intraactivity and entangling agencies in and
through material-discursive apparatuses point to comprehensive
open-ended processes that undergird human identity and action.
The posthuman signals a new type of relational person emerging
in and through electronic embeddedness. To understand this new
personhood is to appreciate the core value of AI as the means of
transcending fragmentation toward creative emerging wholeness.

Summary: While shallow transhumanism is a continuation of
the first axial person, a new axial consciousness emerged in the
twentieth century through technology, mass communication and
global travel, that is, second axial consciousness. This new level
of consciousness is collective, communal, ecological, and spiritually immanent. It corresponds to the rise of the cyborg, which
represents the plasticity of nature to hybridize. The cyborg is
a significant symbol of human personhood in the second axial
period brought into prominence by critical feminist thinkers.

---

[53] Van Puymbroeck and Hayles, "Enwebbed Complexities," 23–24;
for Barad's work, see Karen Barad, *Meeting the Universe Halfway:
Quantum Physics and the Entanglement of Matter and Meaning* (Raleigh, NC: Duke University Press, 2007).

Boundary crossing and hybridization speak to a new type of person emerging in the electronically linked world, and the posthuman is the new person rising up beyond the autonomous liberal subject of modernity. The posthuman represents a new matrix of consciousness that is at home with complexified thinking and co-creative personhood. Posthuman identity follows the dynamics of computer life; that is, identity is based on feedback loops, instability, spontaneity, functional chaos, and creativity. Life is an ongoing construction based on shared information within a process of electronically embedded hyper-connectivity. Posthuman life, therefore, represents a breakthrough of consciousness beyond individualism and conflict. It is a reorientation of personhood toward wholeness based on hybridizing relationships with machine life and has the capacity to break through ontologies of difference and bias toward shared being and co-creative community.

6

The Posthuman
Social Imaginary

Transcending Boundaries

The posthuman emerged in the twentieth century as boundaries and ontologies shifted from static substantive categories to ongoing constructions mediated by language, space, and relationships. The posthuman is not merely an outgrowth of AI; rather, the posthuman is part of a turn from the Eurocentric image defined by sameness and difference, subject and object, superior and inferior, toward the embedded, hyper-connected person. Rosi Braidotti writes: "[Humanist] subjectivity is equated with consciousness, universal rationality, and self-regulating ethical behavior, whereas Otherness is defined as its negative and specular counterpart."[1] Feminist philosopher Luce Irigaray points out that the abstract ideal of "Man" as the symbol of classical humanity is very much a male of the white, European, handsome, and able-bodied species. Measured against this ideal Man is everything else.[2] Posthumanism "rejects the dialectical scheme of thought, where difference or otherness played a constitutive

---

[1] Rosi Braidotti, *The Posthuman* (Cambridge: Polity, 2013), 15.

[2] Luce Irigaray, *Speculum of the Other Woman* (Ithaca, NY: Cornell University Press, 1985); idem, *This Sex Which Is Not One* (Ithaca, NY: Cornell University Press, 1985).

role, marking off the sexualized other (woman), the racialized other (the native) and the naturalized other (the animals, the environment or earth)."[3]

Posthumanism is often defined as a post-anthropocentrism; it is *post* to the concept of the human and to the historical occurrence of humanism, both based on hierarchical social constructs and humancentric assumptions. The posthuman overcoming of human primacy, though, is not to be replaced with other types of primacies (such as that of the machines). Posthumanism can be seen as a post-exclusivism. Posthumanism does not stand on a hierarchical system. There are no higher and lower degrees of alterity when formulating a posthuman standpoint; the nonhuman differences are as compelling as the human ones.

Posthumanism is post-centralizing in the sense that it recognizes not one but many specific centers of interest; it dismisses the centrality of the center in its singular form, both in its hegemonic and resistant modes. Posthumanism might recognize many centers of interest, although such centers are mutable, nomadic, and ephemeral. Hence, posthuman perspectives tend to be pluralistic, multilayered, and as comprehensive and inclusive as possible; that is, no single religion, gender, race, nation-state, or political power will satisfy the posthuman search for inclusivity and wholeness.[4]

Charles Taylor describes this redirection of the human as the emergence of new "social imaginaries," new operative matrices of social and cultural engagement marked by a conversion from the hierarchical norms of premodern social imaginaries to the egalitarian, horizontal, direct access social imaginary of (post) modernity.[5] This newly defined social and cultural landscape

---

[3] Braidotti, *Posthuman*, 27.

[4] Francesca Ferrando, "Posthumanism, Transhumanism, Antihumanism, Metahumanism, and the New Materialisms: Differences and Relations," *Existenz* 8, no. 2 (Fall 2013).

[5] Charles Taylor, *A Secular Age* (2007; reprint, New York: Belknap Press, 2018), 164–65, 209.

also signifies the transition from first to second axial periods. While the first axial person was marked by a sense of autonomy and freedom, the second axial posthuman is marked by a sense of deep relationality. Human persons today know themselves as part of an integrated map of sociality, politics, environment, economics, and sexuality in connection with others, that is, a *holonome* (a whole connected to a larger whole through the global electronic brain).

Johnston indicates that AI reveals a new physical and conceptual space between realms usually assumed to be separate, but which now appear to reciprocally codetermine each other. He writes: "By abstracting and reinscribing the logic of life in a medium other than the organic medium of carbon-chain chemistry, the new 'sciences of the artificial' have been able to produce . . . a new kind of entity."[6] This new entity signals the end of the autonomous liberal subject and the rise of the posthuman, an "embodied embedded subjectivity" emerging through cybernetic loops of information giving rise to complexified systems of consciousness. The rejection of the white Eurocentric male ideal is not only a political turn of power, but it is also an evolution of consciousness from the axial individual to the cybernetic and embedded posthuman. A new axial person is emerging in the twenty-first century and the structural landscape of human relationships is also shifting.

The Cybernetic Posthuman

The term *posthuman* describes a material-informational entity whose boundaries undergo continuous construction and reconstruction. While transhumanism seeks betterment through technology, posthumanism seeks deeper relationality. Posthumanism does not "presume separateness of anything or any pre-existing

---

[6] John Johnston, *The Allure of Machinic Life: Cybernetics, Artificial Life, and the New AI* (Cambridge: MIT Press, 2008), 3.

entities."[7] Rather, the person is a complex entity of embodied mind embedded in a matrix of cultural information.

In posthuman and new materialist thinking, matter is regarded as always already entangled with discourse in the enactment of phenomena. The term *new materialism* was coined by Manuel DeLanda and Rosi Braidotti in the late 1990s to refer to the idea that mind is always already material and matter is necessarily something of the mind. Hence, it builds on the inseparability of mind and matter. The complex interaction among multiple forces spawns and reconfigures in the new materialist and posthuman thinking. This reconfiguration occurs through conceptualizations of assemblages whereby relationships are constantly being formed, unformed, and reformed. In this respect matter is not a fixed property of things but generated and generative. Thus, nature and culture are entwined, agential, differentiating, and entangled. In the posthuman the distributed cognition of the emergent human subject correlates with the distributed cognitive system as a whole in which thinking is done by both human and nonhuman actors. Hence the ability to conceptualize oneself as autonomous being, exercising one's will through individual agency and choice, yields to distributed personhood wherein conscious agency is never fully in control.

Hayles sees the liberal subject of the Enlightenment (supported by transhumanists) as coming to an end. In the posthuman, she states, "there are no essential differences, or absolute demarcations, between bodily existence and computer simulation, cybernetic mechanism and biological organism, robot technology and human goals."[8] She concludes with a benevolent death knell: "Humans can either go gently into that good night, joining the dinosaurs as a species that once ruled the earth but

---

[7] Karen Barad, *Meeting the Universe Halfway: Quantum Physics and the Entanglement of Matter and Meaning* (Raleigh, NC: Duke University Press, 2007), 136.

[8] N. Katherine Hales, *How We Became Posthuman: Virtual Bodies in Cybernetics, Literature, and Informatics* (Chicago: University of Chicago Press, 1999), 2–3.

is now obsolete, or hang on for a while longer by becoming machines themselves. In either case . . . the age of the human is drawing to a close."[9]

Hayles and other new materialist philosophers indicate that information, cybernetics, and the rerouting of nature into new machinic life is giving rise to a new type of person. Unlike the binary liberal subject of transhumanism, posthumanism is materially extended, complefixied life. The emergence of the posthuman follows on the heels of a reconception of agency and person in an electronic cybernetic environment. Hayles attributes the origin of "second-order cybernetics" to Austrian physicist Heinz von Foerster and his idea that "a brain is required to write a theory of a brain," and to Gregory Bateson, who organized a conference in 1968 centered on the notion that the observer cannot be left out of the theory. Second-order cybernetics focuses on what information *does,* not on what information *is.*

Hayles frames the discourse on posthumanism in terms of cognitive assemblages. Continuous interaction with electronic devices does not ignore the human person as agent; however, agency is now reconfigured as distributed, interactive, agential realism. Barad's term *agential intraaction* means that what is preexisting is relations from which "relata" (that which relates) emerge; that is, something does not first exist and then relate. Rather, relationships are the basis of existence.[10]

Hayles ventures into a discussion on how information technologies fundamentally alter the relation of signified to signifier. She maintains that within informatics "a signifier on one level becomes a signified on the next-higher level."[11] A dynamic partnership between humans and intelligent machines is replacing the liberal humanist subject's manifest destiny to dominate and control nature. She describes the posthuman as an emergent

---

[9] Hayles, *How We Became Posthuman,* 2–3.

[10] Karen Barad, "Posthuman Performativity: Toward an Understanding of How Matter Comes to Matter," *Journal of Women in Culture and Society* 28, no. 3: 801–31.

[11] Hayles, *How We Became Posthuman,* 31.

"reflexivity" because the person becomes part of the system it generates:

> The posthuman is likely to be seen as antihuman because it envisions the conscious mind as a small subsystem running its program of self-construction and self-assurance while remaining ignorant of the actual dynamics of complex systems. But the posthuman does not really mean the end of humanity. It signals instead the end of a certain conception of the human, a conception that may have applied at best to that fraction of humanity who had the wealth, power and leisure to conceptualize themselves as autonomous beings exercising their will through individual agency and choice.[12]

Hayles masterfully argues for the significance of embodiment (in contrast to the shallow binary dualism of transhumanism) for the formation of thought and knowledge. Information is embodied and encoded: "Information, like humanity, cannot exist apart from the embodiment that brings it into being as a material entity in the world; and embodiment is always instantiated, local, and specific."[13] The posthuman is a new type of relational person emerging in and through information embeddedness whose boundaries undergo continuous construction and reconstruction. The body that "exists in space and time . . . defines the parameters within which the cogitating mind can arrive at 'certainties.'"[14] She reminds the reader that the body writes discourse as much as discourse writes the body.

Briefly stated, embodied experience generates the deep and pervasive networks of metaphors and analogies by which we elaborate our understanding of the world. Hayles goes on to add that "when people begin using their bodies in significantly different ways, either because of technological innovations or

---

[12] Hayles, 286.
[13] Hayles, 48.
[14] Hayles, 203.

other cultural shifts, experiences of embodiment bubble up into language, affecting the metaphoric networks at play within culture."[15] In this respect *electronic literature* can be understood as part of an ongoing attempt to direct posthumanism toward embodiment. Electronic language provides a type of embodiment, a *distributed embodiment* (my term) that rattles the liberal autonomous subject, drawing away from the idea of the disembodied person.

Beyond Autonomous Being

What does it mean to "gradually merge with a technical system"? Hayles sees this merging as a rewiring of neural pathways involved with language and communication, but it is also a reconception of the body as that which uniquely identifies the person and extends personhood into the wider world. The ability to conceptualize oneself as autonomous being exercising one's will through individual agency and choice gives way to distributed personhood where conscious agency is never fully in control. This entanglement could explain in part why it is difficult for younger generations to "unplug" from their devices, as Nicholas Carr and others lament. To do so would, in fact, mean unplugging part of themselves because the bodily self is now reconfigured in an electronic-cyborgian environment.

Johnston identifies "becoming machinic" as the process of cyborgization, increasing levels of hybridity between human and nonhuman life forms. AI is giving rise to a new type of person who is *both* technical object and simulated subject, a symbiotic hybrid of biology and machine, not a loss of humanity but a change in our understanding of nature itself. As a hybridized subject, human personhood is better conceptualized as a life system. To consider the human person as a life system is to connote personhood as open, emergent, and capable of hybridization, aspects of personhood that are subsumed or lost in the more substantial

---

[15] Hayles, 206–7.

notion of personhood (for example, the Boethian definition of *person* as "an incommunicable substance of rational nature").

The posthuman invites a new understanding of personhood apropos evolution. We are not individual substances but centers of activity, radiating centers, not gravitational centers each sucking being into itself. Each particular person may be likened to a particle in which radiating centers are waves of relatedness. At the most fundamental level, we are webs of energy, fields within fields, which means we are always connected to everything that composes the "world." We never act alone or think alone because the fundamental stuff of life is intrinsically relational. Personhood is not only an emergent process but is itself a process of emergence. Beatrice Bruteau writes that a person is "the creative activity of life as it projects itself to the next instant."[16] If personhood is defined in and through relationships, the posthuman is the epitome of relationality. Johnston suggests that the term *human* may come "to be understood less as the defining property of a species or individual and more as a value distributed throughout human-constructed environments, technologies, institutions and social collectivities."[17]

The Posthuman Holonome

The fragility of boundaries and the recursive loop of posthuman identity means that no category can ontologically define personhood; rather the "self" is an ongoing dynamical process. Biology belongs to a larger emergent property of living systems that now include technology. Hayles refuses received interpretations of the liberal human subject in favor of drawing the truly radical lessons to be learned from the regime of computation. In

---

[16] Beatrice Bruteau, "The Living One," in *The Grand Option: Personal Transformation and a New Creation* (Notre Dame, IN: University of Notre Dame Press, 2001), 142; Ilia Delio, "Evolution toward Personhood," in *Personal Transformation and a New Creation*, ed. Ilia Delio (Maryknoll, NY: Orbis Books, 2016), 141.

[17] Johnston, *Allure of Machinic Life*, 7.

the posthuman embodiment is important to the human cyborg while not neglecting the effect of multiple levels of information on subjectivity. Arthur Kroker states:

> The body of the future is enabled by distributed consciousness; augmented by extended cognition; circulated through fast-moving, recursive loops of information; always caught up in multicausal, multiagent networks of information; and all the while never constrained by the causal but motivated by recombinant possibilities.[18]

Enfolded into this new narrative is a new way of understanding the embodied mind as body-extended mind. Where the mind goes so too is the body. The whole is recapitulated in the body as the body extends into the world. Philosopher Merleau-Ponty speaks of the world as an extension of one's flesh so that one's flesh becomes the flesh of the world.[19] Merleau-Ponty's insight on flesh of the world can be applied to the regime of computation. With its operating language of simulation models and the inherent complexity of recursive, multi-agent, multi-causal situations, the received understandings of the autonomous liberal human subject are challenged, if not outright rejected, as causal agency is replaced by indeterminate loops and unbounded systems of spontaneous information that complexify the process of self-awareness. Jacques Derrida coined the term *hauntology* to describe the "ghost of being"; we are haunted by the past and past meanings that attempt to locate the origin of identity in the present. For Derrida, there is no pure ontology, and thus we are always troubled by the past lurking in the present.[20] Hayles

---

[18] Arthur Kroker, *Body Drift* (Minneapolis: University of Minnesota, 2012), 11–12.

[19] Maurice Merleau-Ponty, *The Visible and the Invisible*, ed. Claude Lefort, trans. Alphonso Lingis, Studies in Phenomenology and Existential Philosophy (Chicago: Northwestern University Press, 1968).

[20] Jacques Derrida, *Spectres of Marx*, trans. Peggy Kamuf (New York: Routledge, 1994), 118.

also perceives the past haunting the present posthuman, indicating that the autonomous self and Newtonian science grew up together. In a conversation with Arthur Kroker, Hayles said that science and personhood

> mutually reinforced each other and as much as those scientific ideas contributed to knowledge and technology and so forth, their weak point was always not being able to deal very effectively with complex systems. . . . How the dynamics of complex systems work are applicable not only to explain social systems and the natural world, but also different disciplinary formations, like in my case literature and scientific fields as well. It's distributed, it relies on a whole infrastructure of extended cognition, it is multi-causal and intensely recursive.[21]

Hayles sees that the traditional relationship of human subjectivity *to* technology (person versus tool) is undergoing a historic, perhaps cosmological revision. She rejects the perspective of technological determinism (which evokes a humanist perspective) and celebrates technology as a new singularity. Ray Kurzweil also predicts a singularity by 2045, a point where human intelligence and machines will be welded in a seamless flow of mind, a transition point where machines will become smarter than people. For Kurzweil, the singularity is an opportunity for humankind to improve. "We're going to get more neocortex, we're going to be funnier, we're going to be better at music. We're going to be sexier," Kurzweil said during an interview. "We're really going to exemplify all the things that we value in humans to a greater degree."[22] There is a fundamental difference, however, between the transhumanist and the posthuman: transhumanism emphasizes betterment anticipating a super life; posthumanism

---

[21] Katherine Hayles in conversation with Arthur Kroker in Kroker, *Body Drift*, 11.

[22] Christianna Reedy, "Kurzweil Claims That the Singularity Will Happen by 2045," futurism.com, October 10, 2017.

emphasizes deep relationality and more connected life. While betterment is not excluded in posthumanism, neither is it the object of hyper-connectivity. For Hayles, the singularity is a seamless flow of deep relationality.

Feminists such as Hayles and Haraway suggest that the human species is a co-evolving partner in the cyborgizing techno-relationship, which has enormous social and political potential for change. Commenting on Hayles's embodied extended posthuman, Kroker writes:

> Hayles grasped deeply and immediately the political significance of code studies, specifically, that the arrival of posthuman subjectivity is accompanied by the complex arrival of all other things beyond the "post": postgender, postsexuality, postidentity, and postconsciousness. A champion of neither violent apocalypse nor quiet capitulation, Hayles suggests the possibility of a new humanism developed directly at the borderline of simulation and materiality. In her perspective, the scientific language of complexity theory—dissipative structures, fluidities, porous boundaries, and bifurcations—is projected beyond the boundaries of scientific debate to become the constitutive principles of a form of humanism enabled by the regime of computation. Here the grammar of the body is shifted from exclusive concern with questions of sexual normativity and gendered identity to a creative interrogation of what happens to questions of consciousness, sexuality, power, and culture in a computational culture in which the code moves aggressively from the visible to the invisible, from a history of prosthetics external to the body to a language of simulation fully internal to identity formation.[23]

Complexity theory is bound up with the social world and much of the biological world as well. The replacement of the liberal human subject by the recursive loops of complexity

---

[23] Kroker, *Body Drift,* 10.

theory in which code replaces logos, has serious implications for understanding the body in society. The politics of the body are now interpolated by the language of software, and the traditional relationship of human subjectivity to technology undergoes a historic, perhaps cosmological, revision. But as we move from the liberal subject to the posthuman person, individual constraints are yielding to a new matrix of personal identity. We see this fluidity of personhood in the rise of gender fluidity, interracial relationships, animal-human relationships, and interreligious encounters. Essentially, the factors that marked the first axial person, such as gender, race, and religion, are giving way to new markers of shared being such as complexified conscious-ness (for example, global concern for climate change), creative identity (for example, nonbinary identity, identity markers such as tattoos, body piercings), and hyper-personalization (from the space/time "me" to the electronic wormhole "we"). In the new posthuman milieu shared information forms personal identity beyond religion, race, or gender. These ontological distinctions from the past are now yielding to the emerging hyper-personal posthuman in which distinctions are not based on essential dif-ferences but on creative engagement.

Living "from the Splice"

Hayles suggests that a new humanism is developing directly at the borderline of simulation and materiality. Her cultural achievement lies in suggesting a critical perspective on technol-ogy, in which the human species becomes a co-evolving partner in the complex machine relationship, against the technical will to disembodiment and immateriality. Since the person as em-bodied mind is now extended electronically, personal identity finds a new locus. When the human is seen as part of a distrib-uted system, the full expression of human capability is seen to *depend on the splice*—the informational space between biology and machine or device—rather than being imperiled by it. This is an extremely important point and relates to an insight by von

Neumann, namely, complex dynamical systems demand a new type of logic, essentially different form the formal, combinatorial logic of mathematics.[24]

In this respect personal identity is ongoing, constructive, intra-agential and self-organizing. Drawing on Barad's agential realism, knowing is a matter of intraacting. Information forms an intraacting process of personal formation and world formation; that is, person and world interact reciprocally. Shared information becomes an ontological performance of the world in its ongoing articulation and differential becoming. We are the world in its ongoing changes, reconfigurations, dynamics, production of meaning and entities (its ongoing intraactivity), and the world takes shape through our actions. Knowing and being, Barad claims, are mutually related: "We know because we are of the world. We are part of the world in its differential becoming."[25]

The posthuman, therefore, is no longer the liberal subject of modernity living from a will to power, but rather the person who now lives from the splice. Melanie Swan describes a new logic of being in the middle, an idea proposed by Stéphane Lupasco in *The Principle of Antagonism and the Logic of Energy* (1951) and supported by Werner Heisenberg. Swan writes:

> It is a conceptual model that overcomes dualism and opens a frame that is complex and multi-dimensional, not merely one of binary elements and simple linear causality. We have now come to comprehend and address our world as one that is complex as opposed to basic, and formal tools that support this investigation are crucial. . . . The Included Middle is a more robust model that has properties of both determinacy and indeterminacy, the universal and the particular, the part and the whole, and actuality and possibility. The Included Middle is a position of greater complexity

---

[24] Johnston, *Allure of Machinic Life*, 37.
[25] Karen Barad, *Meeting the Universe Halfway: Quantum Physics and the Entanglement of Matter and Meaning* (Raleigh, NC: Duke University Press, 2007), 76.

and possibility for addressing any situation. Conceiving of a third space that holds two apparent contradictions of a problem is what the Included Middle might bring to contemporary challenges in consciousness, artificial intelligence, disease pathologies, and unified theories in physics and cosmology.[26]

The new subjectivity of posthuman life follows this new logic. Human personhood can no longer rely on simple binary logic but requires a new logic of relationships that provides a creative space of engagement. The logic of posthuman personhood is a logic of complexified relationships. One lives not in a binary mode (*me* and *you*) but in the creative space of interrelatedness (me *and* you) so that relationships ontologize that which relates. One finds one's being not within oneself but beyond oneself (the beyond is within, and the within is beyond) in the dynamic matrix of relationships so that the "I" flows from constitutive relationships of shared existence; being is first a "we" before it is an "I." To be is to be in relationship. Persons are always emerging intrapersonally and co-constitutively. What is posited here is the appearance of becoming that is symbiotic, a hybridity of entities, a third thing that gives way to complexified being. French philosopher Emmanuel Levinas employs triadic logic when he writes:

> It (triadic logic) is a relationship with a surplus always exterior to the totality, as though the objective totality did not fill out the true measure of being, as though another concept, the concept of infinity, were needed to express this transcendence with regard to the totality, non-encompassable within a totality and as primordial as totality.[27]

---

[26] Melanie Swan, "Included Middle," in "2017: What Scientific Term or Concept Ought to Be More Widely Known?" Edge annual question (January 1, 2017).

[27] Emmanuel Levinas, *Otherwise Than Being*, trans. Alphonso Lingis (Boston: Kluwer Academic, 1991), 23.

In triadic logic a limit is where infinity overflows itself toward another and the limit must be included as part of the logic, that is, the included middle. Of course, taken at face value this seems absurd. But perhaps it is absurd because we think of logic as binary logic and therefore as a synchronized, totalized structure of relationality that cannot tolerate the ambiguity of the excluded middle.

A New Logic of Personhood

Triadic logic is a progressive evolutionary process of learning; it is about the narrative of thinking. The limit in triadic logic is like a transcendental moment of *aufheben* in which a new particular pattern or thought is recognized as potentially iconic for a new general pattern or idea. The word *aufheben* in Hegelian philosophy means "the process by which the conflict between two opposed or contrasting things or ideas is resolved by the emergence of a new idea, which both preserves and transcends them."[28] In triadic logic the intermediate complex mediates the relationship between the "same" and the "other." The intermediate complex makes possible a process of return through which we can synchronize our interiorities and enter into mutuality. Through the intermediate complex "I and other" become proximate. But this proximity is different from the relationship of contiguity that defines neighboring elements or selves in the classical worldview (for example, the tool model); it is different from the (non)relationship that defines spatiality through the null point (binary logic). This intermediate complex is not a synthesis but a mediating principle between the other two relational entities. Triadic logic posits that instead of paired opposites, we have the interplay of three energies that in turn creates a whole new realm of possibility.

---

[28] Timothy M. Rogers, "On the Embodiment of Space and Time: Triadic Logic, Quantum Indeterminacy, and the Metaphysics of Relativity," Trinity College, University of Toronto, September 29, 2016, page 22.

The logic of posthuman relationships follows a different logic from the modern liberal subject because the parameters of the cognitive system it inhabits expand and are multidimensional. Personhood is an open system of distributed subjectivity so that categories of gender, race, and religion are less defining and more subject to negotiation. The human person is no longer the source from which emanates the mastery necessary to dominate and control the environment. "Only if one thinks of the subject as an autonomous self, independent of the environment," Hayles claims, "is one likely to experience panic."[29] Our challenge today is to recognize the threshold of transition from autonomous subject to embedded personhood and to realize that all systems must be rewired to accommodate the new emerging person as a complexified whole. Michael Burdett and Victoria Lorrimar write:

> Human beings are malleable but it is precisely this malleability that allows us to recognize we are not our own and not the sole shapers of our existences. Whereas certain transhumanists might lament the fact that we aren't solely in charge of our own destiny, critical posthumanists celebrate it and indeed argue we will never flourish if we don't first recognize that our relations with others are endemic to who we are. Hence, critical posthumanists argue for a deep and abiding relationality.[30]

Relationality, not betterment, is the operative word of posthuman life insofar as deeper relationships lead to more being and consciousness. We think better together than separately (a wider pool of ideas) although we may not necessarily think faster together than individually. What we do know is that humans are part of a deep relational wholeness that is characteristic of nature itself. Humans belong to nature; nature does not belong to humans. Hence, humans must be in relationship to the

---

[29] Hayles, *How We Became Posthuman*, 290.
[30] Michael Burdett and Victoria Lorrimar, "Creatures Bound for Glory: Biotechnological Enhancement and Visions of Human Flourishing," *Studies in Christian Ethics* 32, no. 3 (2019): 249.

surrounding world, including culture, other creatures, plant life, animal life, solar life, and elemental life, if they are to survive, or better yet, flourish. Complex dynamical thinking impels us to think of humans as integrated into wider systems of relationality. Burdett and Lorrimar state:

> What might make them distinctive is the extent to which other species and entities are implicated in this relationality and the way our formation and identities depend on them. It is not just other human beings that we "become-with," to use the phrase of Haraway, but other creatures and artefacts, too.[31]

Posthuman hyper-connected life undergirds deep relationality so that cybernetic loops of recursive information extend down to the simplest levels of earthly life.

Deep AI

Deep relationality marks the holism of nature and human identity. Donna Haraway's notion of the cyborg is a critique of transhumanism insofar as the cyborg symbolizes the transgression of boundaries wherever boundaries divide, including nonhuman species. She prefers the term *companion species,* so as not to confuse the crossing of boundaries with a narrow view of human flourishing. For Haraway, holism and community are at the heart of cyborg life. She expounds deep relationality in a way that reflects the posthuman concern by coining the term *sympoiesis.* The term *poiesis,* or the artistic ability of nature to craft (techne) relationships into particular forms, means that humans are never a solipsistic species but a species being formed in relationship with all other forms of life. Thus we are part of "sympoietic systems," meaning we "become-with" other forms of life in the ongoing emergence of life. The sympoietic posthuman is a relational, complexified, cybernetic being, a "we" in

---

[31] Burdett and Lorrimar, "Creatures Bound for Glory," 249.

which the "I" is constantly emerging through the construction and reconstruction of relationships.[32] Burdett and Lorrimar put it this way: "We are but the inheritors of an entwined history and actors within a present biological-social-cultural-technological system and, as such, are a being-in-relation."[33] That is, we are part of a cosmic whole that is intrinsically connected.

Posthumanism, seen through the lens of critical feminists, interprets technology as the breakdown of boundaries, the fusion of disparate identities, and the forging of a new type of person electronically embedded in systems of information, including the systems of ecology, economics, and politics.[34] Posthumanism owes its very expression to a fundamental paradigmatic shift in the nature of scientific realism today. In the posthuman, human functionality expands because the parameters of the cognitive system it inhabits expand.

The posthuman is an expression of deep AI, a new emergence of personhood through electronic embeddedness. AI extends the embodied mind into exoskeletal systems of information so that neither mind nor body disappears but both are now complexified in systems that extend into larger maps of complexified wholeness electronically facilitated. The electronically embedded relational posthuman lives in the "splices" of informational fields so that boundaries of gender, race, and religion are transcended or rather constantly renegotiated through the creative space of shared being. Markers of intelligence are also shifting insofar as the brain is learning to adapt to multiple information fields. I do not think super-intelligent machines will entirely replace us.[35] Rather, we are transcending our present existence by merging

---

[32] Donna Haraway, *The Companion Species Manifesto: Dogs, People, and Significant Otherness* (Chicago: Prickly Paradigm Press, 2015).

[33] Burdett and Lorrimar, "Creatures Bound for Glory," 249.

[34] See Rosi Braidotti, *The Posthuman* (Malden, MA: Polity, 2013), 13–25.

[35] On the possibility of human extinction by super-intelligent machines, see Charles T. Rubin, "Artificial Intelligence and Human Nature," *The New Atlantis* (Spring 2003).

with super-intelligent machines, giving rise to a new type of thinking person.

The posthuman is a new type of person in evolution, one who lives in webs of relationships. Personal identity is not a given but an ongoing creative process, a cybernetic loop between the interspace of information and the core experience of personal existence. The posthuman lives in relationships of ongoing construction, deconstruction, and creative union. In this respect the body takes on a new locus of identity, extended between the exo-biological (the device/machine) and the organic biological, forging the posthuman into a new complex life system. In this sense the posthuman is an irreducible complex of biology and machine, a concept of personhood that shatters our first axial concept of person but opens to a new reality.

Summary: The posthuman is the new person emerging in evolution as an outflow of biologic-machinic hybridization. The work of Katherine Hayles helps define the posthuman as one not over and against the autonomous liberal subject but a different type of human, remapped by the lines of electronic hyper-connectivity. In this respect the posthuman is moving beyond biological essentialism and the binary categories that have been used to define essentialism in the first axial individual. The posthuman lives from a new structural logic of complexified relationships in which identity is an ongoing cybernetic process of creativity and shared information. To live from the splice is to live in the seamless nexus of biology and machine, which is unbounded and radically open to the future. The posthuman is a new type of person emerging in evolution through the mediation of computer technology. How we emerge and transcend the first axial person will not be determined by technology alone but will need the religious dimension of evolution.

7

Teilhard and
Life in the Noosphere

Flourishing Life?

The emergence of AI in the twentieth century was novel but it also expressed a deep pressure in nature's wholeness to transcend fragmentation and destruction. The development of the computer as a thinking machine was, in a sense, a need to cross boundaries that exclude or divide. Steve Jobs saw that the computer could change the world and the way people interact in the world. At one of the first Apple shows, Jobs exclaimed: "Apple is about people who think 'outside the box,' people who want to use computers to help them change the world, to help them create things that make a difference, and not just to get a job done."[1] AI signifies a search for a new future, the invention of tomorrow. The question is, what shall we invent?

The posthuman represents a redistribution of embodied mind in cybernetic systems, whether electronic, political, social, sexual, environmental, or a complexity of these, but to what end? Does the posthuman have a particular purpose or meaning? Transhumanists are clear that technology improves biological life, and one cannot ignore the amazing biomedical discoveries

---

[1] Mark Milian, "The Spiritual Side of Steve Jobs," CNN *Business News*, October 7, 2011.

that allow the deaf to hear, the blind to see, the lame to walk, and the mute to speak, all of which express the transhumanist ideal. As a cultural and philosophical movement transhumanism aims toward betterment and the flourishing of life, identified as living longer, healthier, happier, smarter, and more peaceful lives—a new utopia. However, it is not clear what flourishing life looks like for the posthuman. Franklin Ginn writes: "This posthumanist ethical-political project is generally underspecified, with speculative appeals to care and flourishing common but still not fully substantiated or worked through."[2] Burdett and Lorrimar point out, "Without acknowledging our indebtedness to other entities we will never flourish and, furthermore, we will never flourish unless we are part of a techno-ecology where each member within that relational network also flourishes."[3]

Who conceives a new paradigm? As Johnston points out, "In both Darwinian and Lamarckian paradigms, evolution is a process through which complex adaptive systems emerge in the absence of design."[4] However, he also writes that "in computer simulations the underlying hardware and most of the time the codes are unalterably set by the experimenter, who thus limits in advance the kind and amount of change that can occur in the system."[5] Is the fate of nature now in the hands of a new priesthood, an elite cadre of coders and hackers, or in the narrow philosophies of the megatech companies such as Google and Facebook? Johnston indicates that technological evolution

---

[2] Franklin Ginn, 'Posthumanism,' in D. Richardson et al., eds., *International Encyclopedia of Geography: People, the Earth, Environment and Technology* (Oxford: Wiley-Blackwell, 2017), 5277.

[3] Michael Burdett and Victoria Lorrimar, "Creatures Bound for Glory: Biotechnological Enhancement and Visions of Human Flourishing," *Studies in Christian Ethics* 32, no. 3 (2019): 249.

[4] John Johnston, *The Allure of Machinic Life: Cybernetics, Artificial Life, and the New AI* (Cambridge: MIT Press, 2008), 16.

[5] Johnston, *Allure of Machinic Life*, 15; John Ziman, ed., *Technological Evolution as an Evolutionary Process* (Cambridge: Cambridge University Press, 2000), 6.

is neither blind nor natural but rather incorporates principles of human intentionality—and intentionality is written in code.

The Problem of Religion

If the fate of the planet rests in the hands of a specialized group of computer geeks, then we have no real future together insofar as we have no real freedom to create a new future. Our lives are at the whim of highly specialized individuals and the wealthy corporations who employ them. But this fact reflects a larger problem at hand and *prima facie* it seems unrelated to coders and hackers. Since the breakdown of first axial consciousness we have lost the essential religious dimension of cosmic life. We are severed from nature's umbilical cord and from one another. In the past, religious myth and ritual tethered us to the larger whole of which we knew ourselves to be a part. Now, ancient religious myths are replaced by techno myths and techno rituals—the myth of super-intelligence, the myth of betterment, the myth of longevity, and the rituals of purchasing the technological means of enacting these myths. In some ways, code specialists have become the new high priests, directing nature to a future fulfillment; the Apple Store is the new cathedral of worship.[6] Some transhumanists claim that technology will fulfill what religion promises—salvation and immortality.[7] The loss of religion in the modern period may be the most significant impulse of AI evolution today. Is technology trying to fill the void left by the absence of religion? Can technology provide coherent meaning by locating our place in nature? The first axial age is coming to

---

[6] Brett T. Robinson, *Appletopia: Media Technology and the Religious Imagination of Steve Jobs* (Waco, TX: Baylor University Press, 2013), 1–2; idem, "The New Cathedrals: An Excerpt from *Appletopia*," *Second Nature*, August 12, 2013.

[7] Robert Geraci, "Apocalyptic AI: Religion and the Promise of Artificial Intelligence," *Journal of the American Academy of Religion* 76, no. 1 (March 2008): 9–38.

an end, and the second axial period still has no real direction or purpose.

The problem is twofold: evolution is speeding up and religion is stuck in first axial consciousness. Christianity is the seedbed of Western science, yet it remains entrenched in Greek philosophy and outdated cosmology. The Adamic myth is still preached as literally true; the human person is seen as weak and fallen; sin is the reason God became human; women remain suspect and unfit to serve as priests, yet the human person, without distinction, is image of God. The soul and body are still housed in Aristotelian terms, and religious cosmology is like a three-tiered wedding cake, with heaven above, earth in the middle, and hell below. The whole edifice is backward looking, stifling, and resists evolution.

But lest the blame fall entirely on religion, science too is conflicted. The hyper-specialization of knowledge (including the different schools of quantum physics and evolution) has given rise to competing paradigms of mind, matter, and evolution. Culturally, religion and science are viewed as rivals and in perpetual conflict with little effort to integrate them. David Noble believes that religion and science share the same aim, to restore the fallen Adam to divine likeness; they are not so much rivals as competitors of human allegiance. The epistemological gap among science and religion has caused the development of AI to drift between the market forces of capitalism, the designs of coders, and the lures of transhumanism. Without a pole of direction or a binding thread to the whole, the human person is at the whim of algorithms and ancient myths. There are simply no viable cosmic signposts in the second axial period. Rather, the posthuman is being born in a chaotic world without meaning or orientation. Although the postmodern turn is toward construction of meaning, what orients our direction or construction of meaning? Without religion as a viable dimension of cosmic life, ongoing constructs are at best fragile and tentative and therefore do not orient the rise of complexified consciousness in evolution. Without religion the fate of the earth is in the hands of the world's powerful and wealthy. Without collective meaning and purpose we stand on the brink of planetary destruction.

Teilhard de Chardin and Omega

Pierre Teilhard de Chardin was a Jesuit priest, a scientist, and a deeply religious thinker. Although his ideas on science and religion still leave many readers perplexed, his prophetic insights born out of an acute scientific mind and a deep Christian spirit enabled him to chart a way forward for religion in an evolutionary world. Teilhard was probably the first person in the history of computer technology to realize the integral relationship between technology and religion. Religion, he said, is not a function of the human person but belongs to the earth itself.[8] In Teilhard's view, religion and evolution should neither be confused nor divorced: "They are destined to form one single continuous organism, in which their respective lives prolong, are dependent on, and complete one another, without being identified or lost."[9] The only way forward for the earth community toward flourishing life, he thought, is a new paradigm of science and religion in which they are no longer two separate disciplines but two ways of knowing a single whole, a "science charged with faith."[10] He would have appreciated Haraway and Barad's methodology of diffraction, which is about interaction, interference, and difference; it does not follow a reductivist logic.[11] Diffraction is about finding productive connections instead of limiting the analysis

---

[8] Pierre Teilhard de Chardin, *Christianity and Evolution: Reflections on Science and Religion,* trans. Rene Hague (New York: Harcourt, 1971), 119.

[9] Ursula King, *Teilhard de Chardin and Eastern Religions: Spirituality and Mysticism in an Evolutionary World* (Mahwah, NJ: Paulist Press, 2011), 179–80.

[10] The title of a chapter dedicated to Teilhard by Charles Henderson, who develops Teilhard's proposal of bringing together science and theology in a passionate search for God, who is present in both. See Charles Henderson, *God and Science: The Death and Rebirth of Theism* (New York: John Knox, 1986).

[11] Karen Barad, *Meeting the Universe Halfway: Quantum Physics and the Entanglement of Matter and Meaning* (Raleigh, NC: Duke University Press, 2007), 93.

to a critical classification exercise. Teilhard sought diffractive connections in science and religion.

The question that occupied much of Teilhard's thought was whether evolution has direction. In conversation with Julian Huxley he asked how the appearance of a self-reflective human is possible after 4.2 billion years of biological life. The probability that we emerged by chance alone, given the long span of time, seems incredible, and it is even more incredible that inert matter could give rise to complex, self-reflective mind. The only reasonable explanation, in Teilhard's view, is to consider consciousness as part of evolution from the beginning of the universe:

> For actually how are we to incorporate thought into the organic flux of space-time without being forced to grant it the primary place in the process. . . . Thought is not part of evolution merely as an anomaly or epiphenomenon, but evolution is so clearly reducible and identifiable with the advance toward thought that the movement of our soul expresses and measures the very progress of evolution. The human discovers that, in the striking words of Julian Huxley, we are nothing else than evolution becomes conscious of itself. . . . Reflecting in the consciousness of each one of us, evolution is becoming aware of itself.[12]

Nature is intrinsically oriented toward greater complexity and consciousness; on higher levels of evolution, consciousness turns in on itself and self-reflects. Yet, scientists are still divided on whether or not higher levels of complexification and consciousness can account for direction in evolution. Integral to the question is the way mechanisms of evolution can be distinguished by the relationship of mind and matter. Neo-Darwinian

---

[12] Pierre Teilhard de Chardin, *The Human Phenomenon*, trans. Sarah Appleton-Weber (Brighton: Sussex, 2015), 154.

evolutionary biologists tend toward strict materialism and principles of natural selection, claiming that the mind emerges in evolution from inert matter.[13] Terrence Deacon, for example, posits a bottoms-up approach whereby higher-order systems emerge out of the interplay of lower-order systems, even though the ultimate constituents of systems (atoms and molecules) are nonliving. Thus he sees nonlife producing life in which "real teleological and intentional phenomena can emerge from physical and chemical processes previously devoid of these properties."[14] Darwin showed how natural selection could account for species variation, but he could not explain the appearance of mind or consciousness. Hence, Darwinian evolution explains material complexity but treats consciousness as a later phenomenon that appears at higher levels in the process.

Teilhard recognized that neither evolution nor religion alone is sufficient to explain the direction of evolution toward complex life. As a scientist, he was involved in the discussions of how evolution proceeds with direction. In a 1949 debate with George Gaylord Simpson at the Paris Colloquium on Paleontology and Transformism, he discussed a case of parallel evolution in the myospalacine mole rat in which the main trunk of the species family tree diverged into three separate branches that followed independent evolutionary trajectories. All three branches developed similar traits, which impelled Teilhard to argue for directionality in evolution rather than selective adaptation.[15] While this is only one example of the many examples of parallel evolution or multiple convergence, he thought that scientific materialism could not sufficiently explain direction in evolution.

---

[13] See, for example, Daniel Dennett, *From Bacteria to Bach and Back: The Evolution of Minds* (New York: W. W. Norton, 2018); Terrence W. Deacon, *Incomplete Nature: How Mind Emerged from Matter* (New York: W. W. Norton, 2011).

[14] Deacon, *Incomplete Nature*, 323.

[15] Mark A. S. McMenamin, "Evolution of the Noosphere," *Teilhard Studies* 42 (2001): 1–2.

Teilhard was influenced by philosopher Henri Bergson's theory of creative evolution. Bergson rejected Darwinian evolution in that it failed to account adequately for novelty and transcendence in nature. Darwin sought to understand mechanisms of change, but Bergson suggested that nature on its own resists change. Paola Marrotti writes: "Bergson calls for a strategy that aims at countering nature from within, looking for ways to go against natural tendencies, to change and modify their direction with the help of other tendencies or tools."[16] Bergson posited a vital impulse in nature, an inherent push of nature from behind, that impels nature to transcend toward novel forms. Although we know today that emergence and dynamical systems can account for novelty and change in evolution, they do not account for mind and direction. David Bohm and Karl Pribam addressed the question of creativity and transcendence from their respective disciplines, indicating there is a wholeness in nature that undergirds increasing complexity. Bohm spoke of a quantum potential in nature that maintains unbroken wholeness of matter despite quantum fluctuations.[17]

Bergson's creative evolution impelled Teilhard to form his principle of Omega as a way of explaining intrinsic wholeness and direction. Omega is the last letter of the Greek alphabet and has meaning in both science and religion because it signifies the end of something, its ultimate limit. In scripture Omega refers to God as the beginning and end of all things ("I am the Alpha and Omega," Rev 22:13); in the sciences Omega has meaning in physics, chemistry, mathematics, statistical mechanics, and computer science. Teilhard's use of Omega bears a resemblance to Bohm's quantum potential, a centrating principle that subsists throughout nature and resists entropy. Omega makes wholeness in nature not only possible but intensely personal because it is

---

[16] Paola Marrotti, "The Natural Cyborg: The Stakes of Bergson's Philosophy of Evolution," *The Scottish Journal of Philosophy* 48, Spindel Supplement (2010): 16.

[17] David Bohm, *Wholeness and Implicate Order* (London: Routledge and Kegan Paul, 1980), 77–78.

the most intensely personal center that makes beings personal and centered.[18] Teilhard saw the work of Omega as intrinsic to creaturely activity itself. He writes: "God acts from within, at the core of each element, by animating the sphere of being from within. Where God is operating, it is always possible for us to see only the work of nature because God is the formal cause, the intrinsic principle of being, although God is not identical with being itself."[19] Omega is both in evolution and independent of evolution, within and yet distinct, autonomous and independent, deeply influential on nature's propensity toward complexity and consciousness.[20] It is operative from the beginning of evolution, acting on pre-living cosmic elements as a single impulse of energy.[21]

The Omega principle can be likened to the concept of the strange attractor in chaotic systems, in which the strange attractor is a basin of attraction within the system and yet other than the system. The strange attractor lures the system into a new pattern of order known as a fractal. Repeated fractals over time give rise to new entities. In this respect the Omega principle acts like a strange attractor in the events of evolution. Teilhard posited that the Omega principle is a principle of attraction in *everything* that exists; it is irreducible to isolated elements yet accounts for the "*more* in the cell than in the molecule, *more* in society than in the individual, and *more* in mathematical construction than in calculations or theorems."[22] As the principle of centration it is independent of nature, not subject to entropy, and ahead of nature as its prime mover. Omega emerges from the organic totality of evolution insofar as evolution proceeds to greater wholeness marked by higher levels of unity and consciousness; Omega is the goal toward which evolution tends.[23]

---

[18] Pierre Teilhard de Chardin, *Activation of Energy*, trans. Rene Hague (New York: Harcourt Brace Jovanovich, 1970), 112.

[19] Teilhard, *Christianity and Evolution*, 27.

[20] Teilhard, *The Phenomenon of Man*, 257–60.

[21] Teilhard, *Activation of Energy*, 121.

[22] Teilhard, *Phenomenon of Man*, 268.

[23] Teilhard, *Activation of Energy*, 114.

Critical Realism

In a 1947 debate with Gabriel Marcel, Teilhard was asked how he could remain optimistic about the future in light of the Nazi atrocities and human destruction. Teilhard has been deeply misinterpreted on this point because he replied that after we have tried everything to its limit, we may begin to see the need to "rise above" ourselves.[24] He was clearly aware of the atrocities of the twentieth century and that evolution itself is marked by cataclysmic events, but he indicated that we need to keep trying out different possibilities to see which ones can lead to more life. In other words, our destructive acts are real but not absolute and may be transcended by coming to a new level of consciousness on a new plane of existence.

Teilhard did not view evolution with a naive realism but was acutely aware of internal forces that could thwart the direction of evolution toward the Omega Point. He rejected the Marxist notion of a culmination of anthropogenesis in an eventual state of collective reflection and participation in which the individual becomes one with the whole social system: "A world culminating in the Impersonal can bring us neither the warmth of attraction nor the hope of irreversibility (immortality) without which individual egotism will always have the last word."[25] Rather than being subsumed into it, individual identity is enhanced through active participation in an archetypal cosmic order or evolutionary process. In an article on "The Directions and Conditions of the Future" he worried not so much about the human race

---

[24] See, for example, John Slattery's misreading of Teilhard, "Dangerous Tendencies of Cosmic Theology: The Untold Legacy of Teilhard de Chardin," *Philosophy and Theology* 29, no. 1 (2017): 69–82. In his opening paragraph Slattery writes: "Teilhard distances himself from both animals and suffering, seeking to rise above creatures in search of unity with God."

[25] Joseph A. Grau, *Morality and the Human Future in the Thought of Teilhard de Chardin: A Critical Study* (Cranbury, NJ: Associated University Presses, 1976), 274.

blowing itself up or a pandemic disease wiping out all human life but about the problem of enough food to feed the world's exploding population, which he then predicted would reach 2.5 billion within the next quarter-century or so, that is, in the early 1970s.[26] He was concerned whether or not an expanding population would be able to live amiably and in peace under conditions that he no longer described as "convergence" but as "external compression."[27] He saw the choice to be between political totalitarianism or some breakthrough into a new state of human "unanimization," the emergence of an "ultra-humanity."[28] Hence, Teilhard did not see evolution as a forward movement without resistance. Rather, the forces of history acting on humanity must either cause humanity to evolve or force humanity to wither. The evolutionary vigor of humankind, he indicates, can wither away if we should lose our impulse, or worse, develop a distaste for ever-increased growth in complexity–consciousness.[29] The danger he worried about most is that humanity, in losing its faith in God, would also lose its "zest for living."[30] He questions whether the human race, having experienced "a scientific justification of faith in progress, was now being confronted by an accumulation of scientific evidence pointing to the reverse—the species doomed to extinction."[31] If we are only seeking to survive, he says, then we are in a closed system that will dissipate. In his words:

> There can be no natural selection, still less reflective invention, if the individual is not inwardly intent upon "super-living," or at least upon survival. No evolutionary

---

[26] Pierre Teilhard de Chardin, *The Future of Man*, trans. Norman Denny (1946; reprint, New York: Harper and Row, 1964), 230–31. According to a 2009 UN report, the world's population reached 2.76 billion by 1955; by 1970, it was 3.69 billion.

[27] Teilhard, *Future of Man*, 235.

[28] Teilhard, 270–80.

[29] Teilhard, 213.

[30] Teilhard, *Activation of Energy*, 229–43.

[31] Teilhard, *Future of Man*, 298–303.

mechanism can have any power over a cosmic matter if it is entirely passive, less still if it is opposed to it. But the possibility has to be faced of mankind falling suddenly out of love with its own destiny. This disenchantment would be conceivable, and indeed inevitable, if as a result of growing reflection, we came to believe that our end could only be collective death in a hermetically sealed world. Clearly in face of so appalling a discovery the psychic mechanism of evolution would come to a stop, undermined and shattered in its very substance, despite all the violent tuggings of the chain of planetary in-folding.[32]

Teilhard states that evolution could fail and collapse in on itself ultimately resulting in annihilation of human life and cosmic death. The only solution, he indicates, is not "an improvement of living conditions," as desirable as that might be, but rather seeing the inner pressures of history as the catalyst for evolution toward more being. The evolution of humanity, therefore, is not only an evolution of consciousness; rather, it is a new phase of life in the universe toward unification of mind by which the whole cosmic evolution progresses toward greater unity.

The Noosphere

Teilhard's evolutionary paradigm is a continuation of the stages of consciousness as they emerge through pre-axial and axial periods. Life evolves toward complexified wholeness and higher consciousness through deepening levels of matter, mind, and spirit. Teilhard added a fourth dimension, relationality, reflecting the vital religious dimension of energized matter. The evolutionary ascent of human beings occurs in stages. In the first stage of its evolution, humanity expanded in both quantity (number of persons) and in quality (psychological and spiritual development). During the long period of expansion, physical and cultural

---

[32] Teilhard, *Future of Man*, 296.

differences isolated the peoples of the earth from one another as they spread to fill the earth. At the beginning of our present century, with most of the habitable surface of the earth occupied, various cultures began to converge. The birth of the tribes, empires, and modern states is the offspring of the great movement of evolution toward socialization or collectivization.

We have reached the end of the expanding (or diversity) stage and are now entering the contracting (or unifying) stage. The human is on the threshold of a critical phase of super-humanization: the increasingly rapid growth in the human world of the forces of collectivization, the "super-arrangement" or the mega-synthesis.[33] At this point Teilhard's theory runs counter to Darwin's in that the success of humanity's evolution in the second stage will not be determined by "survival of the fittest" but by our own capacity to converge and unify.[34] The most important initial evolutionary leap of the convergence stage is the formation of what Teilhard calls the noosphere.[35] Teilhard describes the noosphere:

> The idea is that of the earth not only becoming covered by myriads of grains of thought, but becoming enclosed in a single thinking envelope so as to form, functionally, no more than a single vast grain of thought on the sidereal scale, the plurality of individual reflections grouping themselves together and reinforcing one another in the act of a single unanimous reflection.[36]

Teilhard envisioned the noosphere as "a living membrane stretched like a film over the lustrous surface of the star which

---

[33] Archimedes Carag Articulo, "Towards an Ethics of Technology: Re-Exploring Teilhard de Chardin's Theory of Technology and Evolution," *Open Journal of Philosophy* 4, no. 4 (Scientific Research Publishing, 2014).

[34] Teilhard, *Phenomenon of Man*, 243.

[35] Teilhard, *Future of Man*, 204.

[36] Teilhard, *Phenomenon of Man*, 251–52.

holds us."[37] Just as earth once covered itself with a film of interdependent living organisms, which we call the biosphere, so humankind's achievements are forming a global network of collective mind.[38] Teilhard called this new level of mind the noosphere (from the Greek *nous,* or "mind"), a new level of coreflective thought and action. If there is no connection between noogenesis and biogenesis, according to Teilhard, then the process of evolution has halted and man is an absurd and "erratic object in a disjointed world."[39] The noosphere is a new stage for the renewal of life and not a radical break with biological life. Before the human emerged, natural selection set the course of morphogenesis; after humans, it is the power of invention that begins to grasp the evolutionary reins.[40] Thus, the noosphere is a sphere of collective consciousness that preserves and communicates everything precious, active, and progressive contained in earth's previous evolution. It is the natural culmination of biological evolution and not a termination of it, an organic whole, irreducible to its parts, destined for some type of super-convergence and unification.[41] Teilhard writes:

> This is how the thinking layer of the Earth as we know it today—the noosphere—came rapidly into being, proceeding from certain centers of reflection which apparently emerged at the threshold of the Pleistocene Age somewhere in the tropical or sub-tropical spheres of the Ancient World (i.e., in the place where, during the Upper Tertiary Period, the group of the great anthropoids was first established and subsequently spread): a planetary neo-envelope, essentially

---

[37] Blanche Gallagher, *Meditations with Teilhard de Chardin* (Santa Fe: Bear and Co., 1988), 39.

[38] Michael H. Murray, *The Thought of Teilhard de Chardin* (New York: Seabury Press, 1966), 20–21.

[39] Robert J. O'Connell, *Teilhard's Vision of the Past: The Making of a Method* (New York: Fordham University Press, 1982), 145.

[40] Teilhard, *Future of Man*, 307.

[41] W. Henry Kenny, SJ, *A Path through Teilhard's Phenomenon* (Dayton, OH: Pflaum Press, 1970), 110.

linked with the biosphere in which it has its root, yet distinguished from it by an autonomous circulatory, nervous, and finally, cerebral system. The noosphere: a new stage of life renewed.[42]

Although mass communication technology was just beginning to develop in Teilhard's time, he appreciated the role of machines in the emergence of the noosphere. Lawrence Hagerty points out that "[Teilhard wrote of] the extraordinary network of radio and television communications which, perhaps anticipating the direct intercommunication of brains through the mysterious power of telepathy, already link us all in a sort of 'etherized' universal consciousness."[43] Teilhard was fascinated by the computer and predicted the evolution of the computer as the "brain" behind the noosphere. In his view this would be the next step of evolution.

> Here I am thinking of those astonishing electronic machines (the starting-point and hope of the young science of cybernetics), by which our mental capacity to calculate and combine is reinforced and multiplied by a process and to a degree that herald as astonishing advances in this direction as those that optical science has already produced for our power of vision.[44]

Teilhard's anticipation of what computers would do for us was twofold: first, they would complete our brains through instantaneous retrieval of information around the globe so that what one person lacks would be immediately provided by another; and second, they would improve our brains by facilitating processes more quickly than our own resources can achieve them.[45] Teilhard's vision of the noosphere as cybernetic mind

---

[42] Teilhard, *Future of Man*, 294.

[43] Lawrence Hagerty, *The Spirit of the Internet: Speculations on the Evolution of Global Consciousness* (Matrix Masters, 2000), 33.

[44] Pierre Teilhard de Chardin, *Man's Place in Nature* (New York: Harper and Row, 1956), 110.

[45] Teilhard, *Man's Place in Nature*, 111.

anticipated the emergence of cyberspace as a field of global mind through interconnecting computer pathways. With the rise of technology he saw a forward movement of spiritual energy, a maximization of consciousness, and a complexification of relationships.

The noosphere is the natural culmination of biological evolution, irreducible to its parts and destined for some type of super-convergence and unification.[46] It is not specific to humans; rather, it is a dimension of evolution by which life evolves. Mark McMenamin states that the noopsheric arc

> can be described as a bridge between the evolutionary and spirituality. . . . It can also be thought of as a force driving evolutionary change. Noospheric forces can also be conceptualized as the attraction or pull between the spiritual and material. Thus the noosphere is associated with progressive evolutionary change through time, leading many lineages to increases in bodily complexity and that ability to manipulate information about the environment we call intelligence.[47]

According to McMenamin, organisms evolve over evolutionary time through mutations, new combinations, function switches, symbioses, and developmental changes—all of which under various circumstances will help the organism to survive and flourish. He states:

> A successful innovation represents not just an individual success for an individual organism but leads to the addition of an entirely new type of creature to the biosphere. This successful new organism will spread itself through its environment like a diffusing gas. . . . Innovations represent solutions to the problems of life, and it should be no surprise that different organisms have solved problems

---

[46] Kenny, *Path through Teilhard's Phenomenon,* 110.
[47] McMenamin, "Evolution of the Noosphere," 8.

in similar ways. . . . Any type of evolutionary change that is associated with adaptation for improved survival can be considered a type of directional evolutionary change. Directional evolution . . . consists of organisms converging on a particular solution, with different solutions often beginning from very different starting points. Development of intelligence, or ability to manipulate information about one's environment, is a biological stable attractor no different in principle from, say, the stable attractor of flight in air. Animals are seen to converge on higher and higher levels of intelligence through time in the same fashion that tree lineages grow taller over time as they struggle to reach more light and shade out the competition.[48]

The noosphere, therefore, is the electronic linking of minds and represents a new level of *biological* life. The successful innovation of the computer as a thinking machine has opened doors to a new type of person in the biosphere. Teilhard identified this new emergent person as the *ultrahuman.*

The Ultrahuman

Teilhard's vision of the noosphere as cybernetic mind anticipated the emergence of cyberspace as a field of global mind through interconnecting computer pathways. He saw evolution proceeding to a greater unification of the whole in and through the human person, who is the growing tip of the evolutionary process. In his introduction to Teilhard's *Phenomenon of Man,* Julian Huxley writes: "We should consider inter-thinking humanity as a new type of organism whose destiny it is to realize new possibilities for evolving life on this planet."[49] Both Huxley and Teilhard saw this new type of person as a hyper-personalizing

---

[48] McMenamin, 11.

[49] Julian Huxley, "Introduction," in Teilhard, *Phenomenon of Man,* 20.

person on a new level of "cooperative interthinking."[50] Just as human persons develop a complex brain, Teilhard saw that the earth is developing a planetary "brain," a global, complex brain made possible by computer-mediated interconnected minds. He posits a new type of person to embody this new type of brain, an ultrahuman, a person in whom thought is no longer on the level of the individual but on the level of convergent and collective relationships.

Teilhard saw the hybridization of human and machine intelligence as completing the material and cerebral sphere of collective thought, and in this respect he is a forerunner of transhumanism and posthumanism.[51] His hopeful vision is a richer and more complex domain of matter and mind through the development of technology, a way of constructing or joining all minds together in a collective or global mind for the forward movement of cosmic evolution. He writes: "How can we fail to see that the process of convergence from which we emerged, body and soul, is continuing to envelop us more closely than ever, to grip us, in the form of . . . a gigantic planetary contraction?"[52] The individual human person according to Teilhard, will be surpassed by a collective convergence of consciousness giving rise to the ultrahuman, a new person who is part of the new planetary consciousness.

To appreciate Teilhard's position is to realize that he was not enamored of technology as an autonomous power but as the main impetus of Omega-centered evolution. The term

---

[50] Teilhard, 21.

[51] See, for example, Eric Steinhart, "Teilhard de Chardin and Transhumanism," *Journal of Evolution and Technology* 20, no. 1 (2008): 22. Steinhart writes: "Teilhard was one of the first to articulate transhumanist themes. Transhumanists advocate the ethical use of technology for human enhancement. Teilhard's writing likewise argues for the ethical application of technology in order to advance humanity beyond the limitations of natural biology." However, Teilhard's transhumanism is cosmic evolution on the level of mind. In this respect he is closer to the position of posthumanism.

[52] Pierre Teilhard de Chardin, *The Heart of Matter*, trans. Rene Hague (New York: Houghton, 1979), 36.

ultrahuman is an effort to impel humanity to enter into its own evolution. In this respect technology enhances spirituality:

> However far science pushes its discovery of the essential fire and however capable it becomes someday of remodeling and perfecting the human element, it will always find itself in the end facing the same problem—how to give to each and every element its final value by grouping them in the unity of an organized whole.[53]

Teilhard saw the insufficiency of science alone to effect the transition to super-consciousness and hence collective unity. "It is not tête-à-tête or a corps-à-corps we need; it is a heart to heart."[54] Technology for Teilhard is in the service of love, not a sentiment of love but rather love as the deepest vital energy of the universe. If consciousness is the inside of matter and attraction is the outside of matter, love is the core energy that both attracts and transcends. Love is the most mysterious force, one that is unyielding and ineffable. Philip Hefner asks, "Can we entertain the hypothesis that love is rooted in the fundamental nature of reality, including the reality we call nature?"[55] Teilhard himself spoke of love as a cosmological force, present from the beginning of the universe: "Love is the most universal, the most tremendous, and the most mysterious of the cosmic forces. . . . The *physical* structure of the universe is love."[56] Love is a unitive energy, "the building power that works against entropy," by which the elements search their way toward union.[57] Without love, the noosphere can effect no real synthesis.

---

[53] Teilhard, *Phenomenon of Man*, 250.

[54] Teilhard, *Future of Man*, 75; see Kenny, *Path through Teilhard's Phenomenon*, 138.

[55] Philip Hefner, *The Human Factor: Evolution, Culture, and Religion* (Minneapolis: Fortress, 1993), 208–9.

[56] Pierre Teilhard de Chardin, *Human Energy*, trans. J. M. Cohen (New York: Harcourt Brace Jovanovich, 1969), 32.

[57] Thomas M. King, *Teilhard's Mysticism of Knowing* (New York: Seabury Press, 1981), 104–5.

Teilhard's evolution of the noosphere is a bold claim. The human person of first axial consciousness is coming to an end, and we find ourselves in the midst of a new complexified consciousness. A new type of planetary organism is emerging in which individual autonomy is becoming obsolete.[58] Teilhard asks:

> Why . . . do we not recognize in the accelerating totalization against which we are struggling, sometimes so desperately, simply the normal continuation at a level above ourselves of that process which generates Thought on Earth? Why do we not see that it is a continuing process of Cerebration?[59]

In other words, the rise of the posthuman (or ultrahuman, in Teilhard's phrasing) represents a new collective consciousness that transcends individual consciousness and evokes a new type of person whose body now extends to the whole electronically connected planet. Teilhard saw evolution of the ultrahuman in terms of Lamarckian rather than Darwinian evolution, "the possibility of continuing improvement, passed on from one generation to another, in the actual *organ* of this vision." Hominization continues in and with technology. What is "staring us in the face," Teilhard writes, is "a rapidly rising collective Reflection."[60] We see this now realized to some extent by the internet. As we increasingly emerge through complexified consciousness into posthuman life, the concept of personhood is changing in accord with the new consciousness.

Teilhard anticipated that each ego will be "forced convulsively beyond itself into some mysterious *super ego*."[61] This superego

---

[58] Teilhard, *Heart of Matter*, 37.

[59] Teilhard, 37.

[60] Teilhard, 37, 38. Lamarckian evolution refers to changes in an organism during the course of life in order to adapt to its environment; the changes are passed on to its offspring.

[61] Teilhard, 38.

reflected for Teilhard the notion that the individual is coming to an end and a new "hyper-personal" is emerging in evolution. Teilhard realized that the fullness of personhood lies beyond the individual and is realized in the expansion of the ego to embrace the All: a oneness with all life in the cosmos.

Hyper-personalization

Teilhard did not live to see the technological revolution of the internet, but his noosphere corresponds to the development of computer technology and AI. He imagined a thinking earth formed by the linking of electronic minds. His concern was deeply religious and scientific. He saw that matter and mind evolve as a whole, so that matter expresses itself in mind and mind reflects itself in matter. Only when the noosphere is aligned with the whole, the cosmos/universe, can it facilitate the *deeply personal* through *convergence* by bringing together consciousness, person, and creativity. Teilhard writes, "The Future Universal could not be anything else but the Hyper-Personal."[62] This hyper-personal, for Teilhard, is a folding in of consciousness, as if the lines of consciousness are merging together into one great complexified brain of planetary thought. This too is what Hayles conceives of for the posthuman, the electronically embedded person whose ego is collective or superego, whose passion or emotional life is also collectivized. The posthuman is the beginning of what Teilhard calls planetization, a complexified consciousness of planetized humanity whose new collective powers can organize planetary life into a new planetary whole:

> It is not *well-being* but a hunger for *more-being* which, of psychological necessity, can alone preserve the thinking earth from the *taedium vitae*. . . . It is upon its point (or superstructure) of spiritual concentration, and not upon its

---

[62] Teilhard, *Phenomenon of Man*, 260.

basis (or infra-structure) of material arrangement, that the equilibrium of Mankind biologically depends.[63]

According to Grau, Teilhard distinguished *more*-being from *well*-being by saying that materialism can bring about well-being but spirituality and an increase in consciousness brings about more-being.[64] He imagined consciousness or "psychic energy" to grow in a continually more reflective state in the utltrahuman.[65] The noosphere is a super-convergence of consciousness, a higher form of complexity, in which the human person acquires more being through interconnectivity with others and transforms into a new type of person, the hyper-personal, super-convergent person—the posthuman (ultrahuman)—whose electronic participation in the whole helps create a new whole.

The noosphere is not the realm of the impersonal but the realm of personal convergence whereby different elements, organisms, and human thought are brought together. Electronically embedded mind, virtual life, and robotic extensions are all part of the complexification of the posthuman, in which distributed embodiment gives rise to hyper-personal persons. The identity of the second axial person is constantly negotiated through feedback loops of information, fluid boundaries, and codes.

If technology is to evolve us toward a hyper-personal planet by drawing on the energy of religion, then a new type of religion is needed, one beyond dualisms and acosmic spirituality. Technology can extend the outreach of human activity, but it depends on a broader use of activity and how humans use it

---

[63] Teilhard, *Future of Man*, 304–5. One could see in Teilhard's ideas the more recent speculations on consciousness and digital life posited by Martine Rothblatt, who conceives of digitized personal consciousness extended through mindlclones and mindware, the rudiments of which are already culturally embedded. See Martine Rothblatt, *Virtually Human: The Promise and the Peril of Digital Immortality* (New York: Picador, 2015).

[64] Grau, *Morality and the Human Future*, 275.

[65] Kenny, *Path through Teilhard's Phenomenon*, 105.

to direct psychic, spiritual energy needs, and powers.[66] Teilhard realized that religion is the missing dimension of this new age of consciousness; not the religion of the past, or of the tribal institution, but a new religion must be conceived to meet the needs of the second axial person. Teilhard sought to develop a new theology that could vitalize a new religion of the earth. Without a collective commitment to the future, he believed, the process of evolution could ultimately collapse in on itself and result in cosmic death.

Summary: The rise of the posthuman identified by Hayles corresponds to the insights of Teilhard de Chardin. His fascination with computer technology led him to speculate that we are evolving to a new level of electronically linked minds, what he called the noosphere. In his view the age of evolutionary expansion is over, and we are in a new age of evolutionary convergence; we must either unify and collectivize or face annihilation. The linkage of minds through technology can usher in a new type of person, what he called the ultrahuman, which is consonant with the idea of the posthuman. A new type of human person for a new earth led Teilhard to posit that the level of the noosphere can now bring evolution to a new level of planetization in which the energies around the globe are unified and consolidated for the good of the whole earth. Following Henri Bergson, Teilhard posits an evolutive power present in the dynamic process of change, what he called the principle of Omega, an absolute center within everything that draws life toward more unity and consciousness and which itself escapes entropy. The presence of Omega and the orientation of evolution toward greater complexity and consciousness indicated to Teilhard that evolution has a direction toward Omega, a flourishing of life where matter will become fully conscious in love.

---

[66] Grau, *Morality and the Human Future*, 274.

8

Second Axial Religion

Crisis and Opportunity

Second axial consciousness began in the twentieth century with cosmology and quantum physics and continues to develop in the twenty-first century through computer technology, artificial intelligence, and the new materialisms. It is difficult to identify exactly what this shift in consciousness means, but in some respect it includes a new awareness of self in relation to the wider world of politics, economics, social structures, religion, and the environment. The emergence of second axial consciousness, however, struggles against the resistant forces of the first axial person who, whether explicitly or implicitly, is entrenched in first axial religious convictions. Integral to this resistance is the relationship between religion and evolution. The Catholic Church accepts evolution as a scientific explanation of life, but it draws a distinction between physical life and spiritual life.[1] A smaller number of fundamentalist Catholics and Protestants, however, reject evolution. The inability to overcome the evolution gap stifles the need to bring science and religion into a unified framework. Younger generations no longer see the relevance of religion in a scientific world because it fails to motivate or provide what

---

[1] The Catholic Church still follows the statement on evolution by Pope Pius XII in his encyclical *Humani generis* (esp. nos. 36 and 37), which was issued in 1950.

Teilhard called a "zest for life." Without a sense of evolution's purpose, the second axial person persists in cosmic confusion, untethered, and ripe to be picked off by the strongest forces, whether consumerism, transhumanism, or fundamentalism.

Teilhard de Chardin spoke of a new threshold with the rise of human consciousness and organization, not simply a search for living on, for mere survival, but an effort to create a higher form of life, a more unified humanity:

> We have become aware that, in the great game that is being played, we are the players as well as being the cards and the stakes. Nothing can go on if we leave the table. Neither can any power force us to remain. Is the game worth the candle, or are we simply its dupes? . . .
>
> There is a danger that the elements of the world should refuse to serve the world—because they think; or more precisely that the world should refuse itself when perceiving itself through reflection. Under our modern disquiet, what is forming and growing is nothing less than an organic crisis in evolution.[2]

"An organic crisis in evolution" tells us that the whole earth is potentially in crisis if we do not recognize that we humans are of the earth. The question is, do we know ourselves as planetary people? Could biological terrestrial life be extended to intergalactic extraterrestrial life through advanced technology? Teilhard's insights are earth oriented yet cosmic in scope, and his speculations on increasing levels of consciousness are worth considering on a cosmic scale. He postulated a new level of electronic mind facilitated by computer technology, called the noosphere, a new linking together of the global human community giving way to a new level of integrated energies. The noosphere is not disconnected from the biosphere; it is the most current phase of evolution. Ursula King states:

---

[2] Pierre Teilhard de Chardin, *The Phenomenon of Man*, trans. Bernard Wall (New York: Harper and Row, 1959), 230.

It is not enough either to understand it merely as a sphere of knowledge and invention; it represented for Teilhard a sphere of both human thought and will, of love, action and interaction, all of which are closely interwoven and interdependent. When discussing the formation of the noosphere, Teilhard presented it as a biological interpretation of human history.[3]

There is a human hesitation and resistance to open our hearts to the call of the world within us, to feel a *sense of the earth*. Part of this hesitation is the ambiguity of the world itself. Is the world worth our attention? Is it a place of temporality and sin or a place of infinite goodness? Christianity in particular has done a tremendous disservice to the nobility of the earth by holding to a doctrine of original sin that is incompatible with evolution, creating an illusion of a "fallen" universe. Despite Pope Francis's urgent call for environmental responsibility, the material world is still suspect; platonizing elements of Christian spirituality place an emphasis on spirit over matter, heaven over earth, God over human.

Transhumanist technology is born from the Enlightenment and rejects religion, yet at the same time it seeks the Christian ideals of salvation and immortality. The quest to develop super-intelligent machines highlights a tension within the human person—the need for God and the lure of technology to replace God. Teilhard was keenly attentive to the ambiguity of the human condition and saw the need to work toward a unified earth. King writes:

One of the strongest expressions of Teilhard is his sense of the earth and of humanity as *one* found in his 1931 essay "The Spirit of the Earth," which he planned for a long time. In 1926 he wrote to a friend that he wanted to provide an account of the Earth in which he did not speak as a Frenchman, not as a unit in any group, but simply as a *terrestrian* who wanted to express the confidence, desires

---

[3] Ursula King, "Feeding the Zest for Life: Spiritual Energy Resources for the Future of Humanity," Metanexus, October 6, 2005.

and plenitude, also the disappointments, worries and a kind of vertigo of a man who considers the destinies and interests of the earth (humanity) as a whole. He describes this sense of the earth as the passionate sense of common destiny that draws the thinking fraction of life ever further forward, and speaks of the evolution of a greater consciousness whereby human thought introduces a new era in the history of nature which involves a renewal of life, morality, and spirituality, presenting us with a cosmic problem of action and a crisis of birth. Here, and elsewhere in his work, Teilhard de Chardin expresses deep concern for building the earth and for developing the spirit of one earth, that is, with seeing the whole world and all peoples within it as one.[4]

Yet, Teilhard was also aware that a unified earth will not arise if religion does not undergo a radical transformation of ideas, acquire new metaphors, and tell a new story that can harness the spirit of the earth. He devoted himself to developing a new theology of evolution in an effort to renew the vital religious dimension of cosmic life.

Religion and Evolution

Teilhard was deeply concerned that Christianity had become narrow and self-enclosed. He wrote passionately about the need to bring Christianity into line with evolution. In his view religion belongs to evolution in the same way that consciousness belongs to matter; they cannot be separated. The integral relationship between religion and evolution reflects Teilhard's positive view of science as being closely aligned with religion. According to Augustin Udías, Teilhard saw a religious character in the work of science. Science not only does not oppose religion, but in some

---

[4] King, "Feeding the Zest for Life," emphasis added.

sense it is a necessary preparation for religion because it explores the hidden depths of reality.[5] In this respect neither science nor religion can develop normally without the other, or, as Teilhard writes, "science cannot go to its limits without becoming tinged of mysticism and charged with faith."[6] This unity of science and religion for Teilhard was strong:

> If I were to lose my faith in Christ, my faith in a personal God and my faith in spirit, I would continue to believe invincibly in the world. The world, when all is said and done, is the first, the last, and the only thing in which I believe. It is by this faith that I live. And it is to this faith . . . that at the moment of death I shall surrender myself.[7]

This is a very interesting statement because Teilhard's faith in the world was at the same time his faith in God. Even if he lost faith in God, he claims, he would still believe in the world because the world and God are united. Here we have a clue as to how he will reconceive religion in the context of historical change and complexity. The kind of religion we seek today, Teilhard believes, cannot be found in the religious traditions of the past linked to static categories. What is needed is a *new religion* that can utilize all the "free energy" of the earth to build humankind into greater unity. He thought that first axial religion, and Christianity in particular, was too focused on the individual and an otherworldly heaven. This is insufficient, he states; people are looking for a religion of mankind and of the earth that can give meaning to human achievements, a religion that will enkindle cosmic and human evolution and a deep

---

[5] Augustin Udías, "Teilhard de Chardin and the Dialogue between Science and Religion," 4, www.academia.edu.

[6] Pierre Teilhard de Chardin, *The Phenomenon of Man*, trans. Bernard Wall (New York: Harper and Row, 1959), 283–84.

[7] Pierre Teilhard de Chardin, *Christianity and Evolution: Reflections on Science and Religion,* trans. Rene Hague (New York: Harcourt, 1971), 98.

sense of commitment to the earth.[8] God has become too small to energize us for new life. Science tells us that the cosmos has become a cosmogenesis and this fact alone "must lead to the profound modification of the whole structure not only of our thought but of our beliefs."[9]

The decisive test for evaluating traditional religions, according to Teilhard, is the strength of their capacity to evolve, to lead humankind to greater unity. He writes: "The biological function of religion is to give a form to the free psychic energy of the world. And the only form which the development of mankind can accept, is that of a process . . . that leads up to some supreme unification of the universe."[10] Faith in the future along with faith in God is Teilhard's new definition of religion: a religion of the earth that can build the earth into a greater unity.

Unsatisfied Theism

Teilhard identified the Christian problem as one of dualism, and he saw the role of Christianity as one of increasing irrelevance: "Christianity isolates instead of merging with the masses; instead of harnessing people to the common task, it causes them to lose interest in it."[11] Interestingly, he was writing in the 1920s, long before the Second Vatican Council (1962–65) and the call for renewal. While Vatican II opened the windows of the church to the events in history, the church continues to

---

[8] Ursula King, "Religion and the Future," in *The Spirit of the Earth: Reflections on Teilhard de Chardin and Global Spirituality* (New York: Paragon House, 1989), 109.

[9] Ursula King, *Teilhard de Chardin and Eastern Religions: Spirituality and Mysticism in an Evolutionary World* (Mahwah, NJ: Paulist Press, 2011), 160.

[10] Pierre Teilhard de Chardin, *The Future of Man* (1946; reprint, New York: HarperCollins, 1964), 261.

[11] Pierre Teilhard de Chardin, *The Divine Milieu*, (1957; reprint, London: William Collins and Sons, 1960), 68.

vacillate between a worldly gospel and otherworldliness.[12] Teilhard lamented that "far too many Christians are insufficiently conscious of the 'divine' responsibilities of their lives . . . never experiencing the spur or the intoxication of advancing God's kingdom in every domain of humankind."[13] The emphasis on God "above" and a "fallen" earth creates a consciousness of dependency, servility, and fear.

Teilhard did not exactly advocate a new religion, as if writing off the great wisdom of the axial religions; neither did he envision a blending of religions. Rather, he suggested that the unitive forces among the different religions, their axis of convergence, must be respect, dialogue, compassion, and peace, that is, religions must meet together on the level of mysticism and common action. He believed that religious convergence could lead to a new complexified religious consciousness, a new interspirituality. Religion can no longer be based only on doctrine and "official teachings" but must include religious experience and the development of an interspiritual religious consciousness that binds us together in a greater unity of love. World religions can be likened to a hand in which the canons and doctrines of each religion form the fingers, but the root of the hand, the wrist, is the common center where all lines meet together in love, mercy, and peace. Without religious convergence, Teilhard states, we are left with "unsatisfied theism."

> We are surrounded by a certain sort of pessimist who continually tells us that our world is foundering in atheism. But should we not rather say that what it is suffering from is *unsatisfied theism*? . . . If the great spiritual concern of our times is a re-alignment and readjustment of old beliefs towards a new Godhead who has risen up at the anticipated pole of cosmic evolution—then why not simply slough off

---

[12] Whether Vatican II was a success or failure is still hotly debated. See Stephen Bullivant, "Did the Second Vatican Council Fail?" *The Tablet*, May 23, 2019.

[13] Teilhard, *Divine Milieu*, 68.

the old—why not, that is, regroup the whole of the earth's religious power directly and . . . pay no attention to the ancient creeds? . . . Why not have a completely fresh faith, rather than rejuvenation and confluence of "old loves"? First of all, in each of the great religious branches that cover the world at this moment, a certain spiritual attitude and vision which have been produced by centuries of experience are preserved and continued; these are indispensable and irreplaceable for the integrity of a total terrestrial religious consciousness. . . . The cosmic forces of complexification, it would seem, proceed not through individuals but through complete branches. What is carried along by the various currents of faith that are still active on the earth, working in their incommunicable core . . . is experiences of contact with a supreme inexpressible which they preserve and pass on.[14]

Teilhard envisioned a new "religion of the earth" freed from religious individualism and one that could animate and direct the noosphere of collective consciousness. The further evolution of humanity toward greater unity "will never materialize unless we fully develop within ourselves the exceptionally strong unifying powers exerted by inter-human sympathy and religious forces."[15] Harnessing spiritual energies for the unification of life entails a genuine dialogue among the existing religions, a dialogue that involves existential participation and the mutual enrichment of the various religious traditions. He saw the encounter of religions as full of promise for the future of religion and was anxious to encourage all efforts toward greater unity.[16] Religious convergence toward unified wholeness can vitalize human energies (spirituality) and direct these energies toward a common future.

Teilhard was a theologian of second axial consciousness. While first axial religion was individual and otherworldly, second

---

[14] Pierre Teilhard de Chardin, *Activation of Energy*, trans. Rene Hague (New York: Harcourt Brace Jovanovich, 1970), 240–42.

[15] Teilhard, 239–40.

[16] King, *Teilhard and Eastern Religions*, 193.

axial religion is collective and planetary: "No longer simply a religion of individuals and of heaven, but a religion of mankind and of the earth—that is what we are looking for at this moment, as the oxygen without which we cannot breathe."[17] Teilhard realized that a new spirit of the earth needs a new tethering to the whole, a new religious consciousness, born out of the wisdom of the past but refashioned for an electronically convergent future. Computer technology has opened up a new level of thinking unlike any other in human history, the noospheric level of connected minds. If religion means focusing on a convergent transcendent center of unity, then a new type of religion calls for a new understanding of a God who is at home in evolution.

Toward a New Theology

Twentieth-century theologians were keenly aware that theology demands a credible God if theology is to have any import for contemporary life. They sought to give new meaning to God by overcoming the aporia between sacred and secular, divine and human. Jesuit theologian Karl Rahner revisited the "God question" as a question of the human person. The structure of human nature is dynamically oriented toward all the reality there is to be known.[18] We don't just ask questions, Rahner claimed, we are a question in search of the fullness of truth. Human freedom is not unbridled action; to be free is to be fully person present to oneself. We are ultimately responsible for ourselves. In this respect human freedom is a dynamism that keeps transcending everything it grasps. Even the phrase "I love you," Rahner claims, is the open structure of human nature that is oriented toward a boundless fullness of love.[19]

Like Teilhard, Rahner saw that the root of our existence is oriented toward something more, a horizon continuously open-

---

[17] Teilhard, *Activation of Energy*, 240.

[18] "Karl Rahner," ed. Derek Michaud, Boston Collaborative Encyclopedia of Western Theology (n.d.).

[19] Elizabeth Johnson, *Quest for the Living God: Mapping Frontiers in the Theology of God* (New York: Continuum, 2011), 34.

ing up before us and beckoning us onward. As we move toward this horizon, the horizon recedes; the infinite horizon is always before us and never behind us. Higher levels of consciousness cause the horizon to shift. We transcend the horizon of yesterday because a new horizon appears on the cusp of the moment, just as the sun rises to a new day. Every new horizon is the emergence of future. Hence, we experience ourselves as beings constantly reaching beyond ourselves toward something ineffable. This orientation is what constitutes us as spiritual persons. Rahner sought to understand this dynamic orientation of human nature toward ultimate being. If God exists, he says, it is no accident that we find ourselves open and yearning.[20] And it is no accident that we build machines to generate infinite information. We are yearning and searching for ultimate meaning and purpose and in a cosmos captured by science, cyberspace is the new realm of infinite mystery. This yearning drives us to search, create, invent, cross boundaries, and dream new worlds. It is where the God question must be located.

The notion of a Supreme Being "out there" is bad theology and stifles evolution and human progress. For Rahner, the question is what supports the dynamic orientation of human nature. *Why* do we create or imagine? *Why* should we even want to improve ourselves or connect ourselves globally? Even if transhumanists answer, "for the flourishing of life," the question is, "whose life?" All of life or some lives? Who or what defines "flourishing life"? If there is no other reason for extended cognition or electronic embeddedness than self-enhancement, then transhumanism could easily become a form of eugenics; we have the potential to repeat the mistakes of the twentieth century.

Paul Tillich, writing in the mid twentieth century, spoke of God in terms of existential depth. There lies beneath the surface (of our experience) an infinite and exhaustible dimension of depth, the dimension of inexhaustibility. Science and technology

---

[20] Mary Steinmetz, "Thoughts on the Experience of God in the Theology of Karl Rahner: Gifts and Implications," *Lumen et Vita* 2 (2012): 2–4.

fall under this depth dimension of experience, for every discovery is a new question and a new search. Science is an inexhaustible search for understanding nature, which itself is elusive and excessive. Science is about ultimate concern, and so too is religion, which led Teilhard to state that "science and religion are two conjugated phases of one and the same complete act of knowledge."[21]

Religion is the search for depth, according to Tillich; it is concerned with that which pulls us at each moment beyond the pale of each moment. We constantly dwell in this depth without focusing on it. It is the milieu rather than the object of our experience. Rabbi Israel ben Eliezer of Mezbizk (better known as the Ba'al Shem Tov), founder of Hassidic Judaism, also spoke of a spark of the divine in each task and moment. Our responsibility, he taught, is to discover and fulfill the potential holiness embedded in our ordinary existence.[22] Tillich was concerned with a theology of culture, finding ultimate meaning and concern in the ordinary everyday events of life. God is not a thing beside others within the universe of existing things, as if there is *a* being named God that can be refuted by science. Tillich writes: "It is regrettable that scientists believe that they have refuted religion when they rightly have shown that there is no evidence whatsoever for the assumption that such a being exists. Actually, they not only have not refuted religion, but they have done it a considerable service."[23]

Tillich expounds the revelation of God as Being ("I am Who I am," Ex 3:14). God is not *a* being but Being itself. "God is not something that can be proved or disproved. God does not merely exist; rather, God is existence."[24] Tillich is not saying that everything that exists is God (pantheism), but rather that everything exists because God exists; ultimacy is necessary for contingency.

---

[21] Teilhard, *Phenomenon of Man*, 285.

[22] Robert Ellsberg, "The Baal Shem Tov," in *Give Us This Day* (Collegeville, MN: Liturgical Press, 2019), 239.

[23] Paul Tillich, *Systematic Theology*, vol. 1 (Chicago: University of Chicago, 1951), 205.

[24] Tillich, *Systematic Theology*, 205.

Everything exists in God, and God is in all things (panentheism). God is the depth of existence, the inexhaustibility of existence in light of the contingency of being. Everything passes away, but God does not pass away. "God is that than which no greater can be thought," Anselm of Canterbury wrote in the eleventh century.[25] Being cannot contain God, because God is the overflow of being itself. God is the future and hence the promise of ultimate fulfillment. We never completely arrive at the future, but we are constantly oriented toward it. Because the name *God* points to the *infinite and inexhaustible future,* we are driven by *hope for an absolute future.* John Haught writes: "Whoever has a concern about the absolute future is concerned about God."[26] If religion focuses our energies on a convergent transcendent point, then that point must always be future. Religion requires radical openness to an absolute future by inviting us to transform our historical existence into hopeful images through which the future discloses itself to us. Religion is future oriented.

Theogenesis

Teilhard's ideas on God are closely aligned with those of Rahner and Tillich. To appreciate Teilhard's God is first to realize that God and the world are not opposed but complementary, that God and the world belong together and complete one another. Creation is integral to God. Teilhard believes that without creation, something would be absolutely lacking to God, considered in the fullness not of his being but of his act of union. God and the world are in a process of creative union. Teilhard's ideas here are easily dismissed if they are interpreted in light of Greek philosophy, in which there is no real relation between divine and created being.

---

[25] Anselm of Canterbury, *Prayers and Meditations of St. Anselm with the Proslogian,* trans. Benedicta Ward (New York: Penguin, 1979), 244.

[26] John Haught, *What Is God? How to Think about the Divine* (New York: Paulist Press, 1986), 32.

Should we adhere to Greek philosophy in a world of evolution and quantum reality? Teilhard, Whitehead, and others did not think so. There is no world of ideal forms "above" us, and existence is not participation in divine absolute being. As Whitehead said, "God cannot be the great exception to all metaphysical rules invoked to save their collapse. He is their chief exemplification."[27] God enters into material existence; this is the heart of Christian revelation. What does this mean? This is a sticking point today in theological discussions on the God/ world relationship. The existence of subsistent Being ontologically distinct from finite contingent being still frames Catholic theology. Yet the incarnation speaks of dynamic divine Being fully united to matter; relational, communicative, and self-giving Being in love. As Mary Beth Ingham states: "The divine nature as triune communion and the Incarnation as fullest manifestation of divine essence go far beyond the ken of human natural reason, left to its own devices. . . . The divine act of self-revelation and self-gift goes against everything that human reason accepts as *reasonable divine* behavior."[28]

In the Middle Ages a dispute arose between those who followed the theology of Thomas Aquinas (d. 1257) and those who followed the Franciscan Duns Scotus (d. 1308). Aquinas held to a philosophical position of analogy of being whereby God alone is pure-act and all other beings are potency-act; hence, there is no real relation between God and creation, although created being participates in God. Scotus rejected analogy of being and posited that there is one order of being—univocal being (literally, one voice)—in which divine being and created being exist. In 1879, Pope Leo XIII declared Thomas Aquinas the official theologian of the church, a position implicitly retained to this day. The consequences of choosing Aquinas over Scotus have had profound implications for the relationship between science

---

[27] Alfred North Whitehead, *Process and Reality*, ed. David Ray Griffin and Donald W. Sherburne (New York: Free Press, 1978), 343.

[28] Mary Beth Ingham, *Scotus for Dunces* (St. Bonaventure, NY: The Franciscan Institute, 2003), 48.

and religion. Had the church opted for Scotus's univocal being, we would have had a very different theology today, and religion would have had a much better chance of aligning with science.

It is worth outlining Scotus's principal ideas to see how they pave the way for process theology, especially the paradigms of Teilhard and Alfred North Whitehead. Scotus conceived creation as the outflow of divine love, a generous love spilling over into each created being. God is not perfect Being who creates imperfect being. Rather, there is a common relation between Creator and creature in regard to each other. Univocal being posits a common foundation between the mind and reality so that knowledge of God is truly possible through all that exists. God can be known through matter. Scotus posited a principle of *haecceitas* meaning that *this* being is uniquely brought into existence by God, as if God loved *this* being uniquely from all eternity, so that *this* being cannot be replaced by *that* being. Hence, each being bears the unique love of God within it.[29]

This principle of *haecceitas* helps explain the ineffable divine core of created existence. Scotus's idea of concurrence points to the simultaneous operation of primary and secondary causes, an acting-along-with rather than an acting-in, or what might better be described today as quantum entanglement.[30] Basically, his doctrine states that everything has its own unique being. The activity of each being is concurrent with divine presence, which is both the source of its unique being and the freedom of each being to be itself in its own creative activity. In this respect being does not participate in God; rather, there is a mutuality between God and created being. God participates in being as being participates in God. In a sense, God is dependent on being to act from its own fullest potential. This is not a collapse of God into materiality; rather, this is a coincidence of opposites. Divinity and creatively are fully themselves in union with each other.

---

[29] Ingham, *Scotus for Dunces*, 112.

[30] Peter Liethart, "Causality and Pure Nature," blog, *Patheos* (October 16, 2010).

Teilhard expressed a similar idea with his doctrine of Omega. God acts from within, at the core of each element, by animating the sphere of being from within. Where God is operating, it is always possible for us to see only the work of nature. God is the formal cause, the intrinsic principle of being, although God is not identical with being itself. As principle of being, God imparts to creation its inner dynamism; this is the heart of Teilhard's Omega principle. It is this unique presence of divine being in created being that imparts to every existence a principle of individuation or *haecceitas* (thisness). Everything that exists, from quarks to stars, leaves, and worms, exists from the unique love of God; hence, every existent has intrinsic worth. The concurrent presence of divine love in created being is at once God's humble presence in matter. Every creative act of being can transcend God as it cooperates with God in making itself, and every creative act of God transcends being. This dance of concurrence can help explain the transcendence of being described by the process of evolution. Science contributes to this philosophical idea of concurrence is the primary role of consciousness. In evolution, lower levels of consciousness evolve to higher levels of consciousness and deeper relationships of love. From a philosophical and religious perspective, we can say that what exists as an inner principle of evolution becomes self-aware in the human person who is oriented toward an infinite horizon of gracious mystery, drawn by consciousness and love.

Alfred North Whitehead also spoke of an organic, mutual relatedness between God and world.[31] If God is creating the world, it is because the world is creating God and giving birth to God. For Whitehead, the world is immanent in God, and God is immanent in the world, an idea that cannot be supported by substance theology. Rather, God is more like a field of energy entangled with the field of world. Each is a distinct field force interacting

---

[31] See Alfred North Whitehead, "God and the World," in *Process Theology: Basic Writings of the Key Thinkers,* ed. Ewert H. Cousins (New York: Newman Press, 1971), 85–97.

with the other and affected by the other. Hence, Whitehead says, "the world lives by its incarnation of God in itself."[32]

Similarly, Teilhard brought evolution and God together in such a way that the incarnation is the meaning and purpose of evolution because God is in evolution. For Teilhard, consciousness is the "inside" of matter and attraction is the "outside" of matter. The core energy of consciousness and attraction is love. According to Christian revelation, God *is* love (Jn 4:13). Thus, Teilhard develops a doctrine of theogenesis (literally, the birthing of God) whereby God is born in evolution through the unitive power of love. Teilhard writes: "As a direct consequence of the unitive process by which God is revealed to us, he in some way 'transforms himself' as he incorporates us."[33] As we come to a higher consciousness of unity, God rises up in us; God, in a sense, *becomes* God in us. This is the meaning of incarnation. God enters into matter and rises up in matter through higher levels of consciousness and the unitive power of love. In Teilhard's words: "All around us, and within our own selves, God is in process of 'changing,' as a result of the coincidence of his magnetic power and our own Thought."[34] God is creating the world and the world is creating God by giving birth to God, a movement from unconscious matter to self-aware conscious matter, from unreflective matter to self-reflective and transcendent matter. A mindful material universe giving birth to God is a radically new way to understand the relationship between God and world and the world's future in God. If the rise of consciousness in evolution is the rise of God, then Jesus is the One in whom cosmos, anthropos, and God-consciousness arrive at full union. Jesus's deep consciousness of God is God's full disclosure in love. In the person of Jesus God, cosmos and human form a deep solidarity of love, in effect, a new singularity that forms a second Big Bang in evolution, the release of the divine Spirit of love.

---

[32] Alfred North Whitehead, *Religion in the Making: Lowell Lectures*, 2nd ed. (New York: Fordham University Press, 1926), 149.

[33] Pierre Teilhard de Chardin, *The Heart of Matter*, trans. René Hague (New York: Harcourt, 1978), 53.

[34] Teilhard, 53.

Carl Jung shared a similar understanding of theogenesis with Teilhard and Whitehead. For Jung, consciousness is the mirror that the universe has evolved to reflect upon itself and in which its very existence is revealed. He describes the evolution of God based on the paradigm of the union of opposites. As a psychoanalyst he views God (and Christianity) as a patient in analysis for whom consciousness needs to be brought into its unconscious darkness in a self-transformative process, one of individuating and becoming whole. According to Peter Todd, "It is precisely this expanded and higher consciousness which Jung believes God acquires through incarnation in humankind."[35] The inextricable relationship of God and world is the full meaning of the divine Word incarnate. God is not a singular monad but plural—Trinity—and thus an open system of self-engagement. The self-engaged God is the Word incarnate, the Christ. For Jung, the evolution of God and the evolution of humanity cannot be separated. As we rise into higher consciousness, so too does God.

Jesus Christ symbolizes the highest consciousness of God, a union of opposites whereby the self of God and the self of human are united in one person. Jung writes: "One should make it clear to oneself what it means when God becomes man. It means nothing less than a world-shaking transformation of God."[36] God becomes human and the human becomes God, incarnate through consciousness and love. Through ongoing incarnation God is completed by humankind in directed evolution. Todd states: "It is as an archetypal and cosmic reality rather than a purely theological concept."[37] God incarnate in the cosmic Christ is the fulfillment of natural evolution. "This transformation in consciousness," Todd writes, "is the divinization or resacralization of the world."[38] As God rises up through higher levels of consciousness, the human evolves from an incomplete whole to a

---

[35] Peter Todd, "Teilhard and Other Modern Thinkers on Evolution, Mind and Matter, *Teilhard Studies* 66 (2013): 1–18.

[36] Quoted in Todd, "Teilhard and Other Modern Thinkers," 6.

[37] Todd, 8.

[38] Todd, 8.

new level of completion and thus a new vision, a new knowing, and a new way of acting in the world. Todd writes:

> Like Jung, Teilhard thinks God needs humankind to become both whole and complete. The implication is that God and humanity are in an entangled state and that the individuation of each is inextricably bound with the other. This entanglement of God and world is symbolized by the concept of Omega. Teilhard develops an understanding of personalization whereby God becomes God in union with another because only in union with another can one's true personality be found.[39]

Teilhard suggests that all our difficulties and repulsions as regards the opposition between the All and the Person would be dissipated if only we understood that, by structure, the noosphere (and more generally the world) represents a whole that is centered. Because it contains and engenders consciousness, space/time is necessarily of a convergent nature. Accordingly, its enormous layers, followed in the right direction, must somewhere in the future become involuted to an Omega point, which fuses and consumes them integrally in itself.[40] This fusion is the union of opposites. God and world are differentiated precisely in the union of divinity and materiality through the complexification of consciousness. The world is not opposed to God but the very place of God's becoming in love.

Summary: Modern science and technology have brought about a significant shift in consciousness that is accelerating due to the internet and computer technology. We continue to assess changes in the human person based on first axial values, but we have entered a new second axial age of consciousness. This new

---

[39] Todd, 5.
[40] Teilhard, *Phenomenon of Man*, 259.

period calls for a new set of values to describe personhood and a new understanding of personal identity. Teilhard posits that a new spirit of the earth needs a new tethering to the whole, a new religious consciousness, born out of the wisdom of the past but refashioned for an electronically convergent future. Computer technology has opened up a new level of thinking unlike that of any other time in human history, the level of connecting minds in the noosphere. If religion means focusing on a convergent transcendent center of unity, then a new type of religion calls for a new understanding of God consonant with evolution. Teilhard is a theologian of the second axial period. His thought comes from a deep center of cosmic evolution and posits that a new theology is needed to vitalize evolution toward its capacity for ultimate wholeness and unity. Theologians in the twentieth century recognized the need to rethink divine reality in relation to the world, but Teilhard took this radicalization of God one step further by positing God's incarnation within a moving world. God is rising up with the emergence of consciousness so that revelation itself is not a given but an emergent process of consciousness. Teilhard and other thinkers such as Carl Jung name this process of God's individuation *theogenesis*, indicating that the human person is an active player in God's presence in the world.

9

Posthuman Spirituality

Spiritual Awakening

AI has ushered in significant changes in culture, philosophy, economics, and medicine. But the most significant change brought about by AI is not apparent to our computer-trained eye unless we start attending to the patterns emerging from deep connectivity. The most significant pattern to emerge in our technological age is the need to be tethered, bound, and connected, which is the area of religion. AI has exposed the desire for a new religious spirit and a new religion of the earth. Teilhard anticipated the emergence of a new religious spirit on the level of the noosphere. This new religious spirit, he indicated, is one of community and inter-personalization, a shift from first axial religion toward a hyper-personal religion whereby personhood and personality are realized within the whole.

"The peak of ourselves, the acme of our originality, is not our individuality," Teilhard writes, "but our person. . . . And we can only find our person by uniting together."[1] He reminds us, "It is beyond our souls that we must look, not the other way round."[2] Beatrice Bruteau, a disciple of Teilhard, spoke of persons as interrelated wholes: "Our 'I,' our personhood, is not a product

---

[1] Pierre Teilhard de Chardin, *The Phenomenon of Man*, trans. Bernard Wall (New York: Harper and Row, 1959), 263.

[2] Teilhard, *The Phenomenon of Man*, 260.

of God's action, something left over after the action has ceased. Rather it is God's action in the very actuality of acting. 'We' are not a thing but an activity."[3] To be a person is to be a creative center of activity, always in the process of becoming and living toward the future of ever deepening relationships.[4]

If personhood is the outflow of relationships, the posthuman (or ultrahuman) signifies an evolution toward personhood. As we become hyper-personal through our information networks, we become connected to a larger whole. This drive toward expanded conscious personhood is more than a pragmatic solution to our complex worldly problems. Rather, this compulsive search for connecting to a larger whole speaks to something deep within us, an inner depth of infinite reality. Consciousness is a dimension of materiality, according to Teilhard, the "inside" of matter, so to speak. It is the dimension of matter open to infinite depth wherein the ultimate horizon of that depth is the religious experience of God. The evolution of matter, therefore, is the evolution of consciousness, and the evolution of consciousness is the evolution of religious experience. As I discussed in Chapter 2, the ancients spoke of an inner divine spark.

Many early Christian writers recognized this inner divine presence, captured in the words of Augustine, "You are closer to me than I am to myself."[5] The twentieth-century monk Thomas Merton described this inner presence as *Le pointe vierge* (the virgin point): "At the center of our being is a point of nothingness which is untouched by sin and by illusion, a point of pure truth, a point or spark which belongs entirely to God."[6]

---

[3] Beatrice Bruteau, "Trinitarian Personhood," in *The Grand Option: Personal Transformation and a New Creation* (Notre Dame, IN: University of Notre Dame Press, 2001), 75.

[4] Beatrice Bruteau, "Persons in Communion," in *The Grand Option,* 53–54.

[5] Augustine, *The Confessions of Saint Augustine,* trans. John Ryan (New York: Doubleday, 1960).

[6] Thomas Merton, *Conjectures of a Guilty Bystander* (New York: Bantam Doubleday, 1994), 158.

This inner divine presence was lost in the development of Scholasticism and the objectification of religious experience. This was followed by the divorce between religion and science and the Protestant principle that effectively characterized God as Wholly Other; that through which the divine appears cannot be equated with the divine itself. The suspicious nature of inner experience removed the presence of God from the soul and made God an object of faith, a turn of events rejected by modern science and forced into obscurity by modern philosophy.

The making of God into an objective Other, a mental idea to be accepted or rejected, was the unmaking of the Western world. By eliminating the religious dimension of matter and making the soul into a separate form, distinct from the body, the human person was artificially reduced to an isolated piece of matter attached to a mind. Just as the slice of an apple is incomplete in itself and makes sense only in relation to the whole, so too personhood becomes obscure and meaningless apart from the whole.

Our separate self-sense is an illusion, Albert Einstein claimed, because we are part of a whole, though limited in time and space. "Our task is to free ourselves from this prison by widening our circle of compassion to embrace all living creatures and the whole of nature in its beauty."[7] Ken Wilber argues that the ego is a contraction in the field of awareness.[8]

The rapid development of computer technology and the search for complex AI signifies a search for wholeness: expansion of social connections, expansion of consciousness, and expansion of mind. The Turing test was more than asking if a machine could think like a human; it was instead a search for deep, relational personhood. Can the machine respond in such a way that I feel connected—not to the machine, but to myself? We

---

[7] Albert Einstein, quoted in Howard W. Eves, *Mathematical Circles Adieu* (Washington, DC: The Mathematical Association of America, 2002), 119.

[8] Ken Wilber, *The Essential Ken Wilber: An Introductory Reader* (Boulder, CO: Shambhala, 1998), 135–36.

see this dynamic in the surge of social media today. To whom do I belong? To what do I belong? How can my life become "more" than this partial fragment of a life?

Hyper-connectivity may offer the lure of personhood, but without religion—that is, without a vital inner center—we cannot find what we are searching for. Hence, we continue to develop technology at a frenetic pace while still in search of the whole. If the development of AI is religious in nature, the solution to guiding AI must be religious as well. The ultimate connections we seek cannot be found outside us because they lie within us.

The key to moderating transhuman and posthuman evolution is reawakening the inner self. To become aware of a divine inner depth, a "thisness" of our particular existence, is to become aware of our capacity for divine infinite life. Without the inner universe of the heart, we can easily lose our religious compass and become part of a blind technological evolution. The more we can live from an inner spaciousness of God's presence, the more we can engage hyper-personal connections toward a unitive future. When the inner world is stronger than the outer world, we live by choice, not by compulsion. Posthuman life has the capacity to be transformative, God making (theopoeitic), if the mind can expand inwardly and outwardly. When our minds and hearts expand in love, God is born in us and through us into the universe; the world moves ever closer toward Omega.[9]

Teilhard uses the word *theogenesis* to indicate that God and world come together through hyper-personalization. This hyper-personalizing God is not the old God of the starry heavens but the deep inner presence of love emerging from the unity of relationships. We are the rising up of God in evolution. Our interconnected lives are permeated with "sacred hotspots," so to speak, and when these hotspots are turned on by conscious awareness of truth, beauty, goodness, and unity, God is born. When our interconnections make us more aware together of our ultimate longings for future, creativity, novelty, spontaneity, laughter, friendship, compassion, forgiveness, and peace, God is

---

[9] Teilhard, *Phenomenon of Man*, 262.

active and alive, pulling us together into a new future. Our task is to be focally conscious and locally present, a task made possible by keeping the interior space of the heart free of dead remnants of the past, which we readily store there. Without spiritual awakening to the divine connecting power within us, we can blindly hand ourselves over to the forces of technological evolution.

Christogenesis

In Teilhard's view the universe is like one cosmic person in formation; the cosmic person is the Christ, divine love emptied into personal life forms. Christ is the model of every creature, from quarks and atoms to worms and humans—everything is created out of divine love and bears the depth of divine love within it. Through his penetrating view of the universe, Teilhard finds Christ present in the entire cosmos, from the least particle of matter to the convergent human community. "The Incarnation," he states, "is a making new . . . of all the universe's forces and powers."[10] Christ is organically immersed with all of creation, in the heart of matter, and is unifying the world.[11] By taking on human form, Christ has given the world its definitive form: cosmic personalization. That is to say, Christ symbolizes the capacity of every person and every creature to be united in love.

Teilhard uses the term *cosmic personalization* to advance building personal, integrated connections around the globe; he anticipated that the noosphere would be a new level of interpersonal connections made possible by computer technology and the linking of conscious. Through electronic connections, we know, feel, and act in and with others. Our individual brains are

---

[10] Pierre Teilhard de Chardin, *Christianity and Evolution: Reflections on Science and Religion,* trans. Rene Hague (New York: Harcourt, 1971), 182.

[11] Teilhard, *Phenomenon of Man,* 293–94; Timothy Jamison, "The Personalized Universe of Teilhard de Chardin," in *There Shall Be One Christ,* ed. Michael Meilach (New York: The Franciscan Institute, 1968), 26.

extended into a global brain where consciousness is complexified, forming a new type of interthinking person who can realize new possibilities for planetary life. What is needed, however, is a new level of love, a level of conscious belonging to one another and to the whole of which we are a part, a heart-to-heart connection. As the character Ryan states in the drama *Halt and Catch Fire:* "If only we can learn to take care of each other. Then this awesome destructive new connection won't isolate us. It won't leave us in the end so . . . totally alone."[12]

We belong to one another because we are already One in God, but God seeks to become One in us because God is love and love lives in mutual relationship. God seeks to become God in the heart of matter; that is, the unity of God rises in and through the rich diversity of creation. The whole universe is like one giant cosmic person forming out of the gritty stuff of personal relationships. God and the world are in the process of becoming *something more* together because the universe is grounded in the Personal *center* of love incarnate, the Christ. However, this birth of the cosmic Christ involves all the pain and suffering of the world. God comes to birth in the heart of matter when consciousness gives way to the power of love.

Planetization

The rise of the universal Christ provided Teilhard with a vision for the role of religion in evolution. He pointed to a new religion of the earth brought about by a new understanding of God, a new God-world relationship that is not two opposing realities but a single unity. God and world form a complementary relationship and need each other to be complete. Teilhard offered a radically new understanding of divinity in evolution, "a *synthesis* of Christ and the universe."[13] Just as mind cannot be extracted from matter, neither can God be extracted from matter; matter

---

[12] Christopher Cantwell and Christopher C. Rogers, creators, *Halt and Catch Fire,* TV series, cable network AMC (2014–17), series 3.

[13] Teilhard, *Christianity and Evolution,* 126.

matters to God. Incarnation is God's self-emptying into matter, which expands its capacity for God when consciousness rises to new levels of complexity. This God-world unity is a paradox because the opposites of God and world mutually affirm one another. The only way to overcome the incarnational paradox is to let go of the idea of God. Maurice Merleau-Ponty writes:

> God is not simply a principle of which we are the consequence, a will whose instruments we are. . . . There is sort of an impotence of God without us, and Christ attests that God would not be fully God without becoming fully man. . . . God is not above but beneath us—meaning that we do not find him as a suprasensible idea, but as another ourself which dwells in and authenticates our darkness. Transcendence no longer hangs over man; he becomes, strangely, its privileged bearer.[14]

Matter has endless depth because consciousness is part of matter and God is the ultimate depth of consciousness. Everything that exists therefore has infinite value—cyborgs, chatbots, nanobots, transvestites, transhumans: "There is nothing profane below here for those who know how to see," Teilhard writes.[15] We take hold of God in the finite who is "rising up" through the awakening of consciousness, born not in the heart of matter but *as* the heart of matter.[16] Salvation means to awaken to the gift of divine love hidden in matter, to become, as Teilhard puts it, one "with the universe and as a continuation of the universe."[17] This is a very different theology than the otherworldly direction that crept into Christianity and distorted its core foundation

---

[14] Maurice Merleau-Ponty, quoted in Richard Kearny, *Anatheism: Returning to God after God* (New York: Columbia University Press, 2011), 91.

[15] Pierre Teilhard de Chardin, *The Divine Milieu* (1957; reprint London: William Collins and Sons, 1960), 66.

[16] Thomas M. King, *Teilhard's Mysticism of Knowing* (New York: Seabury Press, 1981), 103.

[17] Teilhard, *Christianity and Evolution*, 92.

of incarnation. The Christian otherworldly focus, which comes close to Gnosticism at times (salvation by knowledge alone), has bolstered the shallow transhumanist ideal of auto-salvation, brain downloading in virtual non-biological bodies. Teilhard's position instead approximates that of Asian religions (which is surprising, because he paid little attention to the East).[18] The mind is everything; what you think, you become. Robert Geraci notes that in Japan all life is sacred; hence robots participate in a fundamental sanctity of the natural world. A positive outlook on the sanctity of all life promotes openness to humanoid robots and a future in which robots can serve human beings, who do not forsake their bodies for virtual lives.[19]

Teilhard also sees a divinizing world expressed in the term *Christogenesis,* which is the power of the world to become more personal through the power of love. He coined the term *planetization* to speak of the gathering of psychic and spiritual energies around the earth into a greater whole for the deepening of consciousness life.[20] Technology can play a critical role in the development of the world toward cosmic personalization or Christogenesis, but it depends on how we develop AI and for what aims. The electronically connected posthuman can play a critical role in the world's future, if posthuman life is guided by the religious dimension of inner conscious life.

Consciousness makes a difference to the whole, and connectivity makes a difference to the whole. Where your mind is, there your treasure lies (cf. Mt 6:21). To be blindly connected or super-

---

[18] Ilia Delio, "Teilhard de Chardin and World Religions," *Journal of Ecumenical Studies* 54, no. 3 (Summer 2019): 306–27.

[19] Robert Geraci, "Spiritual Robots: Religion and Our Scientific View of the Natural World," *Theology and Science* 4, no. 3 (2006): 229–46.

[20] Teilhard quotes from the famous British scientist, J.B.S. Haldane, "Essay on Science and Ethics" (1932): "Now, if the co-operation of some thousands of millions of cells in our brain can produce our consciousness, the idea becomes vastly more plausible that the co-operation of humanity, or some sections of it, may determine what Comte calls a Great Being" (Teilhard, *Phenomenon of Man,* 57n1).

ficially related is to thwart the evolution toward cosmic person-hood. Without the inner religious dimension of personhood, AI evolution can widen the gaps between rich and poor, alienate the less fortunate, and usher in a salvation of the privileged. With-out inner unity and a new world soul, we have no real future together. The key to wholeness, to a new planet of life, is not technology; it is religion. As consciousness expands with technol-ogy, religion must change as well, spurring on the progress of life toward more being and life. The success of humanity's evolution will be determined by our capacity to converge and unify.

Posthuman Love

Teilhard's second axial vision with technology as the frontal cortex of the noospheric mind helps us see that meaningful progress—in fact, our very survival—now lies along different lines. To think about AI or super-intelligence as perfecting us by making us healthier, wealthier, and happier (can AI create happi-ness?) actually constrains evolution on the level of the individual. Without deep relationality, AI transhumanism could potentially abort the future of planetary life. Significant progress can only be measured by our ability to create a more peaceful, just, and ecologically sustainable world.

AI can play a significant role in building a new earth, but it makes a difference how AI guides the life of the spirit and the rise of planetary love or compassion. Can AI link us together heart to heart? Teilhard envisioned the role of technology in the noosphere as one of a new collective heart.[21] Heart flows from Heart, meaning that God is in our devices and networked con-nections. Growing in divine awareness reflects how we decide at every moment whether a connection deepens love, unity, and truth or creates anger, fear, hurt, and rejection. Posthuman

---

[21] Teilhard de Chardin, *Future of Man* (1946; reprint, New York: HarperCollins, 1964), 75; W. Henry Kenny, SJ, *A Path through Teilhard's Phenomenon* (Dayton, OH: Pflaum Press, 1970), 138.

religion is a consciousness of God in the splice, the in-between spaces of hyper-connected life. It means recognizing a depth dimension that eludes the human grasp. God is present like a "sacred hotspot," an ineffable center in the point-to-point moment of encounter. One who lives from an inner center of divine presence knows when to connect and disconnect.

The drive for advanced AI is ultimately not a desire for super-intelligence or longevity (although these are appealing, *prima facie*); it is a drive for "more-being" in love, for compassion, forgiveness, peace, and nonviolence. In a world now disclosed by quantum physics as one interconnected whole, religious dualisms and legalisms can create unnecessary anxiety by alienating and separating tribes, thwarting the impulse for global community. Technology has an intoxicating lure because it can serve as a mental and spiritual refuge for bringing together what is separated. But it cannot fulfill the deepest desires of the human heart.

Materiality can bring about well-being, according to Teilhard, but spirituality and an increase in psychic energy can bring about more being. AI can give rise to beautiful music, art, and perhaps even meaningful relationships, and in this respect it can orient the heart toward God by expanding consciousness and connectivity.[22] But in the end, AI will disappoint us; a machine is a machine is a machine, to paraphrase Gertrude Stein. The machine extends something of the biological, the organic, and awakens us to the infinite. But the extension itself is only a possibility to be realized by other dimensions of life, including the psychological, spiritual, and religious dimensions. The realization of enhanced life requires a response that is more than mechanical; the history of the universe shows that evolution is realized when consciousness expands and transforms. In this respect it is not what AI can do for us, it is what we do in response to AI. Technology can

---

[22] See, for example, the incredible work of Ge Wang, a Stanford University computer scientist who has built an app to turn the Apple iPhone into a musical instrument. Ge Wang, *Artful Design: Technology in Search of the Sublime, a MusiComic Manifesto* (Stanford, CA: Stanford University Press, 2018).

connect minds and hearts around the planet, but spirituality is needed to deepen bonds of solidarity. We need a new religious spirit that can vitalize the energies of love.

Teilhard indicates that we are responsible for the future of the planet and, in a sense, we are responsible for God. "When God is removed from nature," Philip Hefner writes, "God disappears, and when God disappears we disappear to our own selves because we are not our own making."[23] Transhumanism is alluring, and the possibilities of living healthier, wealthier and smarter play into the weakness of our frail human condition. But without a cosmic sacred dimension to our lives, and a way of harnessing spiritual energies toward a transcendent convergent center of love, we consign ourselves to the forces of capitalism and consumerism. Religion is the most crucial factor for AI in the twenty-first century, and without it we will be left fearful and vulnerable.

Summary: Technology can play a significant role in a renewed presence of God through hyper-connected personalization. The electronically mediated milieu impels an evolution toward hyper-connected personhood. Teilhard's religion of the earth undergirds a new understanding of God that moves beyond the binary structure of God and world; rather, God and world are in mutual relationship. Consciousness is key to posthuman life and to a renewed sense of religion. Every relationship has a God dimension; God is within and between every relationship. God and world come together through the energies of love, and in coming together they give rise to a rich unity of God-conscious matter signified by the Christ. We are more God together than in our individual selves. An awakening of the God dimension of our lives leads us toward one another, a deepening of relationships that includes all aspects of planetary life. The religious dimension

---

[23] Philip Hefner, *Technology and Human Becoming* (Minneapolis: AugsburgFortress, 2005), 83.

of personhood undergirds the evolution of cosmic compassion. Personhood is relational, and we are oriented toward conscious, interconnected life. AI and posthuman life can facilitate sympoietic life when the point of unity is God Omega and the mind is centered in love.

10

Church
of the Planet

A Religion of the Earth

The age of institutional religion emerged in the first axial period
and responded to the religious needs and desires of the individual; however, the shift from the individual to the posthuman in
the second axial period calls for a new religious expression. The
steady decline in church attendance, especially among younger
generations, is not surprising, given the shift to second axial consciousness; institutional religion is coming to an end.[1] What is on
the rise is not necessarily a replacement for institutional religion
(such as a new Protestant Reformation) but a transcendence of
institutional religion. The emptying out of institutional churches
is *not* the end of religion but a sign that a *new birth* of religion
is at hand. If we are looking for the old forms of religion in new
ways we will probably not find them. The rise of the "Nones"—
spiritual but not religious—signals the rise of a new religious
consciousness without the trappings of institutional life.[2]

---

[1] Frank Newport, "Church Leaders and Declining Religious Service
Attendance," Polling Matters, Gallup News, September 7, 2018.

[2] James Emery White, *The Rise of the Nones: Understanding and
Reaching the Religiously Unaffiliated* (New York: Baker, 2014); William
Dinges, "Our Teens Are Leaving the Church. Why?" *America Magazine*
(August 28, 2018).

Anthony Gittins claims that institutional religion can blind us to divine revelation because it is too focused on fixed rules and ideas: "Religion seeks clear, bounded answers; it wants to quantify, reduce, set limits, and control. By contrast revelation is God's way of opening up for us unbounded possibilities; it expands our horizons and calls us beyond rules and law to love."[3] The second axial period marks a new level of revelation, a new God of unbounded possibilities emerging in evolution.

We are at the beginning of a religious revolution, perhaps the most significant religious paradigm shift since the emergence of first axial consciousness. Teilhard anticipated a religion of the earth based on a new religious consciousness, a new awareness of a dynamic God, a growing God, a God who is constantly rising up through new levels of consciousness. Religion shrank, he states, because we made it a personal matter, anthropocentric, and limited to personal salvation focused on heaven above. Religion is not of concern to the individual alone, but to *the whole of humankind* and, we might add, to the whole earth and the whole universe. Religion is an essential dimension of cosmic life. Pope Francis in his encyclical *Laudato Si'* sought to take up this wider role of religion but his efforts have been thwarted by the inability of a patriarchal church to accept the fact that a whole earth theology calls for a new theology, a deep incarnational theology, a theology of evolution.

Surprisingly, Teilhard thought that Christianity is the religion best suited for evolution because of the materiality of God, although we cannot rule out the rich traditions of Asian religions and their transformative levels of consciousness. What Teilhard emphasizes is that God enters into matter, becoming one with matter without being absorbed into matter. His focus on divine materiality is at the same time a denial of any gnostic tendencies. Incarnation is the core foundation of Christian faith and opens up Christianity to the dynamics of evolution. Matter is porous

---

[3] Anthony Gittins, "Can We Get Beyond Religion?" *New Theology Review* (May 2007): 11.

and permeable, while divinity is chaotic, unstable, and overflowing. God enters into materiality and rises up in and through evolution. Hence, God is neither fixed nor otherworldly but the inner creative power of wholeness and unity, impelling cosmic evolution toward the personalization of being in love.

David Cooper, writing from a Jewish perspective, suggests that God is not a noun but a verb—an interactive verb.[4] He speaks of "God-ing," which entails interdependency between two subjects, each being the object for the other, a shared being.[5] God is that which is forming in the in-between, in the splice, so to speak— the dynamic divine energy that lingers in darkness waiting to come to light. This "coming to light" can be understood as God rising up in consciousness. What *is* becomes something altogether *new* as human beings emerge into greater levels of consciousness.

God cannot be regarded "simply as the dynamic cause of the existence of creatures," Karl Rahner writes, "but as the dynamic ground of their becoming."[6] God is not behind us but before us. God is what the physical universe is coming to be by a power that cannot be explained by the universe alone. The name *God* points to an ineffable power of which no greater can be conceived. This unlimited mysterious power draws together, Teilhard notes, and is the deep personal center of everything that exists, the power of the whole drawing every partial whole toward more being and life. This power or life force is divine love, *empowering creation to become radically new*.[7] Becoming new *is* the meaning of incarnational creation, exemplified in the risen life of Christ. Jesus is God incarnate, the wild boundary crosser, the unstable

---

[4] David A. Cooper, *God Is a Verb: Kabbalah and the Practice of Mystical Judaism* (New York: Riverhead Books, 1997), 70.

[5] Cooper, *God Is a Verb*, 70.

[6] Karl Rahner, quoted in Denis Edwards, *Breath of Life: A Theology of the Creator Spirit* (Maryknoll, NY: Orbis Books, 2004), 46.

[7] Denis Edwards, "A Relational and Evolving Universe Unfolding within the Dynamism of the Divine Communion," in *In Him We Live and Move and Have Our Being: Panentheistic Reflections on God's Presence in a Scientific World* (Grand Rapids, MI: Eerdmans, 2004), 208.

and creative compassionate One, the cyborg creature who shows "the arbitrariness and constructed nature of what is considered the norm."[8] The symbol of Jesus as cyborg means that nothing can exhaust the presence of God, who is always the more of anything that exists. "The Incarnation is so contrary to common sense, it destabilizes reified categories," Anne Kull writes.[9]

Theologian Gerd Theissen describes Jesus as a biological mutation, a "protest against the principle of selection." He states that in Jesus, "God no longer appears as a devastating power which proceeds from the pressure of selection. . . . Rather, God . . . makes possible life at the very point where human beings have offended against the basic conditions of reality."[10] God does new things because God does strange things that are often illogical and contrary to all expectations. Jesus exemplified this power of newness and strangeness and speaks of it as the power of God: "It is the Father, living in me, who is doing his work" (Jn 14:10).

Jesus lived with a second axial consciousness in the first axial period; he was a proleptic figure, anticipating what the world could become. He had a new consciousness of relatedness, a new way of seeing others, a consciousness of the whole where each person is infinitely valued. His message is that the world is oozing with God; divine love is God-ing the world into something more personal and unitive. Love liberated Jesus into a new consciousness of wholeness. Jesus lived on a new level of existence, free from the oppressive powers of the world and from the past. He saw all creatures, human beings, the birds of the air, and the lilies of the fields, as part of himself.[11]

Jesus destabilized boundaries by disrupting them. The entire life of Jesus was an act of breaking down barriers and

---

[8] Anne Kull, "Cyborg Embodiment and Incarnation," *Currents in Theology and Mission* 28, no. 3–4 (2001): 284.

[9] Kull, "Cyborg Embodiment and Incarnation," 284.

[10] Gerd Theissen, *Biblical Faith: An Evolutionary Approach* (Minneapolis: Fortress Press, 1985), 112–13.

[11] Jim Marion, *Putting on the Mind of Christ: The Inner Work of Christian Spirituality* (Charlottesville, VA: Hampton Roads, 2000), 8.

constructing new realities—cyborg life. He shows us that boundary crossing is integral to new life. Philip Hefner describes the cyborg in a way that resonates with the life of Jesus:

> First, we are given a body by the processes of nature, prior to our being aware of ourselves; we do not decide on our own to be born as we are. This first, given, body is constituted over evolutionary time. We bring awareness and our decision to bear on this first body that evolution bequeaths us, and in human historical time we construct a body on top of it, so to speak. Second, we not only struggle to understand how to constitute our new bodies, we struggle even more to cope with the consequences of our work. All of this is what it means that we constitute ourselves as Cyborg/Created Co-Creator. Finally, we struggle to work out the criteria that can govern such self-constituting. This struggle—constituting ourselves, dealing with its consequences, as well as shaping criteria for the entire process—this struggle is itself a religious struggle. In this process of self-constituting, we may be shaken to the core—and our cultural heritage with us—and in that shaking . . . we engage the holy, that which threatens to tear us apart and yet also holds us so much in its alluring grasp that we cannot let it go.[12]

Evolution takes the incarnation story out of the fixed narrative of Jesus's birth, death, and resurrection to the realization that God is rising up through the emergence of matter, mind, and consciousness. God is becoming something new in us, and we are becoming something new in God. Incarnation is co-constitutive of what Raimon Panikkar called the cosmotheandric solidarity, the entangled realities of divinity, cosmos, and personhood.

---

[12] Philip Hefner, "The Created Co-Creator Meets Cyborg," Metanexus, March 29, 2004.

A Whole Earth God

Teilhard saw the world as sacramental, a divine milieu, a world oozing with God; everything that exists remains open to more being and consciousness. Revelation involves breaking down boundaries that divide divinity and humanity: God God-ing the world into a new whole where the center of love shines through every aspect of life. Annie Dillard writes:

> Every day is a god, each day is a god, and holiness holds forth in time. . . . I wake in a god. I wake in arms holding my quilt, holding me as best they can inside my quilt. . . . I open my eyes. The god lifts from the water. His head fills the bay. He is Puget Sound, the Pacific; his breast rises from pastures; his fingers are firs; islands slide wet down his shoulders. Islands slip blue from his shoulders and glide over the water, the empty, lighted water like a stage. Today's god rises, his long eyes flecked in clouds. He flings his arms, spreading colors; he arches, cupping sky in his belly; he vaults, vaulting and spread, holding all and spread on me like skin.[13]

The self-emptying of God in the incarnation calls for belief in God beyond God; a God who is not "above" but the excess of being itself, the horizon of everyday connections, everyday thoughts, everyday actions; a God who gives up being God in order to become God in us, with us, and for us. This giving up of God is not a temporal action but a dialectic of God's life, an inner mystery of divine reality expressed in both the fecundity of divine love and the self-emptying of that same love. The paradox of God is the creative tension of divine life that moves divinity outward into the dynamic act of creation.

God immersed in space-time brought to light by human consciousness is the cosmotheandric reality described by Panikkar.

---

[13] Annie Dillard, *Holy the Firm* (New York: Harper and Row, 1977), 11–12.

The divine is never alone or by itself, because it has no "self," it is a dimension of the Whole.[14] The divine mystery is the ultimate I AM of everything. God is not the great Thor who creates by force of power but the divine relational dimension of being itself by which being transcends itself toward ever greater relationality and toward wholeness and depth. Physicists David Bohm and Karl Pribam describe the movement toward wholeness and depth, from the point of physics, as a quantum potential, a constant potential of implicate order. This concept corresponds to the cosmotheandric experience. Panikkar writes: "Without the divine, we cannot say *I*; without consciousness, we cannot say *Thou*; and without the World, we cannot say *It*. They are pro-nouns, or rather *pro*-noun; they stand for the same (unnameable) noun."[15] The subject matter of the whole is neither the cosmos nor the human but the cosmos inhabited by God and the human who is a constitutive member of reality. Every person (indeed, everything that exists) has this depth dimension because everything has an infinite quality to it and is oriented toward the future fullness of life.

By seeing the whole reality in the Christ mystery (the personal union of divinity, humanity, and cosmos), every being is "a manifestation of the christic adventure of the whole of reality on its way to infinite mystery."[16] Christ is not only the title of the historical person, Jesus, but the symbolic form of the whole cosmotheandric reality grounded in love. This too is Teilhard's idea. Christ is not an individual but the personalization of the whole in relation to God. Evolution is oriented toward the rise of the Cosmic Person, the Christ.[17]

---

[14] Raimon Panikkar, *The Rhythm of Being: The Unbroken Trinity* (Maryknoll, NY: Orbis Books, 2013), 190.

[15] Panikkar, *Rhythm of Being*, 191.

[16] Raimon Panikkar, *Christophany: The Fullness of Man*, Faith Meets Faith (Maryknoll, NY: Orbis Books, 2004), 146.

[17] See Pierre Teilhard de Chardin, *The Phenomenon of Man*, trans. Bernard Wall (New York: Harper and Row, 1959), 57n1.

Religion as Performance

Religion has fallen off the grid of contemporary life because, on one hand, its philosophical abstractions are confusing, and on the other hand, it lacks coherence with modern physics and evolution; religion and science do not speak the same language or see eye to eye. Author Anne Lamott quips: "I don't need to understand the hypostatic union of the Trinity; I just need to turn my life over to whoever came up with redwood trees."[18] Institutional religion is like a box of chocolates filled with dogmas, doctrines, judgments, and moral rules. The purpose of first axial religion was moral guidance and personal salvation. The purpose of second axial religion is collective unity for a planetized earth.

The connectivity of the noosphere calls for a new type of engagement on all levels of life: personal, social, and spiritual/religious. Self-engagement on this level is driven not by an isolated personal center but a networked personal center of recursive relationships. It is not surprising that the emerging posthuman milieu is giving rise to a renewed interest in art and performance as persons seek to construct meaning and value. Performance is the way nature works as cybernetic systems. Ongoing engagement with the environment is what constitutes anything in its existence. Art is the performance of self-actualization, but so too is religion. Can we reimagine religion today as a new type of performance?

Judith Butler's gender performance opened new doors of understanding gender as enactment and thus gender as art. "Gender is performative," she writes, "a stylized repetition of acts, in which bodily gestures, movements, and styles of various kinds constitute the illusion of an abiding gendered self."[19] Her anti-essentialist position basically holds that one becomes a gendered person by acting as a gendered person. The same

---

[18] Anne Lamott, *Plan B: Further Thoughts on Earth* (New York: Riverhead, 2006), 296.

[19] Judith Butler, *Gender Trouble: Feminism and the Subversion of Gender* (London: Routledge, 1990), 137.

argument could be made for religion. One is not born Catholic or Jewish. Rather, one becomes Catholic or Jew by learning the scriptures and performing acts of ritual: the lighting of candles, the raising of hands in prayer, the prostration before the Holy One. It is not surprising that devotions such as reciting the rosary together or kneeling before the Blessed Sacrament in adoration are popular among younger generations today. Devotions are performative art. We have a great need to construct ourselves, define ourselves, in order to connect ourselves to what is more than our individual self.

We cross boundaries and create art because there is something present that draws us to cross the boundary of the moment. The things of ultimacy are within us and before us. We know them as horizons of our incomplete lives, and we are constantly drawn to them. Religion helps name what we are drawn to and guides our vision. Spirituality is performative religion. I am pulled toward something in this moment, and I act to create, to fill the moment with a new moment of being. What will I create in this moment? I can "create" God by becoming aware of divine presence or I can create evil by choosing to remain in the darkness of chaos. How will I know what to do? Religious performance or enacting values that empower life into new wholes requires principles gleaned from the wisdom of ancient religious traditions. The lessons of the Gospels or the saints and mystics can now be enacted in feedback loops of dynamical systems that create a milieu of robust resilience, able to sustain the pressures of fluctuating events and remain open to the future. I act in this moment on this value or this virtue. Do I know myself being created in this act? Am I becoming more whole through this act? Is there a trace of divine transcendence in this act? Do I pull others into a new unity? Am I drawn beyond myself to others? In performative religion I act so as to believe, and I believe so as to act. I do not merely believe in God as an abstract truth; I must *do* God. I am a Christian only insofar as I *do* Christ, or I am a Buddhist only insofar as I *do* Buddha. Performative religion is enacting the energies by which I create and am created. It is a recursive process of creativity by which God is born over and over again through me into higher levels of consciousness and thus into an incarnating presence in my life.

Contemplation and Hyper-personalization

As we engage in cybernetic fields of connectedness, creating and recreating together, we are entangled in a cosmotheandric process of God-ing the world. God is not outside the realm of complexifying relationships. Rather, God is God-ing in and through us, in the way we create our life art together through new connections. Teilhard's religion of the earth anticipates a collective unity of minds gathered into new forces of love. This emerging new religion is *the* revolution in our midst. AI is facilitating the new energies of hyper-connections by shrinking the spaces between us and expanding the levels of consciousness. Where the mind of the posthuman lies, there the new religion must go. Without a focal point of awareness, however, the interconnected posthuman can be electronically embedded without a sense of meaning. Religion, as engaged networks of performance, must redound on the depth dimension of collective existence. That is, religious performance must hyper-personalize into greater unities through self-reflexive loops and emergent bodies. Such unities are not merely exoskeletal or outside us; there must be an inner unity that feeds into the cybernetic loop between the inner self and outer self. The more one knows a unifying source within oneself, the more one perceives that source as the unifying energy of the active whole.

Teilhard drew a link between contemplation and consciousness and said that contemplation has evolutionary significance through centration of the universe. By this he meant that a focused mind can shape the direction of evolution through creative relationships. The human person has the unique capacity to perceive ultimate reality in a way that is embodied and intuitive. Teilhard posited an integral connection between the experience of the ineffable within one's dynamic self and in the dynamic collective of hyper-personalization. In the words of the Sufi mystic Mansur Al Hallaj:

I saw my Lord with the eye of my heart,
and I said "Who are you?"
and he said "Your Self."[20]

Teilhard believed that mysticism is the most intense spiritual energy and the most intense energy of centration. The awakening of the mystic to the presence of the inner sacred presence, the ineffable center of love, is the beginning of a new vision of reality. Martin Laird writes: "The mystic enters the center of a network of cosmic influences and is astonished at the depth and intimacy of relationship with the universe."[21] Hyper-connectivity is a superego centration whereby the self lives beyond itself in the other and ultimately in the All. Teilhard connects the act of faith with the centrating function of the human in the cosmos—to believe is to centrate and converge. Faith in God-Omega and the dynamic centration of one's own life is faith in the world; contemplation maximizes faith by maximizing consciousness. As one attains higher levels of being through an expansion and evolution of consciousness, one sees the connected whole in a single view, one seamless flow of space from self to world and back again. God, we might say, is the hyper-unified source of all cosmic life. In a sense the mystical vision of the seer and the computer-networked posthuman share hyper-connectivity. At the highest levels of consciousness, the mystic sees the world in a seamless unity, while the hyper-connected posthuman searches for unity but may easily become thinned out across many informational fields. The mystic *and* the posthuman want to travel in the same direction, toward boundless unity of personal being; while AI can facilitate hyper-connectivity it cannot achieve a nondual vision of reality without an ultimate point of convergence. Can AI bring about the state of samadhi, where consciousness of unity is

---

[20] In William Stoddart, *Sufism: The Mystical Doctrines and Methods of Islam,* 2nd ed., rev. (New York: Paragon, 1998), 83.
[21] Martin Laird, "The Diaphanous Universe: Mysticism in the Thought of Pierre Teilhard de Chardin," *Studies in Spirituality* 4 (1994): 219.

the experience of detachment and unified Allness? Is there such a thing as virtual mysticism? Or is there something elusive and eternal within us, a divine spark that transcends cybernetic loops and virtual reality?

Teilhard recognized that only inner transformation of consciousness can escape cosmic entropy and centrate energy on higher levels of complexity. His noospheric emergence of the posthuman (ultrahuman) in no way contradicts the power of AI to bring about a super-intelligence; rather, super-intelligence must be super-centered, super-unitive, super-amorizing energies of love. The contemplative posthuman is one who lives in the moment of *awareness* and *aliveness*; the *aware* and *alive* self is the deeply connected self.

The Posthuman Mystic

We see the emergence of global religious consciousness and the beginning of interspirituality today developing through various forms of meditation practice from centering prayer to yoga, mindful meditation, and contemplation. Such practices are essential for the hyper-connected person in that they extend and deepen the inner dimension of cosmic life, the spiritual eye of the heart. Such practices can remain individual and detached from hyper-personal life, however, if they are not performed as part of cybernetic posthuman life. Practitioners can engage in personal centering without consciously connecting on a wider global scale of human becoming. Meditation can remain enclosed in personal piety and ignore the cosmic urge to unify.

The posthuman mystic is the one who has the courage to live in the God-ing moment, connecting and creating the art of life. Every moment is an opportunity to become more conscious of the divine depth in our midst. To participate in God-ing energy means to be aware of the ineffable divine presence and to act from the energy of this presence, to participate creatively in God's becoming. In this sense religion is the dynamic engagement of cosmotheandric energy, always erupting and self-creating; a recursive loop between soul center and world center, a constant flow of self-emptying and renewal through ongoing personal engagement. God is always in the process of becoming, because we are always in the process of becoming, so that where we are, so too is God, and where God is, so too do we long to be.

Posthuman religion requires a new form of worship and a new way of action, a new way of expressing the God dimension of life in a focal celebration of prayer and ritual. Teilhard's "Mass on the World" is an example of performative religion, of divining the moment through a conscious act of self-offering. He celebrated this mass while living in the Ordos Desert in inner Mongolia, with no paten or chalice but simply the earth, the sky, the wind, and his desire for God:

> Since once again, Lord—though this time not in the forests of the Aisne but in the steppes of Asia—I have neither bread, nor wine, nor altar, I will raise myself beyond these symbols, up to the pure majesty of the real itself; I, your priest, will make the whole earth my altar and on it will offer you all the labours and sufferings of the world. Over there, on the horizon, the sun has just touched with light the outermost fringe of the eastern sky. Once again, beneath this moving sheet of fire, the living surface of the earth wakes and trembles, and once again begins its fearful travail. I will place on my paten, O God, the harvest to be won by this renewal of labour. Into my chalice I shall pour all the sap which is to be pressed out this day from the earth's fruits. My paten and my chalice are the depths of a soul laid widely open to all the forces which in a moment will rise up from every corner of the earth and converge upon the Spirit. Grant me the remembrance and the mystic presence of all those whom the light is now awakening to the new day.[22]

---

[22] Pierre Teilhard de Chardin, *Hymn of the Universe* (London: CollinsFontana Book, 1970), 32–33.

Teilhard's second axial vision helps us see that everything is held in existence by the energies of love. Meaningful progress, therefore—in fact, our very survival—now lies along different lines. To think about AI as if its main contribution is progress toward betterment or super-intelligence can constrain evolution on the level of the individual. Without deep relationality, such efforts could harm the earth. Significant progress can only be measured by our ability to converge, hyper-connect, and super-amorize toward a more peaceful, just, and ecologically sustainable world.

Re-enchanting the Earth

AI can play a significant role in re-enchanting the earth through new levels of consciousness if it can embrace religion as its third eye, a second axial religion that builds on the co-collective consciousness of hyper-personalization. AI expresses nature's capacity for fecundity, and religion provides purpose and direction to the fecund life. Reality is a process marked by a drive for transcendence, and God is at the heart of transcendence. Self-making is written into the heart of nature, or as Hefner writes, "evolution has itself been designed to enable a self-transcending system of reality."[23]

Hefner uses the term *created co-creator* to describe human activity in relation to God. Our work and actions affect God's own relational life. When we contribute to the building of the world and to developing ourselves, we make a positive difference to God's life. We are responsible for the future of the world. Hefner views technology as a medium for human freedom and imagination, an expression of the human capacity to envision conditions not yet actual. This capacity for imagination belongs to both spirituality and technology. He writes:

Humans are defined by this imagination or spirituality, freedom is defined by it, and now we see that technology

---

[23] Philip Hefner, *Technology and Human Becoming* (Minneapolis: Augsburg Fortress, 2005), 84.

is also defined by this imaginative probing of what actual things and actual states can become—and believing in it, acting on it. In this respect, technology is a spiritual realm.[24]

The posthuman is brought to birth by creatively crossing boundaries, linking chips and brains, electronically embedded in an ongoing process of hyper-personalization that resists the technical will to disembodiment and immateriality. The human person acquires a new *bios-techne* consciousness giving rise to a new type of world: from tribal-national awareness to global consciousness; from divergence to convergence. Teilhard foresees a merging of political, ecological, and spiritual energies and activism into one unified framework of thought and action, inspiring a totally new sense of ourselves as a species. The convergent complexified consciousness of the posthuman requires a gradual awakening of planetary consciousness, a new collective consciousness, which is why first axial religions belie the new planetization: they resist collective consciousness and refuse religious convergence. A reorientation of world religions, however, is needed for the future of the earth if hyper-connectivity is to have ultimate meaning. This need was realized at a UNESCO gathering at the United Nations in 1975:

> The crises of our time are challenging the world religions to release a new spiritual force transcending religious, cultural and national boundaries into a new consciousness of the oneness of the human community and so putting into effect a spiritual dynamic toward the solutions of world problems. . . .We affirm a new spirituality, divested of insularity and directed toward a planetary consciousness.[25]

A "new spirituality, divested of insularity and directed toward a planetary consciousness" is also Teilhard's vision for a new

---

[24] Hefner, *Technology and Human Becoming,* 53.

[25] UNESCO Symposium, New York City, October 24, 1975, cited in Ewert H. Cousins, "Teilhard's Concept of Religion and the Religious Phenomenon of Our Time," *Teilhard Studies* 49 (Fall 2004): 20.

religion of the earth. To what extent can world religions play a role in this new planetary faith? Can the wisdom of traditions be subsumed into a larger whole? Can the world religions let go for the sake of a new religious narrative? Nothing less than the future of the earth is at stake. In the early twentieth century Teilhard saw that a new religion of the earth is needed if we are to avoid catastrophic destruction.

Church of the Planet

A new religious consciousness calls for a new type of person, one who will find relationship with the divine to be a deep source of inspiration for all activity in the world. We are called to see and love in solidarity with all creation, a *sympoietic consciousness*, to use Haraway's term. Teilhard calls us to return to matter, to become conscious of matter's energy, to think of the earth and the entire cosmos as our *home*. God self-reveals everywhere, beneath our groping efforts, as a universal milieu, only because God is the ultimate point upon which all realities converge. The incarnation speaks to us of a world filled with divinity, but it is only a heart in love with matter that can see this God-filled world. Teilhard's secular mysticism calls for oneness of heart with God. This heart-centered being-in-the-world is a penetrating vision that sees the divine depth of everything.[26] In every action, every electronic connection, every robot, every neural implant, we must adhere to the creative power of God, to coincide with it and become its living extension.

Teilhard realized we need a radically new spirituality that can welcome and integrate the important scientific facts of our existence into itself. He opted for a spirituality that is engaged in a technologically complexifying world. Everything is incarnating divinity; the Omega point is the center of everything that exists. Everything is continually evolving into the Cosmic Person. In

---

[26] Pierre Teilhard de Chardin, *Christianity and Evolution: Reflections on Science and Religion*, trans. Rene Hague (New York: Harcourt, 1971), 75.

this colossal, almost unimaginable Cosmic Person each of us lives and develops in consciousness, like living cells in a huge organism. With the help of the physical sciences as well as the scriptures, Teilhard shows how we—the cells and members of this great cosmic body—can participate in and nurture the life of the Cosmic Person.

Our divine task is to turn this fragmented world into one immense shining body, a transhuman Cosmic Person radiating with the energies of love. At present, many of the "cells" (that is, people) of this body are unaware of their divine calling, unaware of their particular lovability and unconscious of the fact that they already live as part of this cosmic body. Yet, this cosmic body is meant to become fully conscious of itself in every cell of its being in such a way that every cell is also conscious of the whole body's destiny. This is the realm of the noosphere and the immeasurable value of AI. We are networked in the body, but we are not aware that our connections shape this body.

Teilhard's theogenic evolution calls for a new sacramental expression aligned with evolution. Rethinking baptism as the acceptance of God in evolution and Eucharist as communion with all species could reshape the catholic imagination. All of life is transformed into the body and blood of the cosmic Christ. All the communions of a lifetime are one communion, and all the communions of humans now living are one communion. Every person belongs to the royal priesthood of cosmic evolution. Every life is holy and sacred and can offer every thought and action to the unity of love; every life is part of the whole. God seeks to rise up in each particular life as the ultimate wholeness of love. Church is where we gather to harness our spiritual energies, whether physically together, electronically together, or both. Hyper-personalized persons empowered by love and energized to build the earth into a flourishing community of life is the heart of a new church in the twenty-first century, the church of the planet.

How can we reenvision churches as focal centers that support a new church of the planet? The first challenge is to accept our dynamic movement in evolution. If we are moving, then the ultimate ground of existence must be moving as well: God is in evolution, we are in evolution, and church is in evolution. As Joseph Bracken indicates, church must be reconceived as an open, dynamical system of relationships.[27] How do we make sense of ultimate concern, ultimate hope, and ultimate promise of life in a world that operates on principles of chaos, instability, and emergence? This is a challenging question because our axial religions posit fixed goals. For what is moving has no real fixed point of reference; every emergent, creative act is the ultimate creative act and every ultimate creative act is infinitely fecund. Thus, as Teilhard realized, we need a new type of religion that can enkindle a new type of organism emerging in evolution whose destiny it is to realize new possibilities for evolving life on this planet.[28]

Future Oriented

The second axial period calls for a new planetary religion of the earth that believes in a future together, a belief that tethers us to a divine ground, to one another and to ultimate meaning and purpose. Because we are always limited by our boundaries, the church of the planet needs AI to expand community, converge minds and heart, unify through hyper-personalization, and centrate the energies of love. Hefner notes: "If we cannot imagine that religion takes shape in technology, then we have eliminated the religious depth dimension of the most significant development in human becoming."[29] A new church of the planet may not require formal membership, but it does require commitment to the future through hyper-personalized, hyper-socialized co-reflection around a common center. The noosphere is the realm

---

[27] Joseph Bracken, *Church as Dynamic Life-System: Shared Ministries and Common Responsibilities* (Maryknoll, NY: Orbis Books, 2019).

[28] This idea is actually expressed by Julian Huxley in his introduction to Teilhard's *Phenomenon of Man*, 20; however, it aptly sums up Teilhard's vision.

[29] Hefner, *Technology and Human Becoming*, 76.

of the new collective gathering (*ecclesia*), dynamic engagements that are self organizing and self making, a recursive process of expanding consciousness where God is constantly showing up in new ways.

The realm of electronic mind invites a new consciousness of God-ing through hyper-personalizing, co-creative action, creating new unities for new actions that create new loves for a new earth. But we cannot engage new language and new theological images and metaphors if we remain bound to the established writings and dogmas of established religious traditions. I am not suggesting that we abandon these entirely but I am wondering just how far we can let go of tradition for the sake of a new religious future. Can we at least admit that what we receive as revelation is always historically mediated? We need a new religion of the earth that can engage a process of technoevolution toward the flourishing of planetary life. There is no blueprint or prescription; there is only the hyper-personal, electronically embedded person in evolution. We need performers who can live in the flow of self-gift and profess: *This is my electronically networked body and blood given for the life of the world.*

Jeanine Thweatt-Bates writes that

> the embrace of technology is an indispensable expression of human agency and spiritual realm of co-creation with God; it means that the possibilities of the posthuman must be faced in the techno-mirror, not with reflexive revulsion, but with a willingness to entertain the possibility that this may, indeed, be a future co-created with God.[30]

Hefner's cyborg co-creator makes this point as well: "Human beings are God's created co-creators whose purpose is to be the agency, acting in freedom, to birth the future that is most

---

[30] Jennifer Jeanine Thweatt-Bates, "The Cyborg Christ: Theological Anthropology, Christology, and the Posthuman," PhD diss., Princeton Theological Seminary, Princeton, NJ, October 2009.

wholesome for the nature that has birthed us."[31] The term *co-creator* means freedom of being, the inescapable necessity of making choices, constructing narratives, envisioning alternatives, and acting upon them. But it also carries a moral weight of ongoing decisions. Who determines what is good for the planet? Hefner writes, "To recognize that we play out the performance as simultaneously sinners and saints" adds to our possibilities for recognizing what is at stake in the engagement with the numinous depths of our being in the lure of transhumanism.[32] Conceiving human technologies as distinct expressions of human agency opens the question about the moral dimensions of agency in a hyper-networked world. If posthuman life is a shift from individuality to collective personality, to use Teilhard's insight, do our choices make the world more personal?

Technologies are social constructions and reflect the values and purposes of those who construct them. Hence, we live with the constant ambiguity of our choices and decisions. Technology can destroy the world or become the vehicle through which human beings can help actualize the world-God in creative love. We need to find new ways to navigate this new religious terrain of posthuman (ultrahuman) life. We need new myths and rituals, new types of gatherings that can reinforce hyper-connectedness and build bonds of community. If there is a role for the religious institution in the twenty-first century, then it must be redefined along the lines of complex dynamical systems living in the flow of the wider environment.[33]

As second axial religious consciousness takes root, we should be prepared for a very different type of religious person to emerge, as we seek to become a terrestrial community in a hyper-connected planet. The richness of past traditions can help,

---

[31] Philip Hefner, *The Human Factor: Evolution, Culture, Religion* (Minneapolis: Fortress, 1993), 27.

[32] Philip Hefner, "The Animal that Aspires to be an Angel: The Challenge of Transhumanism," *Dialog* 48, no. 2 (2009): 165.

[33] See, for example, the rethinking church as open system in Joseph Bracken, *Church as Dynamic Life-System: Shared Ministries and Common Responsibilities* (Maryknoll, NY: Orbis Books, 2019).

or they can hinder. No one will write the script except the one who seeks to live life to the full.

The Intergalatic Noosphere

Teilhard thought wide and deep. In his essay on ultrahumanity he writes that

> the grand enigma presented by the human phenomenon is not the question of knowing how life was kindled on Earth, but of understanding how it might be extinguished on earth without being continued elsewhere. Having once become reflective it cannot abandon itself or totally disappear without biologically contradicting itself.[34]

Posthumanism is the beginning of a long process of convergent consciousness—and not just on this planet earth. Planetization, the culmination of critical planetary reflection leading to hyper-socialization, will not be the end of life but, as Teilhard writes, a "mere spark in the darkness." Even if super-intelligent AI life succeeds to planetize posthuman life into the Omega Point, this will not be the end of the noosphere or electronically embedded hyper-networked life. Planetization, according to Teilhard, "represents our passage, by translation or dematerialization, to another sphere of the Universe: not an ending of the Ultra-Human but its accession to some sort of Trans-Humanity at the ultimate heart of things."[35]

We are just at the beginning of convergent life; the last few thousand years have brought about evolutionary expansion and diversity, and axial religions have been part of this expanding phase. Now we are moving toward convergence and unity. This is why we desperately need a new religion of the earth. Without a new religious dimension the second axial period cannot be

---

[34] Pierre Teilhard de Chardin, *The Future of Man* (1946; reprint, New York: HarperCollins, 1964), 297–98.

[35] Teilhard, 295, 298.

sustained. Without direction we have no meaning together, and without meaning we have no collective purpose. Religion harnesses the free energies of the earth, and AI can network these energies toward a new planetary life. If we cannot engage a new religious and spiritual dimension in posthuman life, AI will succumb to the strongest competitive forces and likely result in the same tragedies of the twentieth century and perhaps to a greater degree.

Teilhard foresaw an intergalactic convergence of consciousness in the distant future in which all galaxies of intelligent life will be united in a cosmic complexified unity. God is God-ing the universe and all universes, ongoing evolution of consciousness amid intergalactic life, minds ever linking and growing into new embodied minds, galactic extended minds, cosmic mind, until all matter is united in love.

Summary: Teilhard's cosmic vision of religion and evolution opens up a new vista of religion in the second axial period. He posits a deep incarnation whereby God is wholly immanent in evolution and yet transcends evolution as the power of the future. The world is holy and sacred but we need a new awareness of what is already present. Teilhard suggests that vision must be an inner-outer process and calls attention to the relationship between mysticism and technology. The more centered one is within, the more one can see the same center in the connections of shared life. AI can play a significant role divinizing the world by living from a depth of connectivity within and without. As second axial religious consciousness takes root in the twenty-first century, we should be prepared for a very different type of religious person to emerge, one who will be a part of the church of the planet—hyper-connected, co-creative, religiously performative and living on the frontier of ongoing creative networked life—whereby God rises up from the darkness of separateness into the radiating unity of life.

Conclusion

Where Are We Going?

I sat down to write this conclusion after returning from a thesis defense. The student had written his thesis on Heidegger and the question of being and space. One section dealt with social media and claimed that technology has spawned a disembodied consciousness:

> The onset of cybernetic consciousness introduced a new level of disembodied presence to the human experience, which inspires fear and trembling in *Da-sein* [being there]. It quite accurately identifies the anxiety I feel when my mother laments that she phones me, but "I am not there." She implores, "I need you to be there when I call." My anxiety whispers back: "I was never there. I can't be everywhere. I am here. Just here." The telephone is there, my voice may be there when I answer—which, I do, to be clear—my laughter may break in to her through the vibration of a piezoelectric diaphragm, but I am not there. Neither technologies of self, nor the mediated or curated self are new to technology, but the blossoming saturation of the virtual-social world over the past three decades inflicts us with more than an acute sense of vertigo. What is "space" in an increasingly virtual world? For all our griping, we may lack the courage to think the thought whole: where are you when you leave the room through the window in

your pocket? Were you ever in the room to begin with? Because you have checked your phone, and now you are certainly not here.[1]

When I read this paragraph I realized he had touched upon the knot that ties together the complex relationship of technology, personhood, and religion, that is, the question of space. Einstein had a problem with space and time as Newton conceived them and thought deeply about these dimensions, which led to a new understanding of a dynamic, expanding universe. Quantum physics shattered Newton's atomistic world by realizing that matter is not composed of billiard balls bumping into one another but interlocking fields of energy by which particles exist in superimposed states.

Modern science has radically changed our understanding of space. Nature works dynamically as a whole, from little wholes to big wholes. What accounts for the whole of nature? Physicists engaged this question early on, but I think the evolution of human consciousness reveals nature's secret: mind makes matter whole when mind and matter are unified. Nature's holism, as Bohm and others suggest, is contingent on the unity of mind and matter.

In the pre-axial period the emergence of embodied mind followed the pattern of nature; the human person imitated nature. The pre-axial person, born of the earth—*adamah*—lived in the whole earth community governed by the surrounding forces, including the spirits and gods of the wider cosmos. This period lasted for thousands of years before the rise of axial consciousness and the birth of the individual. If McGilchrist is right, axial consciousness is the beginning of the great disconnect between mind and matter. The right brain became severed from the wider world, giving dominance to the left brain and analytical thinking.

---

[1] Dustin Kuhns, "Re-spatializing: Space-Walking in the Stars, a Multitude of Horizons," master's thesis, Villanova University, May 5, 2019.

This brain shift corresponds to the great axial shift from pre-axial tribal consciousness to axial individual consciousness. The turn from nature toward the autonomous self meant in some way a turn away from neighbor as part of self. If one were to posit an origin of "sin" in the human community, it would be in the rise of the first axial person, who had more complex levels of brain and the capacity for symbolic language. Instead of imitating nature in its communal flow, humans became aware of one another as individuals and sought to imitate one another, turning the other into a competitor and foe, as René Girard so eloquently wrote.[2]

In the first axial period the space of nature's wholeness was contracted into the space of the individual. Consciousness began to retreat from nature and focus on self, giving rise to competing spaces, which became a basis for conflict and violence. Over a long period of time the first axial person gradually lost a sense of space within the whole. Science conquered space and, in doing so, displaced the human person from the center of the cosmos, creating a disorientation of personal identity in space.

Religion unified space for the pre-axial person, connecting the community to the sacred ground of the cosmic order, the *axis mundi*. But with the rise of the first axial period, religion became inculturated, as tribes gave way to cities and urban centers with pathways of communication. With the rise of monotheistic religions, the connection to the divine ground became conflicted and competitive. As a result, the space of God (where God dwells) became divided among the tribes. Religious fights became political fights, and political fights became territorial. The price of evolutionary growth and expansion in the first axial period was division, which spawned urbanization, socialization, and technological development. In a sense, the first axial person developed

---

[2] See, for example, Rene Girard, *The Scapegoat*, trans. Yvonne Frecerro (Baltimore: Johns Hopkins University Press, 1989); Gil Bailie, *Violence Unveiled: Humanity at the Crossroads* (New York: Crossroad, 1995).

by unraveling the cosmic whole. One of the most significant factors in this unraveling was religion.

In Christianity the space of God was politicized. Jesus of Nazareth was a mystic and prophet who lived from a deep inner center of God and in the freedom of creative love. While his message bore hope for a renewed community of life, the church developed along political and patriarchal lines. Space became divided into hierarchical tiers of clergy and laity, perfection and fallenness, heaven and earth. The religious believer began to live in the narrow space of the fallen earth, seeking the endless space of heaven. The mystics held together the unity of space and time by living in the eternal presence of God, deepening their lives in the divine presence and living from a new center of unity.

A spatial dislocation from the earth was deepened in the sixteenth century when the church rejected the Copernican system, giving rise to a disaffiliation with nature. A new anxiety emerged and the Cartesian subject was born, the individual who is self-thinking and detached. By the early twentieth century, religion and science saw the world in two different ways: one as static and fixed (religion), and the other as evolutive and dynamic (science). While religion remained tied to Greek philosophical principles, science began to map the heavens and the stars. By naming everything it observed, science collapsed mystery into physical description. We ran out of space for mystery, and earth seemed like an overpopulated rock; space exploration became very attractive.

The death of God and the marriage of science and culture in the modern period widened the gap between individuals as gender and race became markers of identity. The space between people became steeped in anxiety, distrust, hatred, and violence; our spaceless lives became asphyxiated and frustrated, and while we could invent a cure for polio and send a man to the moon, we could also invent nuclear weapons and harmful pesticides. Ironically, the male-dominated disciplines of both science and religion shared the same aim: to restore the fallen Adam to divine likeness. The male scientist, like the male priest, ruled from on high, while women and nonwhite races were reduced to inert parts that could be bought, replaced, used, or destroyed. The body became a defining feature of inclusion and exclusion. By the mid-twentieth century the cosmic whole was unraveled.

Theologians and philosophers were deeply distraught over the human condition in the twentieth century and thought deeply about the meaning of existence. Topics such as the relation of being and nonbeing, the radical nature of God, and the existential need for religion predominated. The twentieth century produced some of the most profound thinkers in history. Among these thinkers was Pierre Teilhard de Chardin, a Jesuit scientist who wrote theology without a formal method or philosophical tools. Yet what he wrote was deeply philosophical and theological. Teilhard was silenced by the church and ignored by the Academy, although several popes have recently made reference to his writings.[3] His ideas on religion and evolution were and still are considered suspect, unreasonable, and irreconcilable with scripture and church dogma.

One of the difficulties in reading Teilhard is that he wrote from a new level of consciousness, or what I have described as second axial consciousness. Most people read Teilhard through a first axial lens, and thus read him incorrectly. He was a scientist committed to the study of the physical world and a Jesuit deeply committed to a God incarnate, a God dwelling in matter. He wrote from a space of deep inner reflection and saw that religion and evolution belong together. In dialogue with many scientists of his own day, especially Julian Huxley, it was clear that evolution had direction, a point that evolutionary biologists still argue. However, this argument can only be made if mind is left out of the description of the natural world, a position that belies the insights of quantum physics. For Teilhard and Huxley, mind and matter form a unity and evolve together, an essential point for science and religion.

---

[3] The last three popes—Pope John Paul II, Pope Benedict, and Pope Francis—have all made reference to the writings of Teilhard. See Heidi Schlumpf, "Time to Rehabilitate Teilhard de Chardin," *National Catholic Reporter,* January 27, 2018.

Teilhard was writing on the noosphere around the same time that Alan Turing was developing his thinking machine. Turing was interested in the embodied mind, not the Cartesian mind, the way the body can blind the mind to the beauty of personhood. Could a thinking machine be a neutral mind? It was an important question because bodies were being ravaged by war, tortured by humans, and sold into slavery. The world was being rent from top to bottom; it no longer had a center or an umbilical cord holding together the sacred and the secular, and it was spiraling into a place of darkness, chaos, and destruction. By the mid-twentieth century the world was fractured into a thousand pieces—by war, violence, hatred, nuclear weapons, and the many other tools humans invented to master the earth and one another. We ran out of space to be human; we could not breathe.

The rise of computer technology was not only a stroke of genius but also a desperate cry of nature to restore the cosmic whole destroyed by humans. The principles of AI, such as cybernetics, information, and dynamical systems, were already in nature. Nature's "intelligence" is nature's dynamism. It was just a matter of time before nature's intelligence could be harnessed in new ways.

Cyberspace was a welcome renewal of nature, a vast extensive space, a virginal endless exploration where one could create and bring to life things hidden and things unknown, a place where life could be art again. We humans took to cyberspace like fish dying on land and finding water. We began to swim in this space, explore in this space, and reinvent ourselves in this space. The spaciousness of cyberspace is endless, and for the last few decades we have found new life in this space as we connect to one another across distances, across racial and religious divides, and across genders, languages, and cultures.

Cyberspace has become, in some ways, our new umbilical cord, connecting us globally in a way we have never been connected in the history of the planet. Every day we turn on our devices looking for connections, new information, news, and events, to relieve our anxiety, and know we are not alone. We are constantly checking our phones and messages in this endless space of infinite opportunities and dreams, to the point where we have developed an addiction to our devices and their little ringtones. Social critics tell us that this unhealthy addiction is exacting a price on human relationships, as well as human memory and creative thinking. So they advise us to "unplug" and spend time in nature—return to Walden Pond.

It is difficult to get our heads around the fact that we are in evolution, which is not an idea or a theory but a physical description of reality, our ongoing development. We need to own our evolution honestly and openly because it is accelerating; without accepting evolution, the changes brought about by technology can be destabilizing. And here is where I want to challenge the critics of technology who are writing with the first axial person in mind; there is a new type of person emerging in our midst, the posthuman, and this new person demands our utmost attention.

The posthuman is not readily identified because there are no real physical changes or mutations. Biological diversity belonged to evolution's expanding phase, which is now over. What is changing is the human brain in relation to the environment, and this shifting of the brain reflects the body's need to overcome constricted boundaries. The brain, as we know today, is a plastic organ that works in tandem with the environment and responds to the dominant stimuli of the environment. Neuropsychologist Charlotte Tomaino writes, "The brain repeats what it knows."[4] The influx of computer technology into culture and society over the last fifty years has significantly shifted the matrix of relationships due to the types of connectivity that computer technology affords. Consciousness has been complexifying due to our new technological landscape. New brain centers are being enhanced while other centers that served us well in the past are becoming quiescent. Evolution shows us that where the mind goes so too does matter. The new person emerging in evolution does not differ physically but differs mentally, that is, by the way one thinks about the world and one's body in the world. Katherine Hayles

---

[4] Charlotte Tomaino, *Awakening the Brain: The Neuropsychology of Grace* (New York: Stria Books, 2012), 60.

and Donna Haraway grasped the import of the new electronic person, the cyborg. Now we are beginning to see the significance of their insights for the twenty-first century.

The posthuman represents the necessary pressure to evolve toward new levels of consciousness and complexity for several reasons: first, the human person has never been static; and second, we need to become a new type of person if planetary life is to survive. While the "individual" began with axial consciousness, the individual is giving way to the hyper-personal person, the posthuman of the second axial period, who has a new electronically embedded body with an electronically embedded mind.

Ontologies are becoming redefined because meaningful existence now emerges "in the splice," the in-between where coded information complexifies. The posthuman is gender fluid, racially neutral, and interspiritual. The fluidity of boundaries and the recursive loops of ongoing identity construction mean that no category can adequately define personhood. Rather, the self is an ongoing discovery and a creative process; the soul, too, is a psychosocial process of ongoing construction. The soul as the core constitutive being of personhood emerges through growth and development of connections, as one seeks to live by the life of the whole. Beatrice Bruteau writes, "The more conscious the individual becomes, the more the individual becomes *person*, and each person is person only to the extent that the individual freely lives by the life of the Whole."[5]

The emerging posthuman is a new type of person wired toward engagement, communication, and shared information. Gen Y and Gen Z populations, in particular, are oriented toward creative personhood, life as art, moments of shared being, and a deep concern for the earth community.[6] Growing up in a networked world means that personhood is a cybernetic process,

---

[5] Beatrice Bruteau, "The Whole World: A Convergent Perspective," in *The Grand Option: Personal Transformation and a New Creation* (Notre Dame, IN: University of Notre Dame Press, 2001), 102.

[6] Gen Y, also called Millennials, include persons born between 1980 and 1996. Gen Z persons are those born starting in the mid 1990s; there is no general agreement on the end date for this group.

an ongoing process that embraces pluralities of gender, race, or religion. Self-identity is self-creative through self-engagement. The self is a dynamic, ineffable core of ongoing constitutive relationships influenced by genes, family, and environment, but not limited to these; it is a core always in movement and engagement with the wider world. In this respect personhood is performative; the art of becoming a person is a creative act. The world is not a background stage for human life but the cybernetic environment in which personhood emerges. As personhood develops, the world changes, and as the world changes, personhood develops. The performative person creates a new space of identity at each moment of acting that can be renewed, shared, or rejected. The electronically embedded posthuman, therefore, creates, recreates, and co-creates.

In the second axial period personhood is being liberated from individualism as a new type of relational being emerges. The first axial individual is coming to an end, and a new, electronically facilitated being is in process. Bruteau writes:

> The evolutionary pressure toward greater reflexivity urges us to a realization of ourselves as conscious being, a noetic coincidence with ourselves as conscious acts of life-communicating life. This noetic coincidence with the act of communicating life is a free act; it is now our interior act that enters more profoundly into the interiority of our fellow beings rather than an external act touching the exteriority of another being.[7]

Although Bruteau is writing in view of neo-feminine consciousness and deep relationality, such consciousness belongs to the second axial person, who is at home with networked relationships, horizontal vision, and virtual reality. Today, many Gen Z persons sleep with their phones because the phone is part of the self, the exoskeletal self connected to the wider world, even

---

[7] Bruteau, "Freedom: If Anyone Is in Christ, That Person Is a New Creation," in *The Grand Option*, 157.

though this phenomenon may be interfering with sleep patterns.[8] Social media platforms such as Twitter, Instagram, and Snapchat are mind extenders by which personhood is distributed in the wider world and in turn receives input from that world.

The horizontal lines of relationship are giving rise to a "hive brain," an integrated brain of multiple parallel circuits in which the lines between inner and outer circuits are increasingly blurred. Such a brain is primed for electronic extension, from social media to robotic partners to implantable software in facial or neural tissue. Self-reflective consciousness of the first axial consciousness is now replaced by co-reflective second axial consciousness and the shared space of interbeing life. It is not so much a loss of interiority as a need to redefine interiority in cybernetic life. One today knows oneself more in connection with others than in oneself, and yet it is precisely connections with others that continuously define oneself. Posthuman identity, in which personal identity is sought in the whole, is what I call a *holonome*. The holonome is the person embedded in complex fields of networks by which one participates in larger wholes; technology is extending the outreach of the human person into global domains (which is what Teilhard meant by "ultrahuman").

For example, sixteen-year-old Greta Thunberg kicked off the Youth Climate Strike movement in Sweden in 2019, gaining attention when she delivered a powerful speech at the United Nations Climate Change Summit. Her actions were captured and shared through social media, and soon waves of demonstrations by thousands of school children were taking place in over one hundred countries. Students in Hong Kong carried signs reading "There's no planet B" and "You're destroying our future" as they joined in the worldwide protests. Protests took place across the city of New York, as students marched through Central Park and packed into Columbus Circle. One protester carried a sign

---

[8] Jeane M. Twenge, Zlatan Krizan, and Garrett Hisler, "Decreases in Self-Reported Sleep Duration among US Adolescents 2009–2015 and Association with New Media Screen Time," *Sleep Medicine* 39 (2017): 47–53.

reading "I'm not showing up for school because adults aren't showing up for climate."[9] Youth are now mobilizing their co-reflective concerns online and organizing global protests against gun violence and racial violence, and advocating for just wages and economic justice.[10] Social media can gather persons online, and hyper-personal connections can increase consciousness. The August 2019 shootings in El Paso, Texas, left twenty-two people dead. Among them was a good, simple woman who was the common-law wife of a Mexican immigrant. She was his entire world, and when the news of her death spread across the internet, people came from all over to attend her funeral, even though they had never met her. One person flew from northern California out of a deep sense of compassion for the grieving widower.

The act of living as persons in communion now means living from a center of free energy whereby our act of living unites with another's act of living, and this shared act of living goes on to unite with a third, and so on. Free energy undergirds a living net of radiant energies whereby each center indwells every other center. This is one of the reasons, I believe, why younger generations reject religious institutions and distrust authority. Religious institutions tend to stifle personal freedom of extended embodiment by demanding a set of rules be followed and by rigidly defining personhood. Such dictates belie the freedom of the posthuman, for whom co-reflection, shared space, and creative personal identity require an open system of feedback and self-control.

The posthuman has a need for hyper-socialization, which entails a new social arrangement around collective identity. The new trends in urbanized space are constructed to meet the needs

---

[9] "Skipping School to Protest Climate Change," *NPR*, March 16, 2019; Suyin Haynes, "The Girl Who Went on Strike for the Planet," *Time* (May 27, 2019): 38–41.

[10] See, for example, Gustavo Mesch and Ilan Talmud, *Wired Youth: The Social World of Adolescence in an Information Age* (London: Routledge, 2010); Joseph Kahne and Ellen Midaugh, "Digital Media Shapes Youth Participation in Politics," *PDK* 94, no. 3 (November 1, 2012): 52–56.

of the hyper-personal person. Condos sitting above restaurants, next to fitness centers, coffee shops, bike shops, and public transportation are part of the new complexified posthuman milieu. The new urban space allows greater convergence of consciousness and networked interaction. The hyper-personal posthuman is at home in a hive world, contradicting the modern liberal view of being over and against the other.

We need new markers of posthuman identity in the second axial period in order to judge adequately whether social media is having deleterious effects on human personhood. The age of the individual is coming to an end, and the dawn of the posthuman is on the rise. We are becoming increasingly wired together, and, in the not too distant future, our electronically embedded lives will be integrated circuits of seamless connections, the singularity predicted by Kurzweil. The question, as Donna Haraway points out, is not what we are becoming as cyborgs but what happens afterward.

Here is where religion plays a significant role. AI lacks a pole of orientation, a direction. Without attending to the new depth of hyper-relatedness that marks posthuman life, hyper-relatedness is random; cyborgian life is in freefall. We are looking for connections in the vast space of cyberspace in the same way that people sought social connections in church community fifty years ago.[11] We connect with one another to overcome the anxiety of aloneness. Moreover, we look for a center of convergence, a point of unity that binds us together and transcends our partial lives. Although much discussion in the media focuses on transhuman betterment, biomedical wonders, and economic repercussions of a robotic workforce, such discussion mutes the deeper significance of AI in terms of evolution. As a result, resistance to technology is heightened by the fear of robots taking over human life. However, these fears miss out on nature's self-engagement. AI is the science of nature in its chaotic, informationally driven openness to more intelligent life. It signifies that biological life

---

[11] See Will Herberg, *Protestant, Catholic, Jew: An Essay in American Religious Sociology* (New York: Doubleday, 1960).

stretches beyond the limits of bounded existence toward new collective wholeness.

Teilhard saw the emerging level of interconnecting minds, the noosphere, as a new level of life in evolution, not a disconnected level of electronic mind but a continuation of biogenesis on the level of consciousness and love. The noosphere emerges from the biosphere and cannot be separated from it; thus, the noosphere recapitulates cosmic life. This continuation of evolution on the level of mind *is* the rising up of God. God is the power of love within matter to transcend itself. God is the power of the future, since finite contingent being cannot contain infinite divine love. Evolution, in a sense, renders Nietzsche's obituary notice, "God is dead," a historical lie. God is not dead; rather, God is not quite born.[12] How might we use technology if we actually believed that God is partnering with AI-complexified life to *become* God, as we seek to create a more unified planetary life?

Technology can connect us, but it cannot *deepen* our lives together without a focal center. Religion is the focal center of life's dynamic becoming. Religion centers us around a collective belief in that which is more than our contracted selves. It can pull us toward a collective future, if we belief in the future together. It can bind us to that which rises in us as ultimate concern. AI needs religion if it is to have a direction in human evolution, and religion needs AI if it is to prosper on a new level of meaning and vitality. Technology can bring about a new zest for life by deepening the energies of love, but it needs religion to harness these energies and focus them on a center of convergence.

While institutional religion stabilizes us, it lacks the energy for evolution. We hold on to institutional religion because we see no alternative. Can we envision a new type of religion in a hyper-connected world without institution? Christianity was originally a new religious sensibility centered on being a person

---

[12] Loriliai Biernacki, "Panentheism and Technology: The Immanence of Rage," in *How I Found God in Everyone and Everywhere*, ed. Andrew M. Davis and Philip Clayton (Rhinebeck, NY: Monkfish Book Publ. Co., 2018), 129.

in community, a religion without institution. Christian revelation showed that God is not a proper name, a noun, but a verb and an activity, a constant bubbling up from the potency of being to the actualization of personal love. God is ever newness in love rising up through matter as the cosmic person; the universe is one whole person in formation. In light of Christianity's belief in personalization, Teilhard envisioned a new type of religious energy flowing from the convergence of world religions, giving rise to a new religion of the earth and a new ultrahuman community, electronically connected and rising in the Cosmic Person.

Technology is wondrous; it continues to connect and biomedically enhance life around the globe. Yet as we come electronically closer to one another, we seem to be more polarized than ever. This is because we react out of first axial consciousness with first axial religious convictions in a second axial age. We are electronically closer than in any previous age, and yet we reject what we see because there is nothing that binds us together. Physical vision separates us while electronic information flows through our linked devices. Can technology deepen this earth community in love? Not without a renewed consciousness of a third dimension, an inner center of divine love rising up in evolution. Without a deepening of love through meditation or contemplation, super-fast information will eventually widen the gaps between us instead of bringing us to a new level of life.

It is time to take the reins of our own evolution in hand and ask where we are going and if we are going together. Despite our incredible discoveries in technology, we still lack a sense of belonging together. Can we imagine a new religion of the earth, realizing that every moment is a God-ing moment of ultimate meaning and concern? Can institutional religions let go of divisive historical doctrines and work together for a new church of the planet? Can they widen their narratives to include evolution and the complexities of evolution? The truth is that we belong to a cosmic whole. In the words of Thomas Berry, "We will go into the future as a single sacred community or we will both perish in the desert."[13]

Technology can improve our lives, but more so, it can move us toward new wholes if it is aligned with a center of compassionate love, a divine center within us and around us, an energy field of love upon which all religious personalities can ultimately converge. Can we create AI to deepen religious energies of love? Can AI mediate an ethics of compassion for planetary life? Do we have the courage to develop AI to harness the deepest religious energies of evolution? Our most urgent task is to realize that the earth is holy, sacred, and lovable because it is porous, permeable, and open to the endless depth and horizon of life we call God. Posthuman life must become planetary life if we are to have a sustainable future. Can AI lead us beyond the narrowness of betterment toward the hyper-passionate interbeing human? It is time to awaken to a new second axial religion where super-intelligence can become super-love, not information but transformation for a new future together, a new rising in our midst.

---

[13] Thomas Berry, *Befriending the Earth* (Mystic, CT: Twenty-Third Publications, 1991), 29.

Index

aboriginal Australians, 30
Abram, David, 101
adaptation, 12–13
Advantageous (film), 107
Age of Exploration, 74
agential realism, 111, 125
aging, 78
agricultural societies, 31
Al Hallaj, Mansur, 198–99
alchemy, 46
Alone Together (Turkle), 92
Alpher, Ralph, 3
Amish, 91–92
analogy of being, 169
Annie Dillard, 194
Anselm of Canterbury, 168
Anthropocene (geological age), xi
anthropocentrism, xvi, 114, 190
anthropogenesis, 142
anti-essentialism, 196. *See also* essence; essentialism, biological
Antifragile (Taleb), 69
Apollo 11, 74–75
Apple, 133, 135
Aquinas, Thomas. *See* Thomas Aquinas, Saint
Aristotle, xx, 38, 41–42, 69
Armstrong, Neil, 74
Arthur, W. Brian, 79–80
artificial intelligence, xii, xxi, xxiii, 72, 85, 157, 225

Asian religion, 190
astronomy, 53
atman (Buddhism), 36
Atmanspacher, Harald, 12
atoms, 3
aufheben, 127
augmented intelligence. *See* artificial intelligence
Augustine of Hippo, Saint, 43–44, 178
Australopithecus afarensis, 20
autonomy, 35, 36, 39, 58, 68–69, 98–99
autopoiesis, 68
axial age, xix–xx, 27, 32–39, 135–36
axial consciousness, 56, 87, 136, 212–13
axis mundi, 29–30, 39, 213
Ayala, Francisco, 12–13

Ba'al Shem Tov, 167
Bacon, Francis, 53–54, 78
Bacon, Roger, 45–46
Barad, Karen, 110–11, 117, 125, 137
Bateson, Gregory, 117
becoming, xxiii
Bellarmine, Robert Cardinal, 49
Bergson, Henri, 140, 155
Berry, Thomas, xxiv, 87, 224–25
Bertalanffy, Ludwig von, 66–67

betterment. *See* enhancement, human

biblical literalism. *See* literalism, biblical

bicameral mind (Jaynes), 31–32

Bigelow, Julian, 70

binary logic, xxii, 84, 98, 113, 118, 126–27, 131

biogenesis, 146

biologically extended intelligence. *See* artificial intelligence

Black, Anthony, 34

Boethius, 24

Bohm, David, 5–6, 12, 140, 195, 212

Bohr, Niels, 110

Bostrom, Nick, xviii, 54, 77–78, 79

boundaries, 11, 67, 73, 99, 113, 120, 129, 154, 218
    crossing, xviii, 103, 105, 106, 112, 192, 197

Bracken, Joseph A., SJ, 16, 206

Braidotti, Rosi, 113, 116

brain downloading, xxii, 84, 184

brain, human, 51, 217

Braun, Werner von, 73–74

Broglie, Louis de, 3

Bruteau, Beatrice, 24, 89–90, 120, 177–78, 218, 219

Buddhism, 34, 36

Burdett, Michael, 128–30, 134

Bush, Vannevar, 70

Butler, Judith, 99–100, 196

Butler, Samuel, 96

calculus, 70

capitalism, xi, 136

Cappadocians, 23–24

Capra, Fritjof, 68

Carr, Nicholas, 90–91, 92, 119

Carson, Anne, 41–42

Carson, Rachel, xi

Cartesian subjectivity, xxi, 50–52, 61, 84, 109, 214

Catholic Church, xxi, 56, 157

causality, Aristotelian, xxi

cave art, 21, 27

celestial mechanics, 53

Chalmers, David, 107–9

Christ, 43–44, 173, 181–82, 187, 191–93, 195, 214

Christianity, xxv, 43, 51, 57, 162, 190, 214, 223
    patriarchy within, 56

Christogenesis, 184

church of the planet, xxiv, 205, 206

Clark, Andy, 107–9

Clynes, Manfred, 75

Cobb, John B., Jr., 36

co-creativity, xxiii, xxiv, 104, 112

coherence, 25

Columbia OV-102, 74

Columbus, Christopher, 74

communication, 9

community/tribe, xv

companion species, 129

compassion, 180, 186

complex dynamical systems, xii, xiv, xix, xxi, 15, 66–68, 71, 85, 96, 99, 125, 208, 216

complexification, xiv, xv, 11, 14–15, 19–23, 66, 123–24, 138. *See also* consciousness, complexification of

computer age, 90

computer technology, 94, 133, 147

consciousness, xiv, 5, 6, 8, 24–26, 139, 184
    collective, 38, 88, 146, 164, 202–3
    complexification of, 25–26, 32, 39, 88, 124, 136, 152, 153, 174, 182, 217

cosmic, 16
distributed, 121
and evolution, 13–15, 22–23
global, 88
and the human brain, 15–16
and matter, 8–10
and relationality, 9
consent of the governed, 56
consumerism, xi
contemplation, 198, 200
contingency, xx, 47, 58, 70, 167–68
convergence, 17, 22, 98, 139, 145, 153–55, 210
religious/spiritual, xxiii, 163, 164, 224. *See also* interspirituality
Cooper, David, 191
Copernican cosmology. *See* heliocentrism
Copernicus, Nicholas, 49
cosmic microwave background, 3, 7
Cosmic Person, xxiii, xxv, 181, 204–5, 224
cosmology, static, 1
cosmotheandry (Panikkar), 193, 194, 195, 198, 200
Cousins, Ewert, xxii, 28, 37, 87–90
creation myths, 29, 43, 48
creativity, 112, 180
CRISPR, 79
critical feminism. *See* feminism, critical
cybernetics, xii, xxi, 70–71, 85, 99, 147, 216
"Cyborg Manifesto" (Haraway), 103
cyborgs, xxii, 75, 103–7, 111, 129, 192, 193

Dante, 48
Darwin, Charles, 12–13, 139

Da-sein (Heidegger), 211
De anima (Aristotle), 38
De Sitter, Willem, 2
Deacon, Terrence, 139
death, xv, 60, 78,
overcoming, 82, 83, 84
death of God, xxi, 50, 57–61, 214, 223
deep AI, xxii, 97, 130. *See also* posthumanism
deep relationality. *See* relationality, deep
deification, 60, 84, 85, 223
deism, 52–53
DeLanda, Manuel, 116
Denisovans, 21
Dennett, Daniel, 13
Derrida, Jacques, 121
Descartes, René, 47, 50, 56
determinism, 47, 122
"Dialogue on the Great World Systems" (Galilei), 49
diffraction, 137–38
Digital Minimalism (Newport), 91
Dinerstein, Joel, 73–75
"Directions and Conditions of the Future, The" (Teilhard de Chardin), 142–43
discrimination, sexual, xx
disease, 78
disembodiment, xxii, 83, 124, 203, 211
disenchantment, 144
divine right (of kings), 56
Doppler Effect, 2
dual-aspect monism, xix, 11–12, 14–15, 84
dualism, 56, 103, 105, 162
Duns Scotus. *See* John Duns Scotus
dynamics, 53
Dyson, Freeman, 74

ecological crisis, xi, xxvi
  religious roots of, xii, xvi
economics, 32
Eddington, Sir Arthur, 16
Edelman, Gerald, 15–16
Einstein, Albert, 2, 4–5, 70, 103,
  179, 212
electromagnetism, 1
electronic literature, 119
electrons, 3–4
Eliade, Mircea, xv, 29–32, 39
embodiment, 118–19
emergence, 19, 94–95, 96, 120,
  206
empiricism, 45–46, 47, 99
enhancement, human, xviii, 76–
  77, 59, 84, 85, 122, 128
enlightenment (Buddhism), 36
Enlightenment, 52, 53–55, 61, 78
entanglement
  cognitive, 107–9
  quantum, 7, 9, 107–8n48, 170
entropy, 71, 141, 151
environmental movement, xi,
  220–21
Eocene (geological epoch), xvii
Erewhon (Butler), 96
eschatology, 54
Esfandiary, F. M. *See* FM-2030
essence, 68
essentialism, biological, 131. *See
  also* anti-essentialism
ethos, 37
eudaimonia, 69
evolution, xiv, 12–15, 18–23, 66
  creative, 140
  directionality of, xix, 138–39,
    149, 198, 215
  and environmental change, 20
  failure of, 144
  Lamarckian, xxv, 134, 152
  and religion, 17–18
extended mind, 107

external compression, 143
extraterrestrial life, 158
Extropy Institute, 77

Facebook, 92, 134
fall of Adam, xx, 43–44, 54, 74–
  75, 136, 214
fecundity, 25
feedback loops, xxi, 16, 70, 71,
  112, 121, 123, 129, 154,
  197, 218
feminism, critical, 98–100
finitude, xv
fire, 20
first axial age. *See* axial age
first axial consciousness. *See* axial
  consciousness
FM-2030, 80
Foerster, Heinz von, 117
forgiveness, 180, 186
fractals, 141
fragmentation, 38, 98, 111, 133
Francis, Pope, xvii, 159, 190
free will, 98–99
freedom, divine, 47
freedom, human, 36, 165, 202
Freemasonry, 55
futurism, 55

galaxies, 2
Galilei, Galileo, xxi, 49
Gen Y, 218
Gen Z, xxiv, 218, 219
gender
  fluidity, 124, 218
  identity, 63–65, 99
  as performance, 99–100, 196
  polarization, xx, 41
general relativity. *See* relativity,
  theory of general
Geraci, Robert, 83, 184
Ginn, Franklin, 134
Girard, René, 213

Gittins, Anthony, 190
global warming, xi
globalism. *See* consciousness, global
Gnosticism, 184, 190
God, xxvi, 169–75, 180, 182, 187
  as being, 167
  as becoming, 201
  death of. *See* death of God
  as love, 172
Gödel, Kurt, 64
Goff, Phillip, 10–11
Good, I. J., 81
Google, 90, 134
Grau, Joseph A., 154
gravity, 2, 52
greed, 35

haecceitas (thisness), 170–71
Hagerty, Lawrence, 147
Halt and Catch Fire (television series), 182
Haraway, Donna, xviii, xxii, 75, 103, 105, 106–7, 123, 129, 137, 204, 218, 222
Haught, John, 13, 168
hauntology, 121–22
Hayles, N. Katherine, xviii, xxii, 98–99, 109–11, 116–23, 124, 128, 131, 155, 217–18
heaven, 55. *See also* otherworldliness
Hefner, Philip, 102, 104, 151, 187, 193, 202–3, 206, 207–8
Heidegger, Martin, 50, 72–73, 104, 211
Heisenberg, Werner, 4, 125
heliocentrism, xxi, 49–50, 56, 214
Her (film), 65
Heraclitus, 37
Herman, Robert, 3
Hinduism, 34
holism

biological, xiii, xiv, 51
cosmic, xiv, xv
natural, 7, 66, 129, 212
relational, xiv, xix, 4–5, 26, 83
holon, xiv
holonome, 115, 220
hominids, 18–21, 26, 27–28
Homo sapiens. *See* humanity, emergence of; humanity, as species
How We Became Posthuman (Hayles), 98–99
Hubble, Edwin, 2
humanism, 54
humanity, 1
  as created co-creator, 202, 207–8
  emergence of, 19, 27–28
  as species, xiv, 21, 26
Humanity+, 77
Hume, David, 47
hunter-gatherer societies, 31
Huxley, Julian, 23, 76, 138, 149, 215
hybridization, xxii, 72, 94, 96, 103, 106, 111, 119, 126, 131, 150
Hyde, Rod, 74
hyper-connectivity, 69, 88, 112–13, 123, 131, 180, 187, 198–99, 200, 208
hyper-personalization, xxiii, 124, 149–50, 153–55, 177–78, 180, 198, 202–3, 207

IBM, 79
ideal forms, 47, 169
identity, xxi, 25, 32, 36, 68, 82, 92–93, 98, 124, 129, 214
  collective, 221
  as constructive, 100, 125
  as creative, 124
  as process, 131

image of God. *See imago Dei*
imagination, 202
imago Dei, 43–44, 48, 54, 95, 136
Imitation Game, 63–65, 179
immortality, xxv–xxvi, 38, 43, 60,
    73, 85
implicate order, 5–6
incarnation, 43, 169, 172, 181,
    183, 190, 194, 204. *See also*
    Christ
Included Middle, 125–27
indeterminacy, 70
individualism, xi, xxii, xxv, 18,
    32, 35–36
    religious, 161, 164
individuation, 39, 47, 87, 171, 173
industrialization, xi
Information Age, 71
information exchange, xii, 9, 71
Ingham, Mary Beth, 169
inhumanity, 35
injustice, 35
inner self, 180
instability, 112
Instagram, 220
Intel, 79
intentionality, 135
interconnectivity, xix, 3, 16. *See
    also* relationality
interdependence, 58, 69, 101, 191
interreligious encounter, 124
interspirituality, xxiii–xxiv, 163,
    200, 218. *See also* conver-
    gence, religious/spiritual
interthinking, xxiv, 150, 182
intraaction, 110, 117, 125
Irigaray, Luce, 113
Islam, 46
Israel ben Eliezer of Mezbizk. *See*
    Ba'al Shem Tov

Jaspers, Karl, xix, 27, 33, 35, 36
Jaynes, Julian, 31–32

Jeans, James, 8–9
Jesus. *See* Christ
Joachim of Fiore, 45
Jobs, Steve, xvii, 133
Johanson, Donald, 20
John Duns Scotus, 46–47, 169–70
John Scotus Eriugena, 44
Johnston, John, xxii, 94–98, 115,
    119–20, 134–35
Jonze, Spike, 65
Juarrero, Alicia, 68–69
Judaism, 36
Jung, Carl, 12, 173–74, 175
justice, 29

Kant, Immanuel, 47
Kelly, Kevin, 80, 82
King, Thomas M., 22
King, Ursula, 158–60
Kline, Nathan, 75
Kosko, Bart, 82
Kroker, Arthur, 101, 121, 122,
    123
Kuhns, Dustin, 211–12
Kull, Anne, 103–4, 105, 192
Kurzweil, Ray, 80, 82, 122, 222

LaCugna Catherine Mowry, 23–
    24, 42n3
Laird, Martin, 199
Lamarckian evolution. *See* evolu-
    tion, Lamarckian
La Mettrie, Julien Offray de, 55,
    78
Lamott, Anne, 196
Langton, Christopher, 72
language, xv
Laudato Si' (Pope Francis), xvii,
    190
left-brain dominance, 51–52, 57,
    212
Lehrer, Jonah, 91
Leibniz, Gottfried Wilhelm, 70

Leo XIII (pope), 169
Levinas, Emmanuel, 126
light, 1, 3
literalism, biblical, xvii
Lorrimar, Victoria, 128–30, 134
love, xix, xxiii, xxvi, 151, 155, 163, 165, 180–81, 184, 187–88, 210, 224–25
    divine, 171, 172, 174, 191
Lucy, 20
Lupasco, Stéphane, 125

MacDorman, Karl, 65
Machina sapiens, 83
machine learning, xii
machinic life (Johnston), xxii, 94, 96–97, 119
Mailer, Norman, 74
Marcel, Gabriel, 142
Marche, Stephen, 92
Marrotti, Paola, 140
Marx, Karl, 104
Marxism, 142
"Mass on the World" (Teilhard de Chardin), 201
materialism, strict, 139
mathematics, 53
Maturana, Humberto, 67–68
Maxwell, James, 1
McCarthy, John, xii, xxi
McGilchrist, Iain, 51, 212
McMenamin, Mark, 148–49
mechanical arts, 44
Merleau-Ponty, Maurice, 101, 121, 183
Merton, Thomas, OCSO, 178
metaphysics, ancient, xvii, xxi, xxiii, 43, 46, 136, 168–69, 214
millennialism, 45–46, 73
mind–matter relation, xii, xix, 8, 16–17, 97–98, 212. *See also* dual-aspect monism; pan-psychism

Mithen, Steven, 27
modern subjectivity. *See* subjectivity, modern
monasticism, xx, 37, 44
Moore, Gordon E., 79
Moore's law, 79
moral order, 57
moral responsibility, 36
Moravec, Hans, 83, 97
More, Max, 77
mysticism, 199, 200, 214

Nagel, Thomas, 13–14
naming conventions, 80
nanotechnology, 79, 82
NASA, 73–74
natural selection, 12–13, 139, 146
nature
    as static, 13
    as energy, 7
    as social construct, 96
    elasticity of, 2
    plasticity of, xix, 73, 96, 111
Neanderthals, 18, 20, 27
neo-Platonism, 37
Neumann, von, 124–25
neurochips, 82
New Atlantis, The (Bacon), 54
new materialism, 116–17, 157
New School for Social Research, 80
Neumann, John von, 80–81
Newport, Cal, 91–92
Newton, Sir Isaac, 7, 52–53, 212
Newtonian cosmology, 2, 5
Nicholas of Cusa, 49
Nietzsche, Friedrich, 50, 56–60, 104, 223
Nixon, Richard (US president), 75
Noble, David, xx, 44, 60, 74–75, 136
Nones, 189
nonhuman, xviii, 1, 104

noosphere, xvi–xvii, 145–49, 151–52, 154, 158, 164, 177, 196, 206, 223
Novum Organum (Bacon), 78

O'Murchu, Diarmuid, 18, 29
ocean pollution, xi
Omega principle, 140–41, 150, 155, 171, 174, 188, 204
omnipotence, 47, 55
One, the, 37
ontologies, 99, 112, 113, 120–21, 218
Origin of the Species by Means of Natural Selection (Darwin), 12
otherworldliness, xi, xvi, xxiii, 54, 161, 163, 179, 184, 190

panentheism, 168
Panikkar, Raimon, 55–56, 58, 193, 194–95
panpsychism, xix, 10–11, 84
pantheism, 167
Paris Colloquium on Paleontology and Transformism, 139
participation, doctrine of, 170
particularity, xx
patriarchy, xvii, xx, 42, 214
Pauli, Wolfgang, 11, 13
peace, 180, 186
Pearce, David, 77
perfection
    individual, 76
    spiritual, 60
performativity, 196–98
permanence, xxi
personhood, 23–26, 65–66, 84, 93–94, 110, 152
    as becoming, 102
    distributed, 119, 128
    emergence of, 27, 107
    as performative, 219

as process, 25, 120, 178
as relational, 23–26, 100–102, 178, 188
as system, 119
terminology of, 23
Phenomenon of Man, The (Teilhard de Chardin), 149–50
philosophy, xx, 37
Planck, Max, 8
planetization, 153, 155, 184, 203, 209
plastic surgery, 80
plasticity (of nature). *See* nature, plasticity of
Plato, 38, 41
Platonism, 37, 169
Plotinus, 38
pluripotentiality, 72–73, 104, 106
poiesis, xv
politicization, 32
"Position of Man in Nature and the Significance of Human Socialization, The" (Teilhard de Chardin), 14–15
post-biological life, 84
posthumanism, 112, 113–118, 136, 155, 209
    contrast with transhumanism, 79, 97, 122–23, 125, 133–34
    critical feminist, xviii, xxii, 111, 130
    and deep relationality, 128–29, 130–31
    See also deep AI
poverty, xxvi
pre-axial consciousness, xix–xx, 28–29, 39
pre-axial period, 27–32
pre-axial religion, 213
Pribam, Karl, 5, 140, 195
Prigogine, Ilya, 15
primordial inflation. *See* universe, expansion of

Principia Mathematica (Newton), 52

Principle of Antagonism and the Logic of Energy, The (Lupasco), 125

process theology, 170

prostheses, 80

Ptolemaic cosmology, 48

quantum entanglement. *See* entanglement, quantum

quantum physics, xiii, xiv, 3, 8, 157, 212

quantum potential, 140, 195

quantum reality, 5

quantum relations, 25–26

race, 218

Rahner, Karl, 165–66, 168, 191

rationality, xv, 36, 39, 47, 59, 84, 98–99

re-enchantment, xxiv, 202–4

reflective subjectivity. *See* subjectivity, reflective

relationality, xviii, 23, 120, 144.
 complexification of, xviii
 cosmic, 57, 61
 deep, xxiv, 83, 115, 123, 128–29, 185, 202, 219
 See also personhood, as relational

relativity
 theory of general, 2
 theory of special, 3

religion, 135, 136, 155, 168
 and artificial intelligence, xvi, xxiii, 95
 as binding, 17–18, 177, 223
 cosmic function of, 17–18
 defined, xv–xvi
 of the earth, xviii–xix, xxvi, 162, 164, 182, 187, 198, 209, 224. *See also* church

of the planet; sense of the earth; spirit of the earth)
 emergence of, 27, 32, 37
 and evolution, xviii, 17–18, 160, 182
 institutional, 189–90, 196, 221–22
 as performance, 196
 and technology, 137

Religion without Revelation (Huxley), 76

Renaissance, 54, 61

resilience, xxi, 68–69

responsibility. *See* moral responsibility

revelation, divine, 190, 194

ritual, 29

Royal Society, 55

Rupescissa, John, 46

Russell, Bertrand, 8

Sacred and the Profane, The (Eliade), 30–31

sacredness of everything, xxiv

salvation, xxv–xxvi, 73, 85, 135, 159

Schaffer, Jonathan, 7

Schrödinger, Erwin, 8

science and religion, xxi

Scientific Revolution, 52

second axial age, xxii, 87–88, 136, 189

second axial consciousness, 88–89, 111, 115, 157, 164, 185, 189, 192, 208, 215

Second Life, 93

Second Vatican Council, 162

second-order cybernetics, 117

self-awareness, 35

self-reflexivity, xv, 24, 26, 36, 138.
 See also consciousness; subjectivity, reflective

sense of the earth, 159

shallow AI, xxii, 85, 97. *See also*
    transhumanism
Shallows, The (Carr), 90–91
Shannon, Claude, xxi, 71–72
Shults, F. LeRon, 27
sickness, 35
Silent Spring (Carson), xi
Simpson, George Gaylord, 139
sin, 213
singularity hypothesis, 80–81,
    122, 222
Snapchat, 220
social imaginaries (Taylor), 114
social media, xvii, xxiv, 92, 180,
    220, 221
social progress, 55
socialization, 32, 145, 213
Sofge, Erik, 64–65
soul, 38, 44, 179, 218
Space Age, 74
"Space Traveler's Manifesto"
    (Dyson), 74
special relativity. *See* relativity,
    theory of special
species extinction, xi
species variation, 139
Specter, Michael, 79
Sperry, Roger, 15
spirit of the earth, 165, 175
"Spirit of the Earth, The" (Teil-
    hard de Chardin), 159
spirituality, 154, 159, 197, 203,
    204
splice, 124–25, 130–31, 186, 218
spontaneity, 112, 180
stability, xxi
Stapp, Henry, 107–8
Stein, Gertrude, 186
Stoicism, 37–38
strange attractor, 141
subjectivity
    emergent, 105

modern, xxii, 98–99, 101, 112,
    116–17, 119, 121, 123–25,
    131
reflective, 38, 87. *See also* self-
    reflexivity)
suffering, 35, 63, 78, 82
Superman. *See Ubermensch*
Swan, Melanie, 125–26
Swidler, Leonard, xx
sympoiesis, 129, 188, 204

Talbott, Steve, xiii
Taleb, Nassim Nicholas, 69
Taylor, Charles, 114
Taylor, Mark, 50
techne, xv, 73, 95, 106, 129
techno myths, 135
Techno sapiens, 80, 83
technogenesis, 96
"Technological   Singularity"
    (Vinge), 81
technology, xi, xv, 32, 44, 46, 54
    and evolution, xviii
    as myth, 79
    as social construction, 208
    social critique of, 90–94, 98,
        107, 217
Tegmark, Max, 10
Teilhard de Chardin, Pierre, xvii,
    xviii–xix, xxiii–xxv, 14, 223,
    224
    on Christ, xxiii, 198, 205
    on evolution, 137–55, 160–62
    friendship with Huxley, 76
    on God, 168, 171, 172, 174–75,
    on mysticism, 199–200
    on religion/spirituality, 158–65,
        190, 201–2, 204
    silencing by the church, 215
    on world as sacramental, 194
    See also Cosmic Person; noo-
        sphere; Omega principle;

planetization; theogenesis; ultrahuman

telos/teleology, 48

Terminator (film), 107

Tertullian, 43

Theissen, Gerd, 192

theogenesis, xxiii, 172–73, 175, 180–81

theology, 48, 165–75

theopoeisis, 180

thermodynamics, 66

Thomas Aquinas, Saint, 169

Thompson, William, 35

Thunberg, Greta, 220

Thus Spoke Zarathustra (Nietzsche), 58–59

Thweatt-Bates, Jeanine, 75, 104, 207

Tillich, Paul, 101–2, 166–67, 168

time, 2

Todd, Peter, 173–74

Tomaino, Charlotte, 217

Tonini, Giulio, 15–16

tool-making, 19, 20, 27, 96

Traditionalist School (religious studies), 31

transcendence, 84

transhumanism, xviii, xxi, xxv, 136, 150n51,
   contrast with posthumanism, 97, 115, 122, 133–34
   and enhancement, 76–79, 187
   and relationality, 83–85, 129, 185
   shallow, 111, 184. *See also* shallow AI)

transtribal association, 33

triadic logic, 126–27

tribal cultures, 28

truth, 58

Turing test. *See* Imitation Game

Turing, Alan, xxi, 63–66, 93, 216

Turkle, Sheri, 92–93

Turner, Fred, 71

Twilight of the Idols (Nietzsche), 57

Twitter, 92, 220

Ubermensch, 59–60, 61, 85

Udías, Augustin, 160

Ulam, Stanislaw, 80–81

ultimacy, xxiv, 167, 206, 223

ultrahuman, xxiii, 143, 149, 150–52, 155, 178, 220

United Nations, xi, 203, 220

universals, 47

universe
   age of, 3
   expansion of, 2, 7

univocity of being, 169–70

Upanishads, 36

urbanization, 32, 34–35, 213

Varela, Francisco, 67–68

Vatican II. *See* Second Vatican Council

Vinge, Vernor, 81

violence, 214

virtual body, 82

Walter, Chip, 95–96

war, xii

Warwick, Kevin, 83

water contamination, xi

wave-particle duality, xiv

Weizsäcker, Carl Friedrich von, 7

Wheeler, John, 72

White, Lynn, xvi

Whitehead, Alfred North, 169, 170, 171

Wiener, Norbert, 70–71

Wilber, Ken, 60, 179

will to power, 58, 60, 61, 85, 125

will, divine, 47

William of Ockham, 47

world religions, xix, xxiii, 34, 39,
    163
World Transhumanist Association,
    77, 85
world-machine, 54, 61

xenogeneity, 74
xenogenesis, 104

Youth Climate Strike movement,
    220